CREATING CAMPUS CULTURES

Many colleges and universities have not engaged in the critical self-examination of their campuses necessary for effectively serving racially diverse student populations. This timely edited collection provides insights into how campus cultures can and do shape the experiences and outcomes of their increasingly diverse college student populations. By cultivating values, beliefs, and assumptions that focus on including, validating, and creating equitable outcomes among diverse undergraduate students, an institution can foster their success. While attention to campus climate is critical for gauging the nature of an institution's culture and how students are experiencing the campus environment, changes in climate alone will not lead to holistic and deep rooted institutional transformation. Moving beyond previous explorations of campus racial climates, *Creating Campus Cultures* addresses the considerable institutionally embedded obstacles practitioners face as they attempt to transform entrenched institutional cultures to meet the needs of diverse student bodies. A broad range of chapters include voices of students, new research, practical experiences, and application of frameworks that are conducive to success. This book will help student affairs and higher education administrators navigate this increasingly difficult terrain by providing practical advice on how to foster success among racial minority students and enact long-term, holistic change at any institution.

Samuel D. Museus is Assistant Professor of Educational Administration at the University of Hawai'i at Manoa.

Uma M. Jayakumar is Assistant Professor of Organization and Leadership in the School of Education at the University of San Francisco.

CREATING CAMPUS CULTURES

Fostering Success among Racially Diverse Student Populations

Edited by Samuel D. Museus and Uma M. Jayakumar

Routledge
Taylor & Francis Group

NEW YORK AND LONDON

First published 2012
by Routledge
711 Third Avenue, New York, NY 10017

Simultaneously published in the UK
by Routledge
2 Park Square, Milton Park, Abingdon, Oxon OX14 4RN

Routledge is an imprint of the Taylor & Francis Group, an informa business

Library of Congress Cataloging in Publication Data
Creating campus cultures : fostering success among racially diverse student populations / [edited by] Samuel D. Museus, Uma M. Jayakumar.
p. cm.
Includes bibliographical references and index.
1. Minorities—Education (Higher)—United States. 2. College environment—United States. 3. Multicultural education—United States. 4. Educational equalization—United States. I. Museus, Samuel D. II. Jayakumar, Uma M.
LC3727.C74 2011
370.1170973—dc23
2011025499

ISBN: 978–0–415–88819–6 (hbk)
ISBN: 978–0–415–88820–2 (pbk)
ISBN: 978–0–203–83241–7 (ebk)

Typeset in Bembo by Prepress Projects Ltd, Perth, UK.

Printed and bound in the United States of America on acid-free paper by Edwards Brothers, Inc.

We dedicate this book to the advocates and the activists who have risked the safety and security of complacency to fight for transformation in higher education and society at large. Their voices and energy motivate us, their legacy informs our scholarship, and their work inspires ours. This book belongs to them.

CONTENTS

FOREWORD

When referring to college students and others in postsecondary institutional contexts, I recently began using *minoritized* instead of *minority* to signify the social construction of underrepresentation and subordination. Persons are not born into minority status nor are they minoritized in every social milieu (e.g., in their families and places of religious worship). Instead, they are rendered minorities in particular situations and institutional environments that maintain an overrepresentation of one racial group and its dominant cultural norms. For example, a Latina student is not a minority when she is in her home environment with numerous same-race others, but suddenly becomes minoritized when she comes to a college campus that sustains a culture that disproportionately confers numerous educational advantages to White students, including a sense of belonging not experienced by others in the numerical minority. This book is about the pervasive institutional norms, beliefs, symbols, and practices that undermine success for minoritized students in American higher education. It essentially calls for changing the cultures of institutions to promote success among diverse populations.

Praiseworthy is the impressive roster of authors whom Samuel D. Museus and Uma M. Jayakumar recruited to contribute thought-provoking chapters to this timely volume. Indeed, they do much to provide a more sophisticated understanding of why racial inequities are repeatedly remanufactured in higher education and how minoritized persons often experience campus environments differently from their White counterparts. I am inspired by what I have read in the 10 chapters that follow, and hope that this book is not reduced to just another "diversity book" that does little to advance our quest for elusive racial justice on college and university campuses. It is clear to me that the editors and authors were thoughtful about producing a text that is distinctive from the dozens of others on related topics. Hence, my concern is not with the architects of this book, but instead with the audience for whom it is intended.

It is critical that diversity-related books, and especially this volume, be read and discussed among higher education professionals, and responsibly implemented into institutional plans designed to bring about racial equity. Nonetheless, at national conferences and during my visits to college campuses, administrators (particularly those in student affairs divisions) publicly confess that they do not consume much research or published scholarship related to their professional work. Explanations for this are typically twofold. First, some rightly argue that researchers often fail to translate findings into useful implications for institutional policy and practice – in other words, they view research as lacking relevance to their roles as practitioners. Second, colleagues attribute their failure to understand the need for and implement necessary changes to insufficient time. Reportedly, administrative responsibilities make reading difficult and at times presumably impossible. In my view, this book has incredible implications for change but will result in meaningful change only if the persons who read it utilize the powerful perspectives offered herein to make campus environments more conducive to the success of minoritized student populations.

At this point, especially with the publication of this new book, there is a great deal that is known about the conditions, policies, and practices necessary for achieving racial equity in higher education. Authors of the chapters that follow propose innovative strategies with implications for faculty and leaders at various levels of postsecondary institutions. Nonetheless, educators, administrators, and policymakers cannot implement something they have not read. Those who claim they cannot read because their schedules do not permit them to do so help preserve educational approaches that are outdated and largely ineffective. To know the scholarship exists, but make decisions that affect students' lives and sense of belonging without reading it, makes numerous postsecondary professionals complicit in the cyclical reproduction of racial inequity.

Throughout this book, most especially in Chapter 1, authors emphasize the importance of distinguishing campus climates from campus cultures. Undoubtedly, it is necessary and important to understand differences between these two terms. However, I think it is also important to recognize one important similarity: Both are difficult to change, and there are toxins in both that undermine success for diverse student populations. Useful implications for addressing the problematic nature of both are offered in the pages that follow. I hope readers will invest their energies into understanding the various racial realities written about in this book; thoughtfully reflect on how their own institutional cultures and educational practices contradict espoused personal and institutional commitments to equity; and partner with colleagues to discuss, collaboratively research, and strategically address institutional factors that lead to disengagement, troubling educational outcomes, and an insufficient sense of belonging among minoritized students.

Scholars who wrote for this book did so with much optimism for a more equitable and inclusive version of higher education in the United States, and I share their hopefulness. Several chapters include in their title something pertaining to various cultures. For example, Keith A. Witham and Estela Mara Bensimon write about the nexus between a *culture of inquiry* and student success, whereas Stephen John Quaye and Stephanie H. Chang grapple with the complexities associated with fostering a *culture of inclusion* in college classrooms. Unfortunately, little of what has been so brilliantly proposed herein will come to fruition if educators, administrators, and students continue perpetuating *cultures of avoidance* that lead them to continually avoid talking about racism and racist institutional norms, other realities of race on campus, and the range of factors that explain inequities that recurrently advantage certain racial groups at the expense of others.

In our 2007 study of campus racial climates, Sylvia Hurtado and I discovered that conversations about race were deliberately avoided because people were afraid of being misperceived as racist or naïve, plus they did not want to make others feel uncomfortable or assume the risk of political backlash. In a more recent study I found that higher education researchers routinely attribute racial differences in student outcomes and experiences to myriad factors – racism and racist campus cultures were rarely offered as plausible explanations. In other words, those who attempt to make sense of race-related issues in higher education often neglect to engage one of the most pervasive realities that exist at many colleges and universities in the United States. For sure, sustaining a culture of silence and avoidance will simultaneously sustain the inequities the editors and authors of this book worked so diligently to address. In sum, creating campus cultures that foster success among racially diverse student populations requires honest dialogue about racism and other racial realities. This is a timely, forward-thinking, and incredibly useful book. I can only hope that postsecondary educators and administrators read, reflect on, talk about, and integrate it into their professional work.

Shaun R. Harper, Ph.D.
Center for the Study of Race and Equity in Education
University of Pennsylvania

ACKNOWLEDGMENTS

We thank several people for their contributions to this volume. We thank the pioneering scholars who have advanced knowledge about diverse students' experiences and success for their work that informed this collection of chapters. We thank Amy McDonald Cipolla-Stickles, Kimberly Glanville, Katia Peña, Joanna Ravello, Kimberly Russell, and Blanca Vega for their assistance with editing the volume. Finally, we express our deepest gratitude for the authors who enthusiastically accepted the invitation to contribute to this volume and have provided important insights for those who take seriously the work of adapting our institutions and practices to serve diverse populations effectively.

1

MAPPING THE INTERSECTION OF CAMPUS CULTURES AND EQUITABLE OUTCOMES AMONG RACIALLY DIVERSE STUDENT POPULATIONS

Uma M. Jayakumar and Samuel D. Museus

Although higher education researchers, policymakers, and practitioners across the nation have acknowledged the importance of increasing rates of success among racial and ethnic minority students, several scholars have pointed to a superficial commitment to diversity and multiculturalism on college campuses that falls short of genuine inclusion of students of color (Bell, 2004; Bensimon, 2005; Ladson-Billings & Tate, 1995; Maldonado, Rhoads & Buenavista, 2005; McLaren, 1995; Sleeter & Grant, 2009). The absence of an authentic commitment to diversity and multiculturalism manifests in several ways. For example, some institutions are replacing efforts to actively recruit underrepresented and disenfranchised domestic students, whom predominantly White institutions (PWIs) have a history of excluding, with initiatives to increase enrollment of high-income students from China, India, and other foreign nations. Such efforts function to increase the numbers of students of color on campus, enhance diversity in the student body, and generate exponentially higher revenues – but they also serve to neglect domestic students of color. Another example of the absence of an authentic commitment to diversity and multiculturalism is the fact that several colleges across the country are currently consolidating and dismantling ethnic studies programs, despite evidence of the profound positive impact that such programs can have on validating the experiences of students of color and promoting their success in college (e.g., Kiang, 2002, 2009). Indeed, as colleges and universities progress toward diversification and face rising costs, there is an increasing trend toward eliminating or diminishing the very practices and efforts originally designed to increase the representation and success of historically excluded and currently underrepresented and marginalized racial and ethnic minority student populations.

Perhaps the most obvious manifestation of a failure of colleges and universities to truly commit to diversity and multiculturalism is the fact that many postsecondary institutions fail to adapt adequately to the increasing racial diversity of their student bodies and instead rely on offering token initiatives dedicated to diversity and multiculturalism. Put another way, many colleges and universities have not engaged in a critical self-examination and transformation of the cultures of their campuses that can lead to most effectively serving diverse student populations. This overreliance on tokenized diversity and multicultural efforts, as well as the failure to cultivate institutional cultures that engage, support, and facilitate success among diverse student populations, hinders institutions' abilities to foster environments where underrepresented students of color can thrive. As a result, institutions continue to perpetuate problematic disparities in persistence and degree attainment among college students of color.

In the following section, we highlight persisting racial and ethnic disparities in degree attainment. Next, we discuss the role of campus cultures in hindering and promoting college success among racially diverse student populations. Then, we offer a typology of campus cultures that can help postsecondary educators conceptualize the status of their institutions and how they can work to transform the cultures on their campuses to maximize success among racially diverse student bodies. In the final section, we discuss the importance of cultural assumptions in hindering such cultural transformation. Finally, we offer these assumptions as a starting point – prompting readers to (re)think the cultures of their own campuses and setting the stage for the remaining chapters, which delve into strategies that college and university leaders can employ to engage in deep and broad institutional transformation.

Racial and Ethnic Disparities in College Degree Attainment

Racial and ethnic disparities in persistence and bachelor's degree attainment have received much attention in higher education over the past two decades, and those inequities are substantial and have proven to be resilient. Indeed, recent nationally representative data suggest that 63% of White students who begin college at a 4-year institution will attain a baccalaureate degree within 6 years, whereas fewer than 43% of their Black, Latino, and Native American peers will attain a 4-year degree in the same timeframe (Figure 1.1). Although Asian Americans and Pacific Islanders (AAPIs) have the highest rates of degree attainment when racial statistics are examined, several ethnic subgroups within this racial category suffer from disparities as well. Although data from nationally representative studies of college students are not sufficient for disaggregating attainment rates among AAPI ethnic subgroups (Museus, 2009), Census data indicate that, among those 25 years of age and older, Southeast Asian American

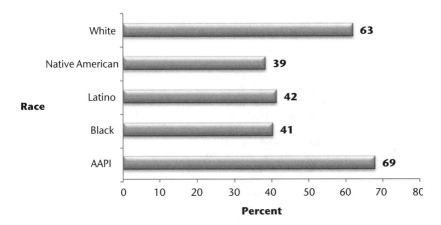

FIGURE 1.1   Six-Year Baccalaureate Degree Completion Rates at 4-year Institutions by Race. Data source: Beginning Postsecondary Students Survey (BPS: 03/09).

(i.e., Cambodian, Hmong, Lao, and Vietnamese), Native Hawaiian, and other Pacific Islander (e.g., Chamorro Islander, Fijian, Guamanian, Micronesian, Samoan, Tongan) groups all hold bachelor's degrees at rates noticeably lower than the national population (Figure 1.2).

Given that racial and ethnic minority students comprise a growing proportion of the student populations entering college campuses, these disparities in success also constitute an ongoing concern and urgent problem that requires the attention of higher education researchers, policymakers, and practitioners (Allen, Jayakumar, & Franke, 2009; Kelly, 2005; Museus, Palmer, Davis, & Maramba, 2011). These racial and ethnic disparities demand attention for multiple reasons. From an equity perspective, higher education has a responsibility to provide its increasingly racially diverse student bodies with equal opportunities to enter and succeed in higher education. Furthermore, it has been noted that persisting racial and ethnic disparities, coupled with a rapidly diversifying population, could lead to an overall decline in levels of educational attainment across the nation and have devastating social and economic consequences for society (Kelly, 2005). Thus, from an economic perspective, higher education also has a responsibility to produce a sufficient number of qualified graduates who can function effectively in the increasingly diverse workforce to secure an economically stable future for generations.

This volume emerged, in part, as a result of our belief that providing access to underrepresented students of color and isolated programmatic efforts to support racially diverse student populations are not enough to move toward equitable outcomes. Rather, we argue that institutional transformation is required to achieve such ends. Institutional transformation is both deep and pervasive, affecting the cultural fabric of college and university campuses

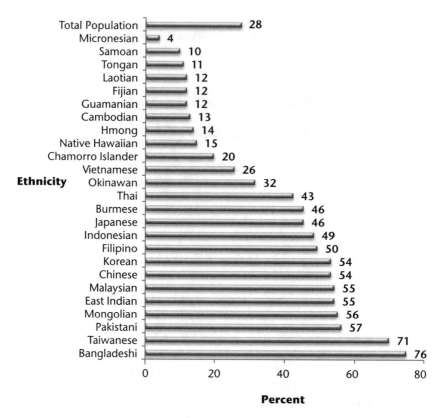

FIGURE 1.2 Baccalaureate Degree Attainment among Asian Americans and Pacific Islanders by Ethnicity. Data source: Public Use Microdata Sample (PUMS: 2007–09). $N = 14,847,168$.

(Eckel, Hill, & Green, 1998). This volume is aimed at better understanding how institutions can cultivate such transformation to better serve their increasingly diverse student bodies.

Campus Culture and the Promise of Holistic Institutional Transformation

Two concepts that have received considerable attention in the higher education literature are campus climate and culture. Although *campus climate* and *culture* are often used interchangeably, there are important distinctions between the two phenomena (Bauer, 1998; Museus & Harris, 2010; Peterson & Spencer, 1990). Such distinctions must be clarified because they are critical to understanding and maximizing the effectiveness of colleges and universities.

Campus climate can be defined as "the current perceptions, attitudes, and expectations that define the institution and its members" (Bauer, 1998, p. 2).

Much of the research on the intersection between institutional environments and racially diverse student populations has examined campus climates as they pertain to race (for review, see Harper & Hurtado, 2007). By and large, analyses of campus racial climates are focused on measuring students' attitudes, perceptions, observations, or interactions within the racial environment of their institutions at a particular point in time (e.g., Cabrera, Nora, Pascarella, Terenzini, & Hagedorn, 1999; Hurtado & Carter, 1997; Museus, Nichols, & Lambert, 2008; Nora & Cabrera, 1996). This campus racial climate research has clarified important realities: it has generated substantial evidence that different racial groups perceive campus environments in disparate ways, students of color encounter prejudice and discrimination at PWIs, and benefits accrue because of cross-racial interactions in college (Ancis, Sedlacek, and Mohr, 2000; Chang, 1999, 2001; Chang, Astin, & Kim, 2004; Chang, Denson, Sáenz, & Misa, 2006; D'Augelli & Hershberger, 1993; Fries-Britt, 1998; Fries-Britt & Turner, 2001; Hurtado & Carter, 1997; Hurtado, Carter, & Spuler, 1996; Jayakumar, 2008; Museus, Nichols, & Lambert, 2008; Museus & Truong, 2009; Rankin & Reason, 2005; Sáenz, Ngai, & Hurtado, 2007; Smedley, Myers, and Harrell, 1993). Aligned with the emphasis on campus racial climates in research, educators at campuses across the nation regularly engage in efforts to address "chilly" climates to improve the college experience for racially diverse student populations. Although the focus on campus racial climates in both research and practice has been invaluable in helping better understand the experiences and outcomes of racially diverse college student populations, we argue that this focus on campus racial climates has at least two important limitations.

First, with few exceptions (e.g., Hurtado, Milem, Clayton-Pederson, & Allen, 1998), the focus on campus climate has failed to generate holistic perspectives regarding how institutions of higher education can and should adapt to increasingly racially diverse student populations. As a result, efforts to positively influence the experiences of students of color often consist of isolated programs and activities designed to make students feel more welcome or feel as if they have a voice on campus. However, the impact of such isolated efforts is often fleeting and fails to stimulate deep, pervasive, and long-lasting systemic institutional transformation. In contrast to campus climate research and discourse, examinations of campus culture seek to understand institutions from a more holistic perspective (Bauer, 1998). The latter takes into account the historical context, rituals and traditions, and other symbolic components of a campus's identity, as well as both the observed and unobserved values and assumptions that shape perspectives, behaviors, and the way education is approached and delivered. In doing so, campus culture research and discourse can help lead to more holistic understandings of the intersection between the deeply embedded and complex elements of institutions and their diverse student bodies.

Second, campus racial climate research has failed to develop an empirical basis for understanding how those deeply embedded elements within the fabric of postsecondary institutions constitute barriers to institutional transformation that is aimed at better serving racially diverse student populations. This is a salient point because, even when college educators enthusiastically advocate for institutional change to address the needs of racially diverse student populations, they encounter systemic cultural and structural barriers. In contrast to the body of knowledge on campus climate in higher education research and discourse, understanding campus cultures can help institutional leaders better comprehend how values and taken-for-granted assumptions that shape behavior and the delivery of education on campuses can inhibit positive institutional transformation. Comprehending campus cultures can also provide institutional leaders with greater flexibility in facilitating institutional transformation (Tierney, 1992, 1993). Such understandings can aid institutional agents in overcoming cultural barriers and leveraging various elements of their campus cultures to make such transformation happen. In sum, our position is that understanding and considering institutional culture is essential for transforming institutions to maximize success among increasingly racially diverse student populations.

Frameworks for Understanding the Impact of Campus Cultures on Racially Diverse Student Populations

Higher education scholars have studied and written about campus culture for decades (e.g., Bauer, 1998; Kuh & Hall, 1993; Kuh & Whitt, 1988; Peterson & Spencer, 1990; Tierney, 1988, 1992, 1993; Whitt, 1996). Although campus culture can be defined in many ways, Kuh and Hall (1993) have offered one of the most useful definitions of organizational culture as it pertains to institutions of higher education. They defined *campus culture* as:

> the collective, mutually shaping patterns of institutional history, mission, physical settings, norms, traditions, values, practices, beliefs, and assumptions that guide the behavior of individuals and groups in an institution of higher education which provide a frame of reference for interpreting the meanings of events and actions on and off campus. (p. 2)

Their definition is particularly valuable because it underscores both the complexity of institutional cultures and value of cultural perspectives in understanding the experiences of individuals and groups on college campuses (Museus, 2007).

Schein (1992) provided a useful framework for understanding the different levels of organizational culture, which can be applied to institutions of higher education and consists of three levels that range from the most to least visible levels of culture: artifacts, values, and assumptions. *Artifacts* are the most visible aspect of an organization's culture, including its history, traditions, stories, and interactions (Schein, 1992). *Values* constitute the next level of organizational culture in Schein's model, and they can both be espoused and enacted. *Espoused values* refer to the shared beliefs about what members of an organization consider important (Whitt, 1996), whereas *enacted values* are those that manifest in the actions of members of that organization (Museus, 2007). Finally, cultural *assumptions* are the most tacit aspects of an organizational culture and constitute the underlying system of beliefs "that influences what people in the culture think about, how they behave, and what they value" (Whitt, 1996, p. 191). The fact that assumptions are the most tacit aspects of a campus's culture means that they can be especially problematic barriers to institutional transformation efforts – a point that we discuss later in this chapter. It should be noted that Kuh and Hall (1993) delineated *perspectives* as a fourth level of culture to this framework. Cultural perspectives are "socially shared rules and norms applicable to a given context," constituting "the way we do things here," and "acceptable behavior" among institutional members in a given setting (p. 6).

In using any cultural framework, it is important to avoid oversimplifying the complexity of campus cultures (Museus, 2007). Indeed, parsing the various elements of a campus's culture for purposes of analysis can hinder one's ability to see that culture in all of its entirety and complexity, and maintaining a holistic perspective of campus culture is important because the many elements of an institution's culture interact in both palpable and implicit ways (Whitt, 1996). For example, the norms, values, practices, beliefs, and assumptions that comprise a campus's culture manifest symbolically in various institutional missions, traditions, language, physical structures, artwork, media representations, interactions, and other artifacts. Together, all of these cultural elements and their symbolic manifestations interact to constitute the "invisible tapestry" that has such a powerful influence on institutional members (Kuh & Whitt, 1988).

Of course, campus cultures are incredibly complicated and, as institutions of higher education have grown and become more diverse, they have progressively increased in complexity. This increasing size and intricacy is accompanied by the emergence of many subcultures that develop within the larger campus. Building on the work of Bolton and Kammeyer (1972), we define *campus subculture* as the distinct culture that is created and perpetuated by a group on campus that (1) is in persisting interaction with each other, (2) has developed distinct values, assumptions, and perspectives that guide behavior of its group members, (3) transmits those values, assumptions, and perspectives to newcomers to facilitate conformity to them, and (4) differs from the dominant culture of the campus.

The cultures of postsecondary institutions shape just about everything that happens on college and university campuses (Kuh, 2001/2002). Although individual student characteristics influence the experiences of undergraduates, the cultures of postsecondary institutions also have an impact on the experiences and outcomes of their students (González, 2002; Guiffrida, 2006; Kuh, 2001/2002; Kuh, Kinzie, Buckley, Bridges, & Hayek, 2006; Kuh, Kinzie, Schuh, Whitt, & Associates, 2005; Kuh & Love, 2000; Kuh, Schuh, Whitt, & Associates, 1991; Kuh & Whitt, 1988; Manning, 1993; Museus, 2007, 2008a,b,c, 2011, in press; Museus & Harris, 2010; Museus & Liverman, 2010; Museus & Maramba, 2010; Museus & Quaye, 2009; Rendón, Jalomo, & Nora, 2000; Strange & Banning, 2001; Tierney, 1999). Moreover, a small body of empirical research provides evidence that institutions of higher education do have some control over the extent to which they foster cultures that are conducive to success among college students in general (Kuh et al., 2005, 2006) and students of color in particular (Museus, 2007, 2008a,b, 2011; Museus & Harris, 2010; Museus & Liverman, 2010; Tierney, 1999).

Research on Campus Cultures and Racially Diverse Student Populations

With regard to college students of color, the vast majority of existing evidence suggests that the campus cultures at PWIs have primarily been associated with negative experiences and outcomes among those undergraduates (Museus, 2011). Indeed, a substantial body of research underscores the fact that racial and ethnic minority students face salient challenges when entering, adjusting to, and finding membership in the dominant cultures of PWIs (e.g., González, 2002; Kuh et al., 2006; Kuh & Love, 2000; Museus & Quaye, 2009). For example, it has been noted that racial and ethnic minority students at PWIs often report experiencing pressure to conform to cultural stereotypes, as well as alienation, isolation, and marginalization from the cultures of their campuses (Feagin, Vera, & Imani, 1996; González, 2002; Lewis, Chesler, & Forman, 2000; Museus, 2007, 2008b; Museus & Truong, 2009; Rendón et al., 2000).

It is possible to make sense of the difficulties that the students of color encounter as they enter and navigate the cultures of PWIs using the concepts of White culture and cultural dissonance (Katz, 1989; Manning & Coleman-Boatwright, 1991; Museus, 2008a). Manning and Coleman-Boatwright explained that, in research and discourse on culture in higher education, culture is often discussed in an objective and nebulous way and questions are rarely asked regarding whose histories, traditions, and experiences are represented and transmitted throughout campus cultures. Drawing on the work of Katz (1989), they underscored the fact that the culture of most institutions of higher education have Eurocentric origins and can therefore be considered "White culture" (Manning & Coleman-Boatwright, 1991, p. 368). The White culture that persists at PWIs validates and reinforces the values and assumptions of the White majority and marginalizes the values and assumptions of racial and ethnic minority populations (Kuh & MacKay, 1989; Manning, 1993; Manning & Coleman-Boatwright, 1991; Museus, 2008a). White culture also shapes the perspectives and behaviors that facilitate daily operations on college and university campuses. Also, White culture is manifest in the artwork, media, rituals, and other symbolic aspects of the campus cultures of postsecondary institutions.

One perspective is that the challenges that students of color face at PWIs can be seen as a function of cultural distance and the consequent high levels of cultural dissonance that they might experience as a result of that distance (Kuh & Love, 2000; Museus & Quaye, 2009). Specifically, given that the policies and practices that permeate most institutions are based on White culture, it makes sense that students of color are more likely to experience greater distance between the cultures from which they come and the cultures of their respective campuses than their White peers (Kuh & Love, 2000; Museus & Quaye, 2009), and that cultural distance is associated with greater *cultural dissonance* – the tension that occurs when they encounter cultural information that is incongruent with their cultural meaning-making systems (Museus, 2008a), which decreases their likelihood of success in college (Museus & Quaye, 2009).

Owing, in part, to experienced cultural distance, cultural dissonance, and the difficulties navigating the cultures of PWIs, college students of color often gravitate toward or intentionally seek out ethnic subcultures on campus (Murguía, Padilla, & Pavel, 1991). Ethnic campus subcultures – such as ethnic studies programs, targeted support programs, cultural and multicultural centers, and ethnic student organizations – can have a powerful positive influence on the experiences and outcomes of students of color in many ways (see, for example, González, 2002; Guiffrida, 2003; Kiang, 2002, 2009; Museus, 2008b, 2010, 2011; Patton, 2006a,b). For example, those subcultures can provide students with safe spaces, serve as vehicles through which students can embrace and express their cultural identities, and help students of color more meaningfully connect to the academic and social subsystems of their institutions.

The concepts of cultural integrity and cultural integration can help explain the potential powerful impact that ethnic subcultures on campus hold. Deyhle (1995) described the notion of *cultural integrity* as it relates to the institution's role in shaping student success or failure in academic endeavors. Tierney (1999) drew upon her work and defined cultural integrity as educational programming that engages the diverse backgrounds of students. In Chapter 6 of the current volume, Museus, Lâm, Huang, Kem, and Tan build on the concept of cultural integrity to discuss *cultural integration*, which they define as the intentional integration of the cultural, academic, and social spheres of students' lives into specific spaces, courses, projects, activities, and activities. Whereas ethnic subcultures on college campuses facilitate such cultural integration, many environments across college and university campuses fail to do so even in the face of compelling evidence that interconnections between these three spheres of college life are important in efforts to maximize success among racially diverse populations (e.g., Kiang, 2002, 2009; Love, Kuh, MacKay, & Hardy, 1993; Museus, 2008c; Tierney, 1999; Tinto, 1998).

Thus, review of the aforementioned literature on campus culture and students of color suggests that the dominant cultures of PWIs have a negative influence on those students, and campus subcultures provide safe spaces that facilitate success among those students. However, there is some indication that institutional leaders can also promote *dominant* organizational values, beliefs, and assumptions that do facilitate the success of diverse student populations (Museus, 2011; Museus & Harris, 2010; Museus & Liverman, 2010). Kuh et al. (1991) and Kuh et al. (2005) have made critical contributions to current levels of understanding regarding how various elements of campus cultures – such as congruence between espoused and enacted values and an unwavering focus on student learning – facilitate engagement and success among college students, but their work did not focus on students of color. Building on that research, Museus (2011) examined three PWIs with high and equitable persistence and graduation rates among underrepresented students of color and found that strong networking values, a commitment to targeted support, a belief in humanizing the educational experience, and an assumed institutional responsibility for racial and ethnic minority student success were the primary cultural factors that contributed to success among racially diverse populations at these institutions. Therefore, there is some evidence that PWIs can cultivate institution-wide values, commitments, beliefs, and assumptions that positively influence the success of diverse student populations, but there is little documentation regarding how such cultures are fostered, what barriers are encountered in cultivating such cultures, and how such barriers can be overcome. The contributors to this volume aim to fill this critical gap in the knowledgebase.

In sum, campus cultures play a fundamental role in shaping the experiences and outcomes of racially diverse student populations and can help better understand several important aspects of the undergraduate experience, including but not limited to (1) the tacit and deeply embedded assumptions and norms that cause cultural dissonance among various racial and ethnic groups entering college, (2) the factors that foster or hinder adjustment to and membership in campus cultures among those diverse populations, and (3) the ways in which specific values, assumptions, and perspectives can be cultivated to validate the cultural identities of and increase success among racially diverse student bodies. We argue that, if institutions are serious about effectively serving and maximizing success among students of color, then they must assess and be open to critiquing, adapting, and transforming the cultures of their campuses.

A Typology of Campus Cultural Orientations

A key complication in understanding the role of campus cultures in facilitating success among students of color is the lack of clarity regarding whether dominant institutional cultures are truly characterized by values of diversity and inclusion. As mentioned, espoused values can be defined as shared beliefs regarding what is important (Whitt, 1996), and enacted values are beliefs that manifest in the actions and behaviors of the group (Schein, 1992; Museus, 2007). The degree to which institutions espouse diversity values varies (Hurtado, Milem, Clayton-Pedersen, & Allen, 1998; Kincheloe & Stenberg, 1997). Moreover, even among institutions that espouse the values of diversity, the extent to which they enact those values – that is, the degree with which diversity values and considerations permeate the behavior and decision-making of institutional actors – varies considerably. Some institutions unapologetically ignore such values. Other campuses espouse a commitment to diversity values but frequently fail to take action that is aligned with those values. Still others have changed or genuinely strive to transform their cultures to incorporate diversity in their missions, curricula, and organizational and physical structures.

Several scholars have proposed frameworks helpful for understanding the extent to which institutions have achieved authentic diversity and multiculturalism (Banks, 2001; Gibson, 1976; Kincheloe & Stenberg, 1997; King, 2004; Manning & Coleman-Boatwright, 1991; McLaren, 1995; Nieto, 2004; Sleeter & Grant, 2003; Valverde, 1998). Although there is a lack of consensus regarding what constitutes "multiculturalism" (Castagno, 2009), Strong (1986) offered one of its earliest conceptualizations, defined in the following way:

> The multicultural organization is one which is genuinely committed to diverse representation of its membership; is sensitive to maintaining an open, supportive and responsive environment; is working toward and purposefully including elements of diverse cultures in its ongoing operations; and. . . is authentic in its response to issues confronting it. (p. 85, as cited in Manning & Coleman-Boatwright, 1991)

It has been two decades since Manning and Coleman-Boatwright (1991) elucidated a monocultural to multicultural continuum that is focused specifically on institutions of higher education. In doing so, the authors discuss struggles, challenges, and processes related to transitioning from monoculturalism to multiculturalism. According to Manning and Coleman-Boatwright (1991), growth toward a state of multiculturalism that is pervasive and institutionalized occurs as "members of the community acquire knowledge about other cultures, gain experience with people different from themselves, and are challenged with structural and systemic change through this effort" (p. 369). Since

Manning and Boatwright offered their continuum, other scholars have offered alternative frameworks. McLaren (1995) provides a typology consisting of four types of multiculturalism: conservative or corporate, liberal, left-liberal, and critical multiculturalism. Kincheloe and Stenberg (1997) extended McLaren's (1995) work and delineated five points on the same continuum: conservative, liberal, pluralistic, left essentialist, and critical multiculturalism. Valverde (1998) offers a similar continuum that includes five stages of "multiculturing a campus" that ends with the "transformed campus," which embodies multicultural perspectives and values in all aspects of the institution.

These frameworks have a couple of things in common. First, they focus on the representation of diversity that exists within and across institutions. Second, they are continua that consist of monocultural institutions on one end, institutions with a representation of diversity that is marginalized along the middle, and transformed institutions that are permeated with diversity on the other end. In the remainder of this section, we draw from literature on campus cultures, the aforementioned continua, and research on equity in higher education to develop and present an alternative typology of campus cultures. Our typology shares the distinguishing feature of Sleeter and Grant's (2003) framework in advocating beyond education for critical awareness and interrogation to promoting social action toward greater equity, but it places a special emphasis on fostering underlying organizational values, perspectives, and assumptions that lead to action toward racial and ethnic equity and the reduction of racial and ethnic disparities in educational outcomes. In developing our typology, we draw from Bensimon's (2005) cognitive frames of institutional participants, which she offers to explicate individuals' underlying personal belief systems and ways of thinking, which shape institutional practices related to diversity and ultimately have implications for equity in student outcomes.

Bensimon (2005) described the cognitive frames of diversity, deficit, and equity. She explains that individuals who adhere to a deficit cognitive frame:

> may value diversity and have positive attitudes toward increasing minority student participation . . . but they are inclined to attribute differences in educational outcomes . . . to cultural stereotypes, inadequate socialization, or lack of motivation and initiative on the part of the students. (p. 102)

Bensimon also states that

> When individuals are guided by diversity as their cognitive frame . . . they focus their attention on demographic characteristics of the student body . . . and interracial contact . . . that promotes learning outcomes and better prepares students for an increasingly diverse workforce and society. (p. 101)

Finally, Bensimon explicates that individuals who operate from an equity cognitive frame are described as those who "focus intentionally on the educational results of outcomes of black, Hispanic, and Native American students" (p. 102). Although excluded, we would add AAPI students – particularly Southeast Asian American, Native Hawaiian, and Pacific Islanders – to that list. Herein, we apply this typology to institutional cultures and posit that such distinctions can be made at the institutional level.

The multicultural frameworks above suggest that institutions can be placed on a continuum from monocultural to multicultural campuses. However, institutions can strive and succeed at becoming more racially diverse and inclusive – thereby moving along the continuum from monoculturalism to multiculturalism – without intentionally addressing racial and ethnic disparities in student experiences and outcomes and while continuing to take actions that undermine an equity agenda (Bensimon, 2005; Bensimon, Hao, & Bustillos, 2006; Chang, Chang, & Ledesma, 2005). The aim then should be not only to work toward diverse and multicultural campuses, but also to cultivate campus cultures that are equity-oriented. Schultz and Hatch (1996) note that "the organizational surface . . . is always hiding a cultural essence, located at the invisible depths of the organization" (p. 541). We believe that the ideal campus is one on which the "cultural essence" of the institution – or core assumptions and values driving organizational behavior – functions to move the institution toward exhibiting more racially and ethnically equitable outcomes.

Bensimon's discussion of cognitive frames promotes this agenda through individual development toward an equity-mindset with values that are necessary for the creation of institutional practices that foster success among racially diverse student populations. We extend this discussion to the institutional level by focusing on the parallel role of organizational culture, which can arguably be described as the shared mindset of members of institutions of higher education, given that culture embodies the shared values, perspectives, and assumptions of those members (Kuh & Hall, 1993). Our application of Bensimon's frames to institutional cultures resulted in a typology of campus cultural orientations toward diversity, which constitutes a tool for identifying and discussing the problem of disparities in success among racially diverse student populations from an organizational culture perspective. The taxonomy includes three different types of diversity orientations of dominant campus cultures that embrace and enact values of diversity in disparate ways: (1) Eurocentric campus cultures, (2) diversity-oriented campus cultures, and (3) equity-oriented campus cultures.

Before we present the taxonomy, at least two disclaimers are in order. We recognize that any typology that is designed to characterize such a complex concept as campus culture is oversimplified, but we offer this taxonomy as a heuristic for those who hope to understand and examine the nature of the cultures of their campuses, as well as future directions for their campuses with regard to diversity and multiculturalism. Second, it might be difficult or impossible to neatly fit an institution into any one of these three categories. Thus, this typology can more effectively be thought of as a continuum from Eurocentrically oriented campus cultures to equity-oriented campus cultures, with a specific focus on the overarching dominant campus culture (as opposed to the many subcultures on campus).

Eurocentric Campus Cultures

On one end of the cultural orientation continuum are Eurocentric campus cultures. The Eurocentric culture is similar to the "White culture" or monoculturism described by previous authors (Katz, 1989; Manning & Coleman-Boatwright, 1991; Valverde, 1998). We define Eurocentric institutional cultures as dominant campus cultures that are racially and ethnically homogenous. Eurocentric campus cultures do not espouse or enact diversity values, and those values do not significantly manifest in the student body, everyday conversation, decision-making, or curricula (Kincheloe & Stenberg, 1997; Manning & Coleman-Boatwright, 1991).

The majority of colleges and universities in the United States, at their inception, employed faculty and staff who were predominantly affluent White men and were designed to serve the needs of that same population (Cohen, 1998). Thus, these institutions and the cultures that developed within them were originally designed to meet the interests and needs of a single dominant and relatively homogenous racial group (Katz, 1989; Manning & Coleman-Boatwright, 1991). As a result, these institutions began as campuses with Eurocentric cultures and norms.

Some college campuses have made little progress or intentional efforts toward diversifying their faculty, staff, and student bodies. On these campuses, the Eurocentric orientation persists, and is deeply embedded in the fabric of the institutions. Norms, values, beliefs, and assumptions, as well as the policies and practices that emerge from them, reflect a commitment to preserving the status quo, homogeneity, and dominant White culture. As Manning and Coleman-Boatwright (1991) explain, these norms are not geared toward inclusion of racially diverse students populations in higher education:

> Organizational structures built on monocultural norms are difficult to penetrate by anyone outside the predominant culture; new groups receive limited resources because of previously established allocation procedures. Selection procedures rarely formally recognize the contributions of people who possess a perspective different from the institutional norm. (p. 371)

Therefore, the expectation is for all college students to fit within or assimilate into the traditional homogenous and Eurocentric culture of the institution. The underlying assumption in Eurocentric institutional cultures is that failure to assimilate or succeed in the environment is attributed to students and their own abilities or capacities to excel, ultimately reflecting a deficit way of thinking about students of color. Scholars have noted that this Eurocentric orientation can be detrimental, given that racial and ethnic minority students' ties to their home communities and cultures can be an important facilitator of their success (Hurtado & Carter, 1997; Jayakumar & Allen, 2007; Museus & Quaye, 2009; Rendón et al., 2000; Tierney, 1999).

Diversity-Oriented Campus Cultures

The second type of campuses in our taxonomy can be viewed as the mid-point on our continuum, between institutions with Eurocentric campus cultures and institutions with equity-oriented campus cultures. Diversity-oriented institutional cultures are ones that have espoused or both espoused and, to a limited degree, enacted diversity values. Furthermore, this cultural orientation and the associated values are manifest in the student body, as well as some areas of everyday conversation, decision-making, or curricula. However, on campuses with a diversity-oriented culture, diversity values are, for the most part, often relegated to subcultures – such as ethnic studies programs, multicultural centers, and ethnic student organizations – at the periphery of the institution but those diversity values do not permeate the dominant culture of the campus.

After institutions of higher education opened their doors to people of color in the mid-twentieth century, there was a gradual increase in the racial and ethnic diversity of student bodies on college campuses across the country (Valverde, 1998) – although those increases vary drastically depending on the location and nature of the institution. This diversification and corresponding diverse viewpoints that accompanied led some institutions to undergo a shift toward multiculturalism. Campuses that diversified and made this shift toward multiculturalism are likely to value numeric racial and ethnic diversity and interracial interactions that enhance the learning environment on college campuses and consequently benefit all students. This focus on acquiring diversity and cross-racial interactions has been embraced by many institutions of higher education and is reflective of diversity-oriented campus cultures. Some have argued that the valuing of racial and ethnic diversity for educational benefits converges with and serves dominant group interests because it disproportionately facilitates developmental outcomes among White students (Bell, 2004).

These diversity values are manifest in efforts that are focused on increasing the number of students of color on campus and facilitating interactions across racial lines. Such efforts do not necessarily holistically address the quality of students' experiences or the racially and ethnically inequitable outcomes that might exist on those campuses. Instead, they most often include activities that celebrate different cultures or curricula and programming that is inclusive of people of color in compartmentalized spaces. These campuses might facilitate programming that is designed to promote interracial interactions and positive race relations. Overall, diverse perspectives and individuals are appreciated and viewed as enhancing the educational environment. Efforts may even be made to improve perceptions of the racial climate. Nonetheless, as with Eurocentric campus cultures, diversity-oriented cultures fail to challenge racial and ethnic inequalities holistically; rather, disparities in outcomes are framed as normal.

Institutions with diversity-oriented cultures are permeated with efforts to offer a service (e.g., higher education) to marginalized communities, but do not sufficiently contribute to uplifting those communities from their oppressed condition. Paulo Freire refers to such efforts as *false generosity*, noting that they serve to alleviate guilt among the privileged, but fail to challenge oppressive structures that produce inequalities (Freire, 1970). In sum, diversity-oriented cultures engage with and include diverse individuals and voices, but they do not address issues of racial and ethnic inequality on a structural level.

Equity-Oriented Campus Cultures

In contrast to the first two cultural orientations, equity-oriented campus cultures reflect guiding values and assumptions that recognize the pervasiveness of persisting institutional racism, historic and current exclusionary institutional practices, and disparities in sense of belonging to the cultures of the campus and educational outcomes. These cultures recognize how institutional practices have historically legitimized and valued the knowledge, perspectives, and strengths of White middle- and upper-class students over students of color, economically disadvantaged students, and other marginalized populations, as well as the reality that they often continue to do so.

To some extent, this cultural orientation is parallel to a critical multicultural perspective, which emphasizes the need for institutions to fully embrace diverse cultural perspectives and values throughout institutional structures and practices (McLaren, 1995; Rhoads & Valdez, 1996). Given this, the voices and interests of diverse student populations, and specifically racially and socioeconomically underrepresented groups, are engaged in decision-making, governance, curriculum, and institutional discourse and thereby instituted through structures and practices that are not fragmented or compartmentalized (Tierney, 1993). From this perspective, "Multiculturalism involves restructuring educational institutions so that all people play a significant role in decision making. Creating critical multicultural institutions involves rethinking the goals of education so that issues of citizenship, social responsibility and democratic participation become central" (Rhoads & Valdez, 1996, p. 48). Integrating this orientation through dominant cultural norms is a necessary step for promoting this type of multiculturalism.

Our concept of equity-oriented campus cultures builds on and diverges from this notion of critical multiculturalism outlined in previous frameworks, with its explicit and pervasive emphasis on promoting an organizational culture characterized by social action toward addressing institutional racism and racial and ethnic inequalities. This cultural orientation bridges the literature on muticulturalism and organizational culture. Equity-oriented campus cultures are characterized by assumptions, values, programs, actions, and other elements of campus cultures that reflect a commitment to address historical legacies and current manifestations of racism and racial exclusion on college campuses and that promote organizational actions aimed at intentionally and holistically targeting and addressing racial and ethnic disparities in educational opportunities, experiences, and outcomes. On college and university campuses with this cultural orientation, diversity efforts are not compartmentalized and not compromised in the face of competing interests. Rather, those diversity efforts are viewed as essential to achieving equitable outcomes, and the focus on diversity and equity is a consistent thread that runs through all elements of the culture of equity-oriented institutions.

Cultural Assumptions that Hinder Institutional Transformation toward Equitable Outcomes

In this section, we offer a list of assumptions that can function to inhibit innovative thinking and institutional transformation aimed at moving toward more equity-oriented campus cultures. Before presenting the list, however, a few disclaimers are in order. First, we do not claim that this list is exhaustive, nor do we argue that these assumptions are salient at every institution of higher education. Rather, we offer these as mere examples of cultural assumptions that can perpetuate institutional racism and hinder transformation toward more equity-oriented cultures on college campuses. If unchecked, these assumptions can hinder efforts to utilize any of the key ideas offered throughout this book. Moreover, we present these assumptions to highlight the importance of institutional leaders introspectively examining the assumptions that shape their behavior and practice. We ask readers to reflect upon these assumptions and consider how they might impede progress toward achieving more equity-oriented cultures at their own institutions.

- *The Natural Occurrence Assumption: "It's the Way We Do Things around Here"*
  As mentioned, cultural perspectives have been described as "the way we do things here" (Kuh & Hall, 1993), and such perspectives exist at most or all institutions of higher education. However, individuals can become

so driven by the "ways of doing business" on their campuses that it can be as if they view those ways of operating as natural or permanent aspects of their institutions and consequently inhibit transformation, even when there is overwhelming evidence that such change is needed to most effectively serve racially diverse student populations. For example, at an urban commuter institution, a group of faculty and staff were having a conversation about how to increase retention in their college. When one of the staff members began talking about the importance of social connections and community, a faculty member responded by saying, "Our students are commuters, and they don't come here looking for community." If that faculty member had read research on collectivism and minority student success (see Chapter 4), accessed the racial climate assessments that had been conducted on his campus, or understood how intentionally or unintentionally finding community had positively transformed the experiences of students of color at his institution, he might have questioned the abovementioned assumption.

Therefore, we believe it is critical that educators question long-standing historical and institutional assumptions about the efficacy of existing policies and practices and engage in systematic reflection and inquiry of those aspects of their campuses' cultures. One method of examining such cultural assumptions is to conduct a cultural audit or assessment (Chapter 3; Museus, 2007; Whitt 1993, 1996). Through these means, institutions can critically examine whether policies and practices that they have always assumed to be ideal ways of doing business actually disadvantage students of color and prevent the achievement of more equitable outcomes.

- *The Displaced Responsibility Assumption: "If We Offer It, They Will Come"*

Postsecondary educators often assume that their responsibility is to maintain and offer support structures that help racially diverse student populations succeed. The assumption is that, when institutions offer sufficient support services, it is students' responsibility to seek out and utilize them when they need assistance. However, creating and maintaining support structures does not guarantee that students will access them (see, for example, Suzuki, 2002), and some students of color might be less likely to actively seek help even if they need it (Museus, 2008b; Suzuki, 2002). Moreover, research shows that more proactive philosophies and the assumption that services need to be *brought to* students might be more effective in efforts to maximize success among undergraduates of color (Museus, 2011; Museus & Neville, in press; Museus & Ravello, 2010). These realities suggest that it is important for college educators to consider whether they are doing a sufficient job at extending their services to racially diverse groups on campus.

- *The Out of Sight, Out of Mind Assumption: "Everything Must Be Okay"*
  Institutional leaders sometimes assume that their experiences in campus environments mirror those of their students, and what they do not experience is absent from students' lives as well. Case in point: a team of institutional leaders on one college campus – consisting of faculty, administrators, and staff – met to discuss how they could increase success rates among underrepresented college students. During the discussion, one of the academic Deans expressed that there were no problems with the campus climate. Because he had not observed any campus climate issues, the Dean assumed that the institution's students did not experience such issues either. However, campus climate assessments revealed that many students of color on campus experienced prejudice and discrimination as racial minorities and English language learners. Thus, it is critical that institutional leaders check their assumptions about how diverse student populations are experiencing their campus environments and conduct systematic assessments of those environments with the assistance of institutional outsiders to excavate and examine those assumptions and their consequences (Museus, 2007; Whitt, 1996).
- *The Specialization Assumption: "I Have My Job to Do, and You Have Yours"*
  Higher education is a highly specialized arena. Historically, college campuses have operated in a relatively fragmented way – teachers teach, academic advisors advise, and student affairs educators engage with students outside the academic sphere. The importance of bridging these divides, however, has been acknowledged (Love et al., 1993; Museus, 2010; Tinto, 1998). Moreover, the importance of college educators providing holistic support has been highlighted as an important factor in serving college students of color in particular (Guiffrida, 2005; Museus, 2010; Museus & Neville, in press; Museus & Ravello, 2010). The idea is that students' problems are often multifaceted, and educators who consider multiple aspects of students' lives can more effectively address their needs or connect them with appropriate services that will do so. Thus, it behooves college educators to ask questions about whether they are expecting students to fragment their lives when they seek help, or whether those students have access to holistic support.
- *The Incompatibility Assumption: "If We Do This, It Compromises Excellence"*
  Debates about the compatibility of equity and excellence have transpired for decades (see Strike, 1985). Many people in higher education still assume that true equity can only be achieved at the expense of excellence. We believe that such assumptions have hindered progress in efforts to maximize the success of racially diverse student populations in higher education. An alternative perspective is that not only are equity

and excellence compatible, but equity is *necessary* to achieve excellence (National Academic of Education, 2009). For institutions to be effective at cultivating equity-oriented cultures, they must shed this assumption and be open to adapting to the rapidly growing diversity of the student bodies entering American colleges and universities.

Conclusion

In the 2003 landmark Supreme Court case that reaffirmed the legality of ensuring more racially diverse student bodies on college campuses through the use of race-conscious affirmative action practices, Justice O'Connor asserted "We expect that 25 years from now, the use of racial preferences will no longer be necessary to further the interest approved today." Underlying O'Connor's statement is an assumption that a racially and ethnically equitable society will be achieved in the near future. However, significant racial and ethnic disparities in educational outcomes persist, and higher education institutions have been widely criticized for exhibiting watered down versions of multiculturalism and inclusion of racially diverse student populations (Bell, 2004; Bensimon, 2005; Ladson-Billings & Tate, 1995; Maldonado et al., 2005; McLaren, 1995; Sleeter & Grant, 2009). Institutions with diversity-oriented campus cultures may achieve diversity in their student bodies and fulfill the charge of facilitating healthy interracial engagement and positive race-relations through intentionally facilitated institutional efforts. These institutionalized efforts are valued within a diversity-oriented campus culture because they provide benefits to all students in increasing critical thinking, the ability to understand diverse perspectives, pluralistic orientations, cultural awareness and understanding, and a host of other outcomes (Antonio, 2001; Chang, 1996; Engberg, 2007; Gurin, 1999; Gurin, Dey, Hurtado, & Gurin, 2002; Hurtado, Engberg, & Ponjuan, 2003; Jayakumar, 2008; Milem, 1994; Pascarella, Bohr, Nora, & Terenzini, 1996).

We argue, however, that, if higher education is to do its part in closing persisting racial and ethnic gaps, institutions of higher education must aim to create the conditions for more equitable outcomes (Bowen, Kurzweil, & Tobin, 2005; Chang et al., 2005) and achieve more equity-oriented cultures. Our hope is that readers will reflect on cultural assumptions that inhibit progress and consider the chapters in this volume as valuable starting points for seeking to make cultural transformation.

In Chapter 2 of this volume, Samuel Museus, Joanna Ravello, and Blanca Vega underscore the intersection between campus culture and race, and discuss how they mutually shape the experiences of students from diverse racial and ethnic backgrounds. The next three chapters examine the ways that institutions can nurture and promote various types of cultures and subcultures on their campuses. In Chapter 3, Keith Witham and Estela Bensimon advocate for creating a culture of inquiry that utilizes data, inquiry into racial inequities in student outcomes, and languages for creating generative dialog about those outcomes. Douglas Guiffrida, Judy Kiyama, Stephanie Waterman, and Samuel Museus discuss the potential benefits of cultivating collectivist cultural orientations in Chapter 4. In Chapter 5, Stephen John Quaye and Stephanie Chang discuss the process of creating classroom cultures of inclusion.

The final four chapters focus on the process of fostering institutional transformation and the role of collective and individual institutional agents in facilitating such transformation. Samuel Museus, Sơn Ca Lâm, ChuYu Huang, Pratna Kem, and Kevin Tan discuss how ethnic subcultures can foster cultural integration in Chapter 6. In Chapter 7, Uma Jayakumar underscores the role that college students of color can play in creating more inclusive campus cultures. Adrianna Kezar utilizes data and evidence to argue that shared or collaborative leadership is critical in efforts to foster campus cultures that are more supportive of racial and ethnic minority students in Chapter 8. In Chapter 9, Jay Dee and Cheryl Daly emphasize the role that faculty can play as cultural change agents in efforts to support students of color. Finally, Glenn Gabbard and Sharon Singleton discuss a multi-institutional change initiative and lessons learned from the preliminary stages of that project.

Our view is that colleges and universities that engage in inquiry aimed at achieving equity, create and maintain collectivist values, integrate students' backgrounds and communities into campus life, and construct inclusive educational environments will move closer to attaining equity-oriented campus cultures. If this happens, then we will begin to see progress in eliminating the racial and ethnic inequities that have remained so persistent across generations.

References

Allen, W. R., Jayakumar, U. M., & Franke, R. (2009). *Till Victory is Won: The African American Struggle for Higher Education in California*. University of California, Los Angeles: CHOICES.

Ancis, J. R., Sedlacek, W. E., & Mohr, J. J. (2000). Student perceptions of campus cultural climate by race. *Journal of Counseling and Development, 78*(2), 180–185.

Antonio, A. L. (2001). The role of interracial interaction in the development of leadership skills and cultural knowledge and understanding. *Research in Higher Education, 42*, 593–617.

Banks, J. (2001). Multicultural education: Characteristics and goals. In J. Banks & C. Banks (Eds.), *Multicultural education: Issues and perspectives* (4th ed., pp. 3–30). New York: John Wiley and Sons.

Bauer, K. W. (1990). Editor's notes. *New Directions for Institutional Research, 98*, 1–5.

Bell, D. (2004). *Silent covenants: Brown v. Board of Education and the unfulfilled hopes for racial reform*. New York: Oxford University Press.

Bensimon, E. M. (2005). Closing the achievement gap in higher education: An organizational learning perspective. *New Directions for Higher Education, 131*, 99–111.

Bensimon, E. M., Hao, L., & Bustillos, L. T. (2006). Measuring the state of equity in higher education. In P. Gandara, G. Orfield & C. Horn (Eds.), *Leveraging promise and expanding opportunity in higher education* (pp. 143–166). Albany: SUNY Press.

Bolton, C. D., & and Kammeyer, K. C. W. (1972). Campus cultures, roles orientations, and social type. In K. Feldman (Ed.), *College and student: Selected readings in the social psychology of higher education* (pp. 377–391). New York: Pergamon Press.

Bowen, W. G., Kurzweil, M. A., & Tobin, E. M. (2005). Race in American higher education: The future of affirmative action. In *Equity and excellence in American higher education* (pp. 139–160). Charlottesville: University of Virginia Press.

Cabrera, A., Nora, A., Pascarella, E. T., Terenzini, P. T., & Hagedorn, L. (1999). Campus racial climate and the adjustment of students to college: A comparison between White students and African-American students. *Journal of Higher Education, 70*, 134–160.

Castagno, A. E. (2009). Making sense of multicultural education: A synthesis of the various typologies found in the literature. *Multicultural Perspectives, 11*(1), 43–48.

Chang, M. J. (1996). *Racial diversity in higher education: Does a racially mixed student population affect educational outcomes?* Unpublished doctoral dissertation, University of California, Los Angeles.

Chang, M. J. (1999). Does racial diversity matter? The educational impact of a racially diverse undergraduate population. *Journal of College Student Development, 40*(4), 377–395.

Chang, M. J. (2001). Is it more than about getting along? The broader educational relevance of reducing students' racial biases. *Journal of College Student Development, 42*(2), 93–105.

Chang, M. J., Astin, A. W., & Kim, D. (2004). Cross-racial interaction among undergraduates: Some consequences, causes and patterns. *Research in Higher Education, 45*(5), 529–553.

Chang, M. J., Chang, J. C., & Ledesma, M. C. (2005). Beyond magical thinking: Doing the real work of diversifying our institutions. *About Campus, 10*(2), 9–16.

Chang, M. J., Denson, N., Sáenz, V., & Misa, K. (2006). The educational benefits of sustaining cross-racial interaction among undergraduates. *Journal of Higher Education, 77*(3), 430–455.

Cohen, A. (1998). *The shaping of American higher education: Emergence and growth of the contemporary system*. San Francisco, CA: Jossey-Bass.

D'Augelli, A. R., & Hershberger, S. L. (1993). African American undergraduates on a predominantly White campus: Academic factors, social networks, and campus climate. *Journal of Negro Education, 62*(1), 67–81.

Deyhle, D. (1995). Navajo youth and Anglo racism: Cultural integrity and resistance. *Harvard Educational Review, 65*(3), 403–444.

Eckel, P., Hill, B., & Green, M. (1998). *On change: En route to transformation*. Occasional Paper, No. 1. Washington DC: American Council on Education.

Engberg, M. E. (2007). Educating the workforce for the 21st century: A cross-disciplinary analysis of the impact of the undergraduate experience on students' development of a pluralistic orientation. *Research in Higher Education, 48*(3), 283–317.

Feagin, J. R., Vera, H., & Imani, N. (1996). *The agony of education: Black students at White colleges and universities*. New York: Routledge.

Freire, P. (1970). *Education for critical consciousness.* New York: Continuum Publishing Company.

Fries-Britt, S. (1998). Moving beyond Black achiever isolation: Experiences of gifted Black collegians. *Journal of Higher Education, 69*(5), 556–576.

Fries-Britt, S., & Turner, B. (2001). Facing stereotypes: A case study of Black students on a White campus. *Journal of College Student Development, 42,* 420–429.

Gibson, M. (1976). Approaches to multicultural education in the United States: Some concepts and assumptions. *Anthropology and Education Quarterly, 7*(4), 7–18.

González, K. P. (2002). Campus culture and the experiences of Chicano students in a predominantly White university. *Urban Education, 37*(2), 193–218.

Guiffrida, D. A. (2003). African American student organizations as agents of social integration. *Journal of College Student Development, 44*(3), 304–319.

Guiffrida, D. A. (2005). Othermothering as a framework for understanding African American students' definitions of student-centered faculty. *Journal of Higher Education, 76*(6), 701–23.

Guiffrida, D. A. (2006). Toward a cultural advancement of Tinto's theory. *Review of Higher Education, 29*(4), 451–472.

Gurin, P. (1999). Expert report of Patricia Gurin, in the compelling need for diversity in higher education. Gratz et al. v. Bollinger et al., No. 97–75321 (E.D. Mich.) Grutter et al. v. Bollinger et al., No. 97–75928 (E.D. Mich.). Ann Arbor: University of Michigan.

Gurin, P., Dey, E. L., Hurtado, S., & Gurin, G. (2002). Diversity in higher education: Theory and impact on educational outcomes. *Harvard Educational Review, 72*(3), 330–366.

Harper, S. R., & Hurtado, S. (2007). Nine themes in campus racial climates. In S. R. Harper & L. D. Patton (Eds.), *Responding to the realities of race on campus: New Directions for Student Services* (pp. 7–24). San Francisco: Jossey-Bass.

Hurtado, S., & Carter, D. (1997). Effects of college transition and perceptions of the campus racial climate on Latina/o college students' sense of belonging. *Sociology of Education, 70,* 324–345.

Hurtado, S., Carter, D., & Spuler, A. (1996). Latina/o student transition to college: Assessing difficulties and factors in successful college adjustment. *Research in Higher Education, 37,* 135–157.

Hurtado, S., Engberg, M. E., & Ponjuan, L. (2003). *The impact of the college experience on students' learning for a diverse democracy.* Paper presented at the Annual Meeting of the Association for the Study of Higher Education, Portland, OR.

Hurtado, S., Milem, J. F., Clayton-Pedersen, A. R., & Allen, W. R. (1998). Enhancing campus climates for racial/ethnic diversity: Educational policy and practice. *Review of Higher Education, 21*(3), 279–302.

Jayakumar, U. M. (2008). Can higher education meet the needs of an increasingly diverse and global society? Campus diversity and cross-cultural workforce competencies. *Harvard Educational Review, 78*(4), 615–651.

Jayakumar, U. M., & Allen, W. R. (2007). *Cultural integrity and successful college transitions: Countering the miseducation of young Black scholars.* Report to the College Access Project for African Americans and the Ford Foundation.

Katz, J. (1989). The challenge of diversity. In C. Woolbright (Ed.), *Valuing diversity* (pp. 1–22). Bloomington, IN: Association of College Unions-International.

Kelly, P. J. (2005). *As America becomes more diverse: The impact of state higher education inequality.* Boulder, CO: National Center for Higher Education Management Systems.

Kiang, P. (2002). Stories and structures of persistence: Ethnographic learning through research and practice in Asian American Studies. In Y. Zou & H. T. Trueba (Eds.), *Advances in ethnographic research: From our theoretical and methodological roots to post-modern critical ethnography* (pp. 223–256). Lanham, MD: Rowman & Littlefield.

Kiang, P. N. (2009). A thematic analysis of persistence and long-term educational engagement with Southeast Asian American college students. In L. Zhan (Ed.), *Asian American voices: Engaging, empowering, enabling* (pp. 59–76). New York: NLN Press.

Kincheloe, J., & Stenberg, S. (1997). *Changing multiculturalism.* Philadelphia, PA: Open University Press.

King, J. (2004). Culture-centered knowledge: Black studies, curriculum transformation, and social action. In J. Banks & C. Banks (Eds.), *Handbook of research on multicultural education* (2nd edn., pp. 349–378). San Francisco: Jossey-Bass.

Kuh, G. D. (2001/2002). Organizational culture and student persistence: Prospects and puzzles. *Journal of College Student Retention: Research, Theory & Practice, 3*(1), 23–39.

Kuh, G. D., & Hall, J. E. (1993). Using cultural perspectives in student affairs. In G. D. Kuh (Ed.), *Cultural perspectives in student affairs work* (pp. 1–20). Lanham, MD: American College Personnel Association.

Kuh, G. D., Kinzie, J., Buckley, J. A., Bridges, B. K., & Hayek, J. C. (2006). *What matters to student success: A review of literature.* A commissioned report for the National Symposium on Postsecondary Student Success: Spearheading a dialogue on student success. Washington, DC: National Center for Education Statistics.

Kuh, G. D., Kinzie, J., Schuh, J. H., Whitt, E. J., & Associates (2005). *Student success in college: Creating conditions that matter.* San Francisco: Jossey-Bass.

Kuh, G. D., & Love, P. G. (2000). A cultural perspective on student departure. In J. M. Braxton (Ed.), *Reworking the student departure puzzle* (pp. 196–212). Nashville, TN: Vanderbilt University Press.

Kuh, G. D., & MacKay, K. A. (1989). Beyond cultural awareness: Toward interactive pluralism. *Campus Activities Programming, 22*(4), 52–58.

Kuh, G. D., Schuh, J. H., Whitt, E. J., & Associates (1991). *Involving colleges: Successful approaches to fostering student learning and development outside the classroom.* San Francisco: Jossey-Bass.

Kuh, G. D., & Whitt, E. J. (1988). *The invisible tapestry: Culture in American colleges and universities.* ASHE-ERIC Higher Education Report Series, No. 1. Washington, DC: Association for the Study of Higher Education.

Ladson-Billings, G., & Tate, W. F. (1995). Toward a critical race theory. *Teachers College Record, 97*(1), 47–68.

Lewis, A. E., Chesler, M., & Forman, T. A. (2000). The impact of "colorblind" ideologies on students of color: Intergroup relations at a predominantly White university. *Journal of Negro Education, 69*(1/2), 74–91.

Love, P. G., Kuh, G. D., MacKay, K. A., & Hardy, C. M. (1993). Side by side: Faculty and student affairs cultures. In G. D. Kuh (Ed.), *Cultural perspectives in student affairs work* (pp. 59–80). Lanham, MD: University Press of America and American College Personnel Association.

Maldonado, D., Rhoads, R., & Buenavista, T. (2005). The Student-Initiated Retention Project: Theoretical contributions and the role of self-empowerment. *American Educational Research Journal, 42*(4), 605–638.

Manning, K. (1993). Properties of institutional culture. In G. D. Kuh (Ed.), *Cultural perspectives in student affairs work* (pp. 21–36). Lanham, MD: University Press of America and American College Personnel Association.

Manning, K., & Coleman-Boatwright, P. (1991). Student affairs initiatives toward a multicultural university. *Journal of College Student Development, 32,* 367–374.

McLaren, P. (1995). *Critical pedagogy and predatory culture: oppositional politics in a postmodern era.* London: Routledge.

Milem, J. F. (1994). College, students, and racial understanding. *Thought and Action, 9*(2), 51–92.

Murguía, E., Padilla, R. V., & Pavel, M. (1991). Ethnicity and the concept of social integration in Tinto's model of institutional departure. *Journal of College Student Development, 32*(5), 433–454.

Museus, S. D. (2007). Using qualitative methods to assess diverse institutional cultures. In S. R. Harper, & S. D. Museus (Eds.), *Using qualitative methods in institutional assessment* (New directions for institutional research, no. 136, pp. 29–40). San Francisco: Jossey-Bass.

Museus, S. D. (2008a). Focusing on institutional fabric: Using campus culture assessments to enhance cross-cultural engagement. In S. R. Harper (Ed.), *Creating inclusive environments for cross-cultural learning and engagement in higher education.* Washington, DC: National Association of Student Personnel Administrators.

Museus, S. D. (2008b). The model minority and the inferior minority myths: Inside stereotypes and their implications for student involvement. *About Campus, 13*(3), 2–8.

Museus, S. D. (2008c). The role of ethnic student organizations in fostering African American and Asian American students' cultural adjustment and membership at predominantly White institutions. *Journal of College Student Development, 49*(6), 568–586.

Museus, S. D. (2009). A critical analysis of the exclusion of Asian Americans from higher education research and discourse. In L. Zhan (Ed.), *Asian American voices: Engaging, empowering, enabling* (pp. 59–76). New York: NLN Press.

Museus, S. D. (2010). Delineating the ways that targeted support programs facilitate minority students' access to social networks and development of social capital in college. *Enrollment Management Journal, 4*(3), 10–41.

Museus, S. D. (2011). Generating Ethnic Minority Success (GEMS): A collective-cross case analysis of high-performing colleges. *Journal of Diversity in Higher Education.* Retrieved on May 25, 2011 from http://psycnet.apa.org/index.cfm?fa=buy.optionToBuy&id=2011-05316-001.

Museus, S. D. (in press). Using cultural perspectives to understand the role of ethnic student organizations in Black students' progress to the end of the pipeline. In D. H. Evensen & C. D. Pratt (Eds.), *The end of the pipeline: A journey of recognition for African Americans entering the legal profession.* Durham, NC: Carolina Academic Press.

Museus, S. D., & Harris, F. (2010). The elements of institutional culture and minority college student success. In T. E. Dancy II (Ed.), *Managing diversity: (Re)visioning equity on college campuses* (pp. 25–44). New York: Peter Lang Publishing.

Museus, S. D., & Liverman, D. (2010). Analyzing high-performing institutions: Implications for studying minority students in STEM. In S. R. Harper, C. Newman, & S. Gary (Eds.), *Students of color in STEM: Constructing a new research agenda* (New directions for institutional research, no. 148, 17–27). San Francisco: Jossey-Bass.

Museus, S. D., & Maramba, D. C. (2010). The impact of culture on Filipino American students' sense of belonging. *Review of Higher Education, 34*(2), 231–258.

Museus, S. D., & Neville, K. (in press). The role of institutional agents and social capital in the experiences of minority college students. Manuscript accepted for publication in the *Journal of College Student Development*.

Museus, S. D., Nichols, A. H., & Lambert, A. (2008). Racial differences in the effects of campus racial climate on degree completion: A structural model. *Review of Higher Education, 32*(1), 107–134.

Museus, S. D., & Palmer, R., Davis, R. J., & Maramba, D. C. (2011). *Racial and ethnic minority student success in STEM education*. ASHE-ERIC Monograph Series, 36(6). San Francisco: Jossey-Bass.

Museus, S. D., & Quaye, S. J. (2009). Toward an intercultural perspective of racial and ethnic minority college student persistence. *Review of Higher Education, 33*(1), 67–94.

Museus, S. D., & Ravello, J. N. (2010). Characteristics of academic advising that contribute to racial and ethnic minority student success at predominantly White institutions. *NACADA Journal, 30*(1), 47–58.

Museus, S. D., & Truong, K. A. (2009). Disaggregating qualitative data on Asian Americans in campus climate research and assessment. In S. D. Museus (Ed.), *Conducting research on Asian Americans in higher education* (New directions for institutional research, no. 142, pp. 17–26). San Francisco: Jossey-Bass.

National Academic of Education (2009). *Equity and excellence in American education*. Washington, DC: Author.

Nieto, S. (2004). *Affirming diversity: The sociopolitical context of multicultural education* (4th edn.) Boston: Pearson.

Nora, A., & Cabrera, A. (1996). The role of perceptions of prejudice and discrimination on the adjustment of minority students to college. *Journal of Higher Education, 67*, 119–148.

Pascarella, E., Bohr, L., Nora, A., & Terenzini, P. (1996). Is differential exposure to college linked to the development of critical thinking? *Research in Higher Education, 37*, 159–174.

Patton, L. (2006a). Black culture centers: Still central to student learning. *About Campus, 11*(2), 2–8.

Patton, L. (2006b). The voice of reason: A qualitative examination of Black student perceptions of their Black culture center. *Journal of College Student Development, 47*(6), 628–646

Peterson, M. W., & Spencer, M. G. (1990). Understanding academic culture and climate. In W. G. Tierney (Ed.), *Assessing academic climates and cultures* (New directions for institutional research, no. 68, 3–18). San Francisco: Jossey-Bass.

Rankin, S. R., & Reason, R. D. (2005). Differing perceptions: How students of color and White students perceive campus climate for underrepresented groups. *Journal of College Student Development, 46*(1), 43–61.

Rendón, L. I., Jalomo, R. E., & Nora, A. (2000). Theoretical considerations in the study of minority student retention in higher education. In J. Braxton (Ed.), *Reworking the student departure puzzle* (pp. 127–156). Nashville, TN: Vanderbilt University Press.

Rhoads, R., & Valdez, J. (1996). *Democracy, multiculturalism, and the community college: A critical perspective*. New York: Garland Publishing.

Sáenz, V. B., Ngai, H. N., & Hurtado, S. (2007). Factors influencing positive interactions across race for African American, Asian American, Latino, and White college students. *Research in Higher Education, 48*(1), 1–38.

Schein, E. H. (1992). *Organizational culture and leadership* (2nd edn.) San Francisco: Jossey-Bass.

Schultz, M., & Hatch, M. J. (1996). Living with multiple paradigms: The case of paradigm interplay in organizational culture studies. *Academy of Management Review, 21*(2), 529–557.

Sleeter, C. & Grant, C. (2003). *Making choices for multicultural education: Five approaches to race, class, and gender* (4th edn.). Hoboken, NJ: John Wiley and Sons.

Sleeter, S., & Grant, C. (2009). *Making choices for multicultural education: Five approaches to race, class and gender* (6th edn.). Hoboken, NJ: John Wiley & Sons.

Smedley, B. D., Myers, H. F., & Harrell, S. P. (1993). Minority-status stresses and the college adjustment of ethnic minority freshmen. *Journal of Higher Education, 64*(4), 434–452.

Strange, C. C., & Banning, J. H. (2001). *Educating by design: Creating campus learning environments that work.* San Francisco, CA: Jossey-Bass.

Strike, K. A. (1985). Is there a conflict between equity and excellence? *Educational Evaluation and Policy Analysis, 7*(4), 409–416.

Suzuki, B.H. (2002). Revisiting the model minority stereotype: Implications for student affairs practice and higher education. *Working with Asian American college students* (New directions for student services, no. 97, pp. 21–32). San Francisco: Jossey-Bass.

Tierney, W. G. (1988). Organizational culture in higher education. *Journal of Higher Education, 59*, 2–21.

Tierney, W. G. (1992). Cultural leadership and the search for community. *Liberal Education, 78*, 16–21.

Tierney, W. G. (1993). *Building communities of difference: Higher education in the twenty-first century.* Westport, CT: Bergin and Garvey.

Tierney, W. G. (1999). Models of minority college-going and retention: Cultural integrity versus cultural suicide. *Journal of Negro Education, 68*(1), 80–91.

Tinto, V. (1998). College as communities: Taking the research on student persistence seriously. *Review of Higher Education, 21*, 167–178.

Valverde, L. A. (1998). Future strategies and actions: Creating multicultural higher education campuses. In L. A. Valverde & L. A. Castenell, Jr. (Eds.), *The multicultural higher campus: Strategies for transforming higher education* (pp. 19–29). London: Sage.

Whitt, E. J. (1993). Making the familiar strange: Discovering culture. In G. D. Kuh (Ed.), *Cultural perspectives in student affairs work* (pp. 81–94). Lanham, MD: University Press of America and American College Personnel Association.

Whitt, E. J. (1996). Assessing student cultures. In M. L. Upcraft and J. H. Schuh (Eds.), *Assessment in student affairs: A guide for practitioners.* San Francisco: Jossey-Bass.

2

THE CAMPUS RACIAL CULTURE

A Critical Race Counterstory

Samuel D. Museus, Joanna N. Ravello, and Blanca E. Vega

At an institution that we call Research University, the Department of Modern Languages has a tradition of posting national flags that correspond with each one of the languages that they teach on a wall. In 2008, when the department began offering a course in Vietnamese, it decided to post the Vietnamese national flag on its wall. The Việt Minh national flag is red with a large five-pointed yellow star in the center, and was officially adopted by North Vietnam in the mid-twentieth century. Until the fall of Saigon and the end of the Vietnam War in 1975, South Vietnam had used a very different flag, which displayed three horizontal red stripes on a yellow background. Thus, for many South Vietnamese Americans who lived in the surrounding communities and some students who attended Research University, the Việt Minh flag was an offensive symbol – an artifact that suggested that the institution supported North Vietnamese communist ideologies and made the campus less welcoming for those who opposed such ideologies. Following the posting of the flag, there was protest and conflict among students surrounding the flag controversy.

This opening story is true. It is also complex. Embedded within it are issues of perceived hostility in the climate because, as noted, some individuals in the community and the institution felt that the flag was symbolic of communism. Also, given the fact that many Vietnamese American refugees fled their country after the Vietnam War ended because they were being persecuted by the communist regime that won the conflict (Hsu, Davies, & Hansen, 2004), many probably associated the flag with oppression.

Also embedded in this story, however, are complex issues of cultural conflict. The department's culture perpetuated a tradition of posting flags that symbolized the diversity of their department and the breadth of their curricular offerings. The department, however, did not fully understand that the Việt Minh flag would embody an entirely different meaning for some people on or around campus. Leaders in the department did not fully comprehend or appreciate the fact that the flag symbolized a long history and a set of values and beliefs that some of its own students deemed unwelcoming. We believe it is quite common for institutions and agents within them to act based on their own cultural values, beliefs, and assumptions, without fully understanding or taking into account the impact that such actions can have on students of color who come from cultures that are very different from those that predominate on their campuses.

In the remainder of this chapter, we underscore the importance of understanding the intersection between campus culture and race, as well as how they mutually shape the experiences of students of color. First, we review literature on campus racial climate, campus culture, and racial minority students in higher education. Then, we offer the concept of the campus racial culture, which can provide a framework for race-conscious examinations of the cultures of postsecondary institutions. Finally, using Critical Race Theory (CRT) – critical race counterstorytelling in particular – we illustrate how students of color can experience the campus racial culture of a predominantly White institution (PWI) and provide implications for institutional leaders who wish to better understand how the cultures of their campuses shape the experiences of the diverse student populations whom they serve.

Campus Climate and Culture Research

A plethora of research has analyzed the role of campus climate and culture in the experiences of college students in general and students of color in particular (Harper & Hurtado, 2007; Hurtado, Milem, Clayton-Pederson, & Allen, 1999; Museus & Harris, 2010; Pascarella & Terenzini, 2005; Strange & Banning, 2001). Although the two concepts are often conflated in higher education discourse, campus climate and culture differ in both meaning and the ways that they have been examined in educational research. Campus climate can be defined as the "*current* perceptions, attitudes, and expectations that define the institution and its members" (Bauer, 1998, p. 2), and it is often used to understand how people *feel* within a particular environment. Although climate can be used to understand how any identity group (e.g., low-income or lesbian, gay, bisexual, transgendered students) experiences the campus environment, it has most frequently been applied to understand the experiences of students of color, and, as a result, scholars have coined and defined the term *campus racial climate*, which has been referred to as "the overall racial environment" of an institution (Solórzano, Ceja, & Yosso, 2000, p. 62). Moreover, much of the existing literature that examines campus racial climates focuses on understanding how students of color experience racial prejudice and discrimination on their campuses, how welcoming racial and ethnic minority students perceive their campus environments to be, differences in White and racial minority students' perceptions of the environment, and students' interactions across racial lines (for thorough reviews of this research, see Chang, 2007; Harper & Hurtado, 2007).

The aforementioned body of research has been invaluable to advancing current levels of understanding regarding the experiences of students of color (e.g., Hurtado & Carter, 1997; Museus, Nichols, & Lambert, 2008; Nora & Cabrera, 1996). However, that research has been less effective at generating a complex understanding of how history and culture shape the experiences of those students. This is a crucial gap in the higher education literature because such contexts are important in efforts to understand how diverse populations experience college. Indeed, in addition to the psychological and behavioral dimensions of the campus climate, considering historical legacies and campus cultural context is critical (Hurtado, et al., 1999).

In addition, community cultural contexts – that is, the culture of racial and ethnic minority communities external to the institution – are also a critical element in understanding the experiences of students of color on campus. Not only can focusing on historical, campus cultural, and community cultural contexts help shift the perceived responsibility for success from diverse students to their institutions, but it can also prompt more in-depth examination and understanding of how campus cultures and students' cultural and racial backgrounds interact to shape the experiences of students of color. Such analyses can lead to better understandings of how educators can shape campus cultures so that they are more inclusive and supportive of students from diverse cultural and racial backgrounds. In the story at the opening of this chapter, for example, understanding how Vietnamese undergraduates perceived the racial environment on campus is important, but comprehending and appreciating the historical, campus cultural, and community cultural contexts that converged to create the conflict are equally necessary to understand how diverse groups make meaning of the symbolic flag and to prevent the flag conflict and improve the experience for all students on that campus.

Toward a Definition of Campus Racial Culture

Higher education scholars have long acknowledged the importance of the campus culture in understanding the experiences of students in higher education (Bauer, 1998; Kuh & Hall, 1993; Kuh, Kinzie, Schuh, Whitt, & Associates, 2005; Kuh & Love, 2000; Kuh & Whitt, 1988; Magolda, 2000, 2003; Manning, 2000; Manning & Colman-Boatwright, 1991; Museus, 2007, 2008c, 2011; Museus & Harris, 2010; Museus & Quaye, 2009). Kuh and Hall (1993) defined campus culture in the following way:

the collective, mutually shaping patterns of institutional history, mission, physical settings, norms, traditions, values, practices, beliefs, and assumptions that guide the behavior of individuals and groups in an institution of higher education which provide a frame of reference for interpreting the meanings of events and actions on and off campus. (p. 2)

This definition underscores the more tacit elements of a campus's culture (e.g., values, beliefs, assumptions, norms), as well as the artifacts and symbols (e.g., mission, physical setting, traditions) that embody those cultural elements in institutions of higher education. Those artifacts and symbols enable individuals to create and communicate knowledge about life (Geertz, 1973, p. 89). On a related note, as Kuh and Whitt (1988) explain, those symbols also provide students with tools to understand the college experience:

institutional culture helps students make meaning of various events and activities, teaches them some important information about what the institution stands for and how it works, and encourages them to perform in ways that will enable them to success academically and socially. (p. 25)

It is also important to note, however, that this description does not explain how different groups might perceive, make meaning of, and experience various components of a institution's culture in disparate ways. Also, the deracialized nature of this description is congruent with much of the work on culture, which has improved our understanding of college students' experiences in the campus context in general but is limited in its clarification of how different groups – such as various racial groups – experience particular elements of a campus culture in varied ways (e.g., Kuh & Whitt, 1988; Kuh & Hall, 1993; Kuh et al., 2005; Strange & Banning, 2001).

A few scholars have begun to expand our understanding of how cultural values, beliefs, assumptions, and artifacts within an institution might positively or negatively influence the experiences of students of color specifically (e.g., González, 2002; Guiffrida, 2006; Kuh & Love, 2000; Museus, 2007, 2008a, 2008b; Museus & Quaye, 2009; Rendón, Jalomo, & Nora, 2000). This body of literature, however, is relatively small and more scholarship in this area would greatly benefit institutional policymakers and practitioners as they contemplate ways to create environments that positively influence the experiences of all students. Indeed, as evident in the story at the beginning of this chapter, elements of campus culture, such as symbolic artifacts, can be perceived by and shape the experience of different groups in drastically disparate ways. As this example illustrates, such artifacts can create community or identity among one group (the modern languages department), while cultivating a hostile environment for another (the Vietnamese American Community). If educators hope to avoid such conflicts, they must understand how campus culture differentially impacts those groups.

This chapter emerged, in part, from our belief that higher education research needs to move beyond campus racial climate research to develop deeper understandings of how history, culture, and race jointly shape the experiences of students of color to advance current levels of understanding about and transform institutions to maximize the success of those students. As one step toward such deeper comprehension, we offer the concept of campus racial culture, define it, and illustrate how it can be used to gain a more in-depth understanding of the experiences of racial and ethnic minority college students.

Building on the work of several scholars who have written about culture, campus culture, race, and the role of race in higher education (e.g., Delgado & Stefancic, 2001; Hurtado et al., 1999; Kuh & Hall, 1993; Kuh & Whitt, 1988; Museus, 2007, 2011; Museus & Harris, 2010; Museus & Quaye, 2009; Peterson & Spencer, 1990; Rendón et al., 2000), we define the campus racial culture as the collective patterns of tacit values, beliefs, assumptions, and norms that evolve from an institution's history and are manifest in its mission, traditions, language, interactions, artifacts, physical structures, and other symbols, which differentially shape the experiences of various racial and ethnic groups and can function to oppress racial minority populations within a particular institution. Under this definition, different racial groups experience and make meaning of elements of the campus culture in disparate ways. The campus racial culture is disproportionately shaped over time by the racial majority at a given college or university and consequently is congruent with, engages, reflects, and validates the values of the culture from which the individuals from the racial majority come. At the same time, that culture is often less congruent with, engaging of, reflective of, and validating of the cultural backgrounds of racial and ethnic minority populations.

Two salient examples of an element of the campus racial culture that differentially shape the experiences of different racial groups are the model minority and inferior minority myths (Museus, 2008b). The racial stereotype that Asian Americans and Pacific Islanders (AAPIs) are all model minorities who achieve unparalleled and universal success might be harmless to some groups, while leading to institutions neglecting the needs of AAPIs (Museus, 2009; Museus & Kiang, 2009; Suzuki, 2002). Similarly, the racial stereotype that Black and Latino students are academically inferior may be harmless to other racial groups while having adverse effects on the confidence and academic performance of Black and Latino undergraduates (Steele, 1999).

Understanding the concept of the campus racial culture is crucial because faculty, administrators, and staff at many institutions throughout the country are disproportionately White and therefore must be conscious of the fact that students of color might perceive the same elements of their campus's cultures in ways that are very different from themselves. If the administrators in the opening scenario, for example, took the time to question how their actions would be perceived by students and communities of color, considered the potential consequences, and truly appreciated the diverse perspectives around this issue, they might have avoided the conflict that followed the posting of the flag by, for example, posting both Vietnamese flags – the Việt Minh flag and the flag that was associated with South Vietnam.

A Critical Race Theory Framework

In the remainder of this chapter, we utilize CRT to demonstrate how the concept of the campus racial culture can help excavate the experiences of students of color and generate a better understanding of their experiences navigating the cultures of a PWI. In doing so, we underscore how one component of CRT – counterstorytelling – can be used to excavate the voices of students of color and illuminate their perspective regarding various elements of the culture of a PWI, as well as how those perspectives might differ from those of faculty, administrators, and staff.

Critical Race Theory originated in the mid-1970s from the work of progressive educators, activists, and legal scholars who felt strongly that the Critical Legal Studies (CLS) movement was not doing enough to address issues of race and racism in U.S. jurisprudence (DeCuir & Dixson, 2004; Delgado & Stefancic, 2001). Scholars such as Derrick Bell, Robert Williams, Richard Delgado, Mari Matsuda, and others wanted to place race and racism at the center of social, political, and economic discourses, and they searched for and created critical spaces to examine how social constructions of race contributed to racial inequities in America (Delgado & Stefancic, 2001; Iverson, 2007; Yosso, Parker, Solórzano, & Lynn, 2004). According to Solórzano and Yosso (2002), there are five major CRT tenets used in educational research: (1) the intercentricity of race and racism with other forms of subordination, (2) the challenge to dominant ideology, (3) the commitment to social justice and social transformation, (4) the transdisciplinary perspective, and (5) the centrality of experiential knowledge through counterstorytelling (Buenavista, Jayakumar, & Misa-Escalante, 2009; Harper, Patton, & Wooden, 2009; Solórzano, Villalpando, & Oseguera, 2005; Solórzano & Yosso, 2001).

The first tenet of CRT is the intercentricity of race and racism with other forms of subordination. Critical Race Theorists argue that race and racism are an endemic, permanent aspect of American society (DeCuir & Dixson, 2004). Specifically, they assert that race has no basis in biological or genetic reality; instead, the dominant group creates, manipulates, or eliminates race to advance its ideological notions of superiority (Delgado & Stefancic, 2001). Moreover, CRT recognizes that race intersects with other forms of identity (e.g., gender, class, sexuality, language, culture, immigrant status, phenotype, accent, and surname) (Delgado & Stefancic, 2001; Solórzano & Yosso, 2001; Yosso, Smith, Ceja, & Solórzano, 2009). This is relevant to the current discussion because, as we highlight in the following sections, students' multiple identities – including race, ethnicity, gender, and socioeconomic status – shape the ways that they experience the campus cultures of PWIs.

The second tenet of CRT is the challenge to dominant ideology. Critical Race Theory challenges the historical record of research, policy, and practice (Cobham & Parker, 2007; Villalpando, 2004). A premise of CRT is that majoritarian conceptualizations of historical events are inaccurate and contribute to majoritarian ideologies (Howard-Hamilton, 2003; Morfin, Perez, Parker, Lynn, & Arrona, 2006). Theorists counter majoritarian interpretations with reinterpretations aligned with the lived experiences of communities of color (Harper et al., 2009). Critical Race Theorists argue that racism materially benefits White elites and psychically benefits White working-class people, who have little incentive to see it dismantled (Delgado & Stefancic, 2001). This tenet makes CRT useful because campus cultures consist of the values, beliefs, assumptions, and stories of the dominant majority. Thus, CRT can be used to call those cultural elements into question.

The third tenet of CRT is the commitment to social justice and social transformation. Proponents have a strong commitment to equalizing the playing field and eliminating all forms of oppression (Howard-Hamilton, 2003; Morfin, Perez, Parker, Lynn, & Arrona, 2006; Solórzano et al., 2005). They stand against overt forms of racism and racial microagressions. Racial microaggressions are the more subtle insults experienced by people of color (e.g., verbal, nonverbal, and visual) (Harper et al., 2009; Sue, Bucceri, Lin, Nadal, & Torino, 2007; Yosso et al., 2009). Theorists work to expose and eliminate these subtle, insidious forms of racism within higher education, which have a number of negative outcomes for students of color (Sue et al., 2007). Applying this tenet to the campus racial culture, it can be argued that campus racial cultures can function to oppress students of color at PWIs, and CRT can be utilized to understand campus racial cultures and how to transform them so that they are more reflective of the diverse home ethnic communities and corresponding cultures from which students come.

The fourth tenet of CRT is the transdisciplinary perspective. Critical Race Theory incorporates multiple intellectual traditions and forms of scholarship, including ethnic studies, women's studies, sociology, history, critical legal studies, Marxist and neo-Marxist perspectives, and internal colonial traditions (Delgado & Stefancic, 2001). Using multiple methodological and epistemological approaches, Critical Race Scholarship challenges the ahistorical, undisciplinary focus of many analyses on race and racism and transcends disciplinary boundaries to analyze historical and contemporary views of race and racism (Howard-Hamilton, 2003; Morfin, Perez, Parker, Lynn, & Arrona, 2006; Solórzano et al., 2005; Solórzano & Yosso, 2001; Yosso et al., 2009). As demonstrated by the opening vignette, historical context illuminates how diverse groups perceive and interpret elements of the campus racial culture differently.

The fifth tenet of CRT is the centrality of experiential knowledge. Critical Race Theory recognizes and legitimizes the lived experiences of people of color as key to understanding, analyzing, and exposing racial subjugation (Harper et al., 2009; Howard-Hamilton, 2003; Solórzano & Yosso, 2001). In higher education, Critical Race Theorists highlight the importance of the perspectives of students of color (Solórzano et al., 2005; Solórzano & Yosso, 2001). Critical Race Methodology takes on a variety of forms including storytelling, family histories, proverbs, biographies, scenarios, parables, testimonies, chronicles, and narratives (Harper et al., 2009; Morfin, Perez, Parker, Lynn, & Arrona, 2006; Villalpando, 2004; Yosso et al., 2009). In the following sections, we offer a detailed discussion and example of the role of storytelling – and more specifically counterstorytelling – in understanding the campus racial culture at PWIs.

Critical Race Counterstorytelling

Love (2004) argues that the United States has historically denied people of color the language or means to express their injuries from experienced oppression. Counterstories can be used to respond to this denial of voice and oppression. Counterstories serve several purposes. First, counterstorytelling can be used in research and discourse to highlight the role of race and racism on multiple levels: individual, system, institutional, and societal (Love, 2004). Second, counterstories expose, analyze, and challenge the dominant stories and discourse that reinforce privilege and power that have historically been denied to marginalized groups (DeCuir & Dixson, 2004; Love, 2004; Solórzano & Yosso, 2001, 2002). Third, counterstories aim to build a community among marginalized groups and strengthen the social, political, and cultural survival and resistance traditions of people of color (Solórzano & Yosso, 2001, 2002). Finally, counterstories can put a human face on educational theory and practice.

Many communities of color have had a rich and continuing tradition of counterstorytelling to share experiences that are essential to their survival and liberation (Delgado, 1989). Communities of color have had different histories and experiences with oppression and members of these communities can share their counterstories with Whites to bring those stories to the awareness of the majority (Delgado & Stefancic, 2001). In higher education, counterstorytelling enables students of color to produce their own narratives that have historically been manipulated by the dominant discourses at PWIs (Howard-Hamilton, 2003). These powerful narratives can help teach others the importance of combining the story and the current reality into a constructed new world (Solórzano & Yosso, 2001).

Methods for counterstorytelling include personal stories or narratives, other people's stories or narratives, and composite stories or narratives (DeCuir & Dixson, 2004; Solórzano & Yosso, 2001). Personal counterstories or counternarratives recount a student's individual experiences with subjugation. These stories are often autobiographical accounts of students' encounters with racism, sexism, and classism. Writers may juxtapose these lived experiences with a critical race analysis of a particular case within the larger sociopolitical context (Solórzano & Yosso, 2001). Other people's counterstories or counternarratives recount another person's narrative describing their experiences with various forms of oppression. Told in the third voice, these stories offer biographical analyses of the lived experiences of students of color with U.S. institutions in the sociohistorical context (Solórzano & Yosso, 2001). Composite counterstories or counternarratives use various forms of data that shed light on the racial, sexual, and class oppression of people of color. In these narratives, several data elements can be combined to create composite characters and pose them in social, historical, and political situations to examine multiple forms of subjugation (Solórzano & Yosso, 2001).

In the remainder of this section, we primarily build on the work of Delgado (1989) and Solórzano and Yosso (2001) to demonstrate the utility of counterstorytelling in efforts to help illuminate how educators' and students' experiences in the campus racial culture can differ, how the campus racial culture can function to exclude and oppress students of color, and how the campus racial culture can hinder educators' abilities to meet the needs of their racial and ethnic minority students. In constructing our stories, researchers draw from multiple sources, including (1) interview data gathered from over 90 students of color across 10 PWIs, (2) extant research on campus culture, and (3) our personal and professional experiences.

In analyzing the data, we used a three-step process (Solórzano & Yosso, 2001). First, we reviewed the transcripts from our interviews with racial and ethnic minority college students, which served as our primary source of data, to identify examples of the ideas that we sought to convey – experiences navigating the culture of a PWI. Second, we reviewed literature on campus culture and CRT, drawing connections between the data from our interviewees of color and the literature. We listened both to our racial and ethnic minority interview participants' voices and the minority researchers and participants' voices in extant literature. Also, we added our own personal and professional experience to provide context and make meaning of the experiences of these individuals. Third, we created composite characters to help us tell a story that illuminates some of the key concepts that emerged from our data sources. We acknowledge that some readers may find these methods unconventional. However, although the characters in the story are contrived, the events that take place in it are real – drawn from the voices of our interview participants, the literature, and our own experiences. Thus, we ask them to suspend judgment, be open to considering the utility of counterstorytelling for understanding the experiences of students of color, and listen to the voices that are engaged in the two conversations within the story. After the story is told, we discuss the utility of the story in understanding the salience of the campus racial culture in the experiences of students of color.

The Dominant Story and the Counterstory

We present two conversations. The first conversation is a discussion between Provost Shirley Stone and Professor Terry Jones. Provost Stone is a White female Provost of a prestigious public university on the East Coast and Professor Jones is a mixed-race Black/Native American male Assistant Professor of sociology in the College of Liberal Arts at the same university. Through this conversation, we are exposed to the dominant story. The second conversation is between Linda Tran and Celina Gomez. Linda is a first-year multiracial White/Vietnamese American female undergraduate in the College of Liberal Arts and Celina is Linda's peer and a fourth-year Latina student in the same college. These two students' conversation presents the counterstory. The first conversation takes place in the Provost's office, where she is discussing the rejection of a recent proposal for a new Ethnic Studies Program with Professor Jones.

Provost Stone: Given how tough things are economically right now, the university just didn't see approving a new Ethnic Studies Program as feasible.

Professor Jones: Don't you think the students who have been advocating for the program have a good point, though – that they want to have courses that address the social issues and inequities that they find important to them?

Provost Stone: Well, diversity is a key component of our mission. We already have courses throughout the curriculum that address diversity issues related to race, class, and gender. So the issues important to minority students are addressed in those courses and they can take as many of them as they would like.

Professor Jones: What about the view that an Ethnic Studies program would create community among faculty and students of color?

Provost Stone: I'm not sure how relevant that really is. Over half of our students are commuters. They don't really come here looking for community on campus.

Professor Jones: Well, some students have expressed that they would like courses that focus on the needs of their specific ethnic communities. Don't you think that is valid, since we are a public institution and are supposed to serve the public?

Provost Stone: Yes, it's true that we are supposed to serve the public, but honestly, sometimes I think we are too focused on local communities. Higher education is supposed to be about getting students to step outside of their comfort zones and learning about other communities and about the world. Our work is about teaching students to become global citizens.

In this first conversation, Provost Stone's perspective represents the dominant or stock story, filled with values, beliefs, and assumptions held by the majority at the institution. The story picks, chooses, and emphasizes the values, beliefs, and assumptions that support the resistance to Ethnic Studies, while failing to consider the potential positive benefits that such a program could bring to the campus. The Provost and institution, for example, emphasize the institutional value of diversity and the incorporation of diversity throughout the curricula, but do not question whether her conceptualization of diversity might be different from others. To the Provost and institution, it appears that the courses that cover race, class, and gender issues are symbolic of a genuine commitment to diversity, but no one brings up the fact that these might be token symbols of an espoused, but not enacted, institutional value. The Provost and the institution makes assumptions about whether students would want or benefit from a community on campus, without critically questioning whether those assumptions are biased. She imposes her belief about what constitutes a valid purpose of higher education and never asks if valuing knowledge of identity and local communities is mutually exclusive or contradictory to teaching college students to be global citizens.

Most important is the seeming neutrality of the Provost and institution's dominant story. Throughout the dialogue, the Provost's dominant narrative is presented as if it is race-neutral – it is presented as if it conveys the best interests of the institution and all of its members. The implication is that the cultural values, beliefs, and assumptions that are espoused by the Provost and the institution represent all members of that university, regardless of their racial or ethnic backgrounds. The dominant story avoids calling the actions or integrity of the institution into question, and it avoids blaming the institution for neglecting and failing to respect and meet the needs of undergraduates of color on its campus.

The second conversation takes place in the lounge of the campus's student union between Linda and her friend Celina. Linda was one of the student advocates for the Ethnic Studies Program and is disappointed in the negative outcome.

Linda: I feel like this university is racist.
Celina: Why do you say that?
Linda: Well, they are always saying that they value diversity, but it's all talk. I looked through the entire course catalog and I can't even find one course that explicitly covers Asian American *or* multiracial history

or issues. We have courses that talk about diversity, but everything is presented as Black and White. Don't get me wrong, those issues are important too and all.

[Celina nods in affirmation.]

Celina: I know exactly what you mean. On the East Coast, Latino issues are always overlooked too. It's almost like we don't even exist sometimes.

Linda: Do you know that, one time, I asked my American literature professor why there were not any Asian American authors included in the course and he actually said, "That's what Asian Studies courses are for." He didn't even know that there was a difference between Asian *American* and Asian! That's why I was so hoping that we could establish an Ethnic Studies Program here – because we are excluded from the curriculum. I went to take an Ethnic Studies course at another university last fall, and it was so eye-opening. It made me realize how deprived I have been. I finally had a chance to learn about Asians in America. I finally had a chance to learn about *my* history, *my* community, *my* family, *my* identity, and myself and my place in the world.

Celina: Yeah. Sometimes it doesn't seem like we have come very far from the days when public educational institutions were designed to force Native Americans to forget their culture and assimilate.

Linda: Exactly. I really connected and felt a sense of community with people in that Ethnic Studies course too – unlike any of my courses here. I mean, I wasn't looking for one, but when I found that community, it was a great experience. It felt like I had a second family in college.

Celina: I hear you. The Ethnic Studies Program that we had in my high school served a similar purpose for me back then. I'm not even sure if I would have graduated high school if it weren't for that program. Anyway, it's great that you found that community. I think that's a minority thing. I mean, everybody wants some kind of community, but I think it's even more critical for us to feel like we belong here.

Linda: And, we actually talked about Vietnamese communities in that course. But here, this is supposed to be a *public* institution, but it doesn't serve our communities. The Vietnamese community that I come from is very underresourced and has all kinds of educational, economic, and health disparities that need to be addressed. But, when they talk about social inequities and problems here, they never talk about our community, even though it's just 10 minutes away from campus.

Celina: So, what are you going to do now?

Linda: Fight. We have to keep fighting for the Program so that future students here have the opportunity to be represented in the curriculum.

This second conversation – the counterstory – is obviously very different than the dominant story told by the Provost and espoused by the institution.

Linda's perspective underscores the ways that racial and cultural bias permeates the campus racial culture. Her story also highlights how various elements of the campus racial culture can be perceived by and influence the experience of various groups differentially. Whereas the Provost underscores the diversity values embedded in the campus's mission, Linda does not perceive it as an authentic and enacted value of the institution. In fact, at one point, she calls the university "racist."

Whereas the provost is quick to point out the diversity embedded in the curricula of the university, Linda and the Vietnamese American communities from which she comes are not represented in the courses offered by the institution. Linda uses a key cultural artifact of the campus – the course catalog – to highlight how Asian Americans and multiracials are excluded from the institution's curricular offerings. She talks about a professor who makes an assumption that Asian American literature is not a part of American literature – another cultural assumption that functions to exclude certain groups from the curricula.

The Provost also uses her and the university's belief about global citizenship being a primary purpose of higher education as a tool to diminish the importance of incorporating the backgrounds and communities of particular racial and ethnic minority groups into the curricula of the university. Alternatively, Linda explains how the Ethnic Studies course that she took at another institution engaged her racial and cultural background and community, gave her space to learn about her Vietnamese American community and her own identity, and allowed her to develop a better understanding of her place in the world – thereby enhancing, rather than diminishing, her development as a global citizen.

In sum, the counterstory told by Linda highlights the salience of the campus racial culture and how it can be perceived by and influence the experiences of various racial and ethnic groups differentially. When juxtaposed with Linda's story, the neutrally framed dominant story of the institution appears one-sided and culturally biased. Rather than representing all members of the campus, it represents the people in power at the institution and neglects the needs and desires of particular racial and ethnic minority groups at the university.

Implications for Institutional Policy and Practice

In this chapter, we highlight the intersection between campus culture and race in higher education. We also demonstrate the utility of critical race counterstorytelling in illuminating and understanding the campus racial culture. We conclude by offering a set of recommendations for institutional leaders who are interested in understanding how the cultures of their respective campuses shape the experiences of racially diverse student populations.

Assess and Understand the Campus Racial Culture

First and foremost, institutional leaders must commit to making continuous efforts to understand the campus racial culture. This continuous commitment is critical, given the often taken-for-granted nature of campus racial cultures. Embracing such a commitment is not easy. It means that college and university leaders must question their own dominant narratives, which may have historically guided their understandings and actions with regard to delivering education. It means that postsecondary educators must take time to question whether the values, beliefs, and assumptions that drive thought and behavior across their institutions might inadvertently function to oppress racial and ethnic minority student populations.

If institutional leaders wish to fully understand the culture of their campus – or, in this case, the campus racial culture – they can either view their cultures as an outsider or conduct a systematic assessment of the cultures of their campus (Whitt, 1993). However, it has been argued that both understanding campus cultures from an external perspective and conducting systematic assessments of those cultures are important (Museus, 2007). Indeed, because elements of an institution's culture are often taken for granted, they can be invisible to insiders, and both external perspectives and systematic inquiry are important components to developing an accurate understanding of the cultures that exist on a particular campus – especially the deeply embedded assumptions that shape perspectives and daily behavior at those institutions.

Think Critically about Key Elements of the Campus Culture

Even when institutional leaders identify a particular element of their campus's racial culture that is conducive to the success of diverse populations, they could be misinterpreting that cultural element. Case in point: the value of diversity might be espoused by an institution to foster success among diverse student populations, but instead have a negative influence on the experiences of students of color by fueling assumptions that the institution is sufficiently responding to the diversity of its student body even though students of color on that campus feel neglected. Indeed, through the counterstory above, we demonstrate how institutional leaders can perceive the diversity values of their respective institutions as authentic, whereas racial and ethnic minority students see it as misleading.

Thus, college and university leaders must be able to think critically about the most salient elements of their campus's culture and be sensitive to the different ways that diverse groups within the institution can perceive those elements of the culture. It is important to note that fragmenting the elements of a campus's culture for the purpose of analysis can prevent institutional leaders from seeing that culture in a holistic way (Whitt, 1996). Nevertheless, understanding specific elements of an institution's culture, as well as the way they shape the experiences of various racial and ethnic groups in different ways, is critical.

Provide Space and Opportunities for Sharing and Analyzing Counternarratives

The discussion above highlights the valuable insights that can result from listening to stories and perspectives that differ from those of the dominant majority. Unfortunately, however, giving due attention to counterstories is an insufficiently utilized practice at postsecondary institutions. College educators should provide safe spaces for faculty and students – especially those from marginalized groups – to share their stories and voice their concerns. This could, for example, manifest in the form of town hall forums during which people from marginalized racial and ethnic groups can volunteer their perspectives.

Institutional leaders can provide opportunities for students from marginalized racial and ethnic groups to share their stories in other venues related to important institutional decision-making as well. They can, for example, include students of color on strategic planning committees, faculty and staff hiring committees, or curriculum committees. If those in power are truly open to valuing students' opinions and listen to the voices of marginalized groups, then they can have a powerful impact on their institutions and the cultures within them.

References

Bauer, K. (Ed.). (1998). *Campus climate: Understanding the critical components of today's colleges and universities* (New directions for institutional research, no. 98). San Francisco: Jossey-Bass.

Buenavista, T., Jayakumar, U., & Misa-Escalante, K. (2009). Contextualizing Asian American education through critical race theory: An example of U.S. Pilipino college student experiences. In S. D. Museus (Ed.), *Conducting research on Asian Americans in higher education* (New directions for institutional research, no. 142, pp. 69–81). San Francisco: Jossey-Bass.

Chang, M. J. (2007). Beyond artificial integration: Reimagining cross-racial interactions among undergraduates. In S. R. Harper & L. D. Patton (Eds.), *Responding to the realities of race on campus* (New directions for student services, no. 120, pp. 25–37). San Francisco: Jossey-Bass.

Cobham, B. A., & Parker, T. L. (2007). Resituating race into the movement toward multiculturalism and social justice. In S. R. Harper & L. Patton (Eds.), *Responding to the realities of race on campus* (New directions for student services, no. 120, pp. 85–93). San Francisco: Jossey-Bass.

DeCuir, J. T., & Dixson, A. D. (2004). "So when it comes out, they aren't that surprised that it is there": Using critical race theory as a tool of analysis of race and racism in education. *Educational Researcher, 33*(5), 26–31

Delgado, R. (1989). Storytelling for oppositionists and others: A plea for narrative. *Michigan Law Review, 87*, 2411–2441.

Delgado, R., & Stefancic, J. (2001). *Critical Race Theory: An introduction*. New York: New York University Press.

Geertz, C. (1973). *The interpretation of cultures*. New York: Basic Books.

González, K. P. (2003). Campus culture and the experiences of Chicano students in a predominantly White university. *Urban Education, 37*(2), 193–218.

Guiffrida, D. A. (2006). Toward a cultural advancement of Tinto's theory. *Review of Higher Education, 29*(4), 451–472.

Harper, S. R., & Hurtado, S. (2007). Nine themes in campus racial climates and implications for institutional transformation. In S. R. Harper & L. D. Patton (Eds.), Responding to the realities of race on campus (New directions for student services, no. 120, 7–24). San Francisco: Jossey-Bass.

Harper, S., Patton, L., & Wooden, O. (2009). Access and equity for African American students in higher education: A critical race historical analysis of policy efforts. *Journal of Higher Education, 80*(4), 389–414.

Howard-Hamilton, M. (2003). Theoretical frameworks for African American women. In M. F. Howard-Hamilton (Ed.), *Meetings the needs of African American women* (New directions for student services, no. 104, pp. 19–27). San Francisco: Jossey-Bass.

Hsu, E., Davies, C., & Hansen, D. (2004) Understanding mental health needs of Southeast Asian refugees: Historical, cultural, and contextual challenges. *Clinical Psychology Review, 24*, 193–213.

Hurtado, S., & Carter, D. (1997). Effects of college transition and perceptions of the campus racial climate on Latina/o college students' sense of belonging. *Sociology of Education, 70*, 324–345.

Hurtado, S., Milem, J. F., Clayton-Pedersen, A. R., & Allen, W. R. (1999). *Enacting diverse learning environments: Improving the climate for racial/ethnic diversity in higher education*. ASHE ERIC Higher Education Report 26(8). San Francisco: Jossey-Bass.

Iverson, S. (2007). Camouflaging power and privilege: A critical race analysis of university diversity policies. *Educational Administration Quarterly, 43*(5), 586–611.

Kuh, G. D., & Hall, J. E. (1993). Using cultural perspectives in student affairs. In G. D. Kuh (Ed.), *Cultural perspectives in student affairs work* (pp. 1–20). Lanham, MD: American College Personnel Association.

Kuh, G. D., Kinzie, J., Schuh, J. H., Whitt, E. J., & Associates. (2005). *Student success in college: Creating conditions that matter*. San Francisco: Jossey-Bass.

Kuh, G. D., & Love, P. G. (2000). A cultural perspective on student departure. In J. M. Braxton (Ed.), *Reworking the student departure puzzle* (pp. 196–212). Nashville, TN: Vanderbilt University Press.

Kuh, G. D., & Whitt, E. J. (1988). *The invisible tapestry: Culture in American colleges and universities*. ASHE-ERIC Higher Education Report Series, 1. Washington, DC: Association for the Study of Higher Education.

Love, B. (2004). Brown plus 50 counter-storytelling: A critical race theory analysis of the "majoritarian achievement gap" story. *Equity & Excellence in Education, 37*(3), 227–246.

Magolda, P.M. (2000). The campus tour ritual: Ritual and community in higher education. *Anthropology and Education Quarterly, 31*(1), 24–46.

Magolda, P. M. (2003). Saying good-bye: An anthropological examination of a commencement ritual. *Journal of College Student Development, 44*(6), 779–796.

Manning, K. (2000). *Rituals, ceremonies, and cultural meaning in higher education.* Westport, CT: Greenwood.

Manning, K., & Coleman-Boatwright, P. (1991). Student affairs initiatives toward a multicultural university. *Journal of College Student Development, 32*, 367–374.

Morfin, O. J., Perez, V. H., Parker, L., Lynn, M., & Arrona, J. (2006). Hiding the politically obvious: A Critical Race Theory preview of diversity as racial neutrality in Higher Education. *Educational Policy, 20*(1), 249–270.

Museus, S. D. (2007). Using qualitative methods to assess diverse institutional cultures. In S. R. Harper & S. D. Museus (Eds.), *Using qualitative methods in institutional assessment* (New directions for institutional research, no. 136, pp. 29–40). San Francisco: Jossey-Bass.

Museus, S. D. (2008a). Focusing on institutional fabric: Using campus culture assessments to enhance cross-cultural engagement. In S. R. Harper (Ed.), *Creating inclusive environments for cross-cultural learning and engagement in higher education* (pp. 205–234). Washington, DC: National Association of Student Personnel Administrators.

Museus, S. D. (2008b). The model minority and the inferior minority myths: Inside stereotypes and their implications for student involvement. *About Campus, 13*(3), 2–8.

Museus, S. D. (2008c). The role of ethnic student organizations in fostering African American and Asian American students' cultural adjustment and membership at predominantly White institutions. *Journal of College Student Development, 49*(6), 568–586.

Museus, S. D. (2009). A critical analysis of the exclusion of Asian American from higher education research and discourse. In L. Zhan (Ed.), *Asian American voices: Engaging, empowering, enabling* (pp. 59–76). New York: NLN Press.

Museus, S. D. (2011). Generating Ethnic Minority Success (GEMS): A collective-cross case analysis of high-performing colleges. *Journal of Diversity in Higher Education.* Retrieved on May 25, 2011 from http://psycnet.apa.org/index.cfm?fa=buy. optionToBuy&id=2011-05316-001.

Museus, S. D., & Harris F. (2010). The elements of institutional culture and minority college student success. In T. E. Dancy II (Ed.), *Managing diversity: (Re)visioning equity on college campuses.* New York: Peter Lang Publishing.

Museus, S. D., & Kiang, P. N. (2009). The model minority myth and how it contributes to the invisible minority reality in higher education research. In S. D. Museus (Ed.), *Conducting research on Asian Americans in higher education* (New directions for institutional research, no. 142, pp. 5–15). San Francisco: Jossey-Bass.

Museus, S. D., Nichols, A. H., & Lambert, A. (2008). Racial differences in the effects of campus racial climate on degree completion: A structural model. *Review of Higher Education, 32*(1), 107–134.

Museus, S. D., & Quaye, S. J. (2009). Toward an intercultural perspective of racial and ethnic minority college student persistence. *Review of Higher Education, 33*(1), 67–94.

Nora, A., & Cabrera, A. (1996). The role of perceptions of prejudice and discrimination on the adjustment of minority students to college. *Journal of Higher Education, 67*, 119–148.

Pascarella, E. T., & Terenzini, P. T. (2005). *How college affects students: A third decade of research* (2nd edn.). San Francisco: Jossey-Bass.

Peterson, M. W., & Spencer, M. G. (1990). Understanding academic culture and climate. In W. G. Tierney (Ed.), *Assessing academic climates and cultures* (pp. 3–18). San Francisco: Jossey-Bass.

Rendón, L. I., Jalomo, R. E., & Nora, A. (2000). Theoretical considerations in the study of minority student retention in higher education. In J. Braxton (Ed.), *Reworking the student departure puzzle* (pp. 127–156). Nashville, TN: Vanderbilt University Press.

Solórzano, D. G, Ceja, M., & Yosso, T. (2000). Critical race theory, racial microaggressions, and campus racial climate: The experiences of African-American college students. *Journal of Negro Education, 69*(1), 60–73.

Solórzano, D. G., Villalpando, O., & Oseguera, L. (2005). Educational inequities and Latina/o undergraduate students in the United States: A critical race analysis of their educational progress. *Journal of Hispanic Higher Education, 4*(3), 272–294.

Solórzano, D., & Yosso, T. (2001). Critical race and LatCrit theory and method: Counter-storytelling. *International Journal of Qualitative Studies in Education (QSE), 14*(4), 471–495.

Solórzano, D., & Yosso, T. (2002). A critical race counterstory of race, racism, and affirmative action. *Equity & Excellence in Education, 35*(2), 155.

Steele, C. (1999). A threat in the air: How stereotypes shape intellectual identity and performance. *American Psychologist, 52*(6), 613–629.

Strange, C. C., & Banning, J. H. (2001). *Educating by design: Creating campus learning environments that work*. San Francisco, CA: Jossey-Bass.

Sue, D. W., Bucceri, J., Lin, A. I., Nadal, K. L., & Torino, G. C. (2007). Racial microaggressions and the Asian American experience. *Cultural Diversity and Ethnic Minority Psychology, 13*(1), 72–81.

Suzuki, B. H. (2002). Revisiting the model minority stereotype: Implications for student affairs practice and higher education. In M. K. McEwen, C. M. Kodama, A. Alvarez, S. Lee, & C. T. H. Liang (Eds.), *Working with Asian American college students* (New directions for student services, no. 97, pp. 21–32). San Francisco: Jossey-Bass.

Villalpando, O. (2004). Practical considerations of Critical Race Theory and Latino Critical Theory for Latino college students. *New Directions for Institutional Research, 105*, 41–50.

Whitt, E. J. (1993). Making the familiar strange. In G. D. Kuh (Ed.), *Cultural perspectives in student affairs work* (pp. 81–94). Lanham, MD: University Press of America and American College Personnel Association.

Whitt, E. J. (1996). Assessing student cultures. In M. L. Upcraft and J. H. Schuh (Eds.), *Assessment in student affairs: A guide for practitioners* (pp. 189–216). San Francisco: Jossey-Bass.

Yosso, T., Parker, L., Solórzano, D., & Lynn, M. (2004). From Jim Crow to affirmative action and back again: A critical race discussion of racialized rationales and access to higher education. *Review of Research in Education, 28*, 1–25.

Yosso, T., Smith, W., Ceja, M., & Solórzano, D. (2009). Critical race theory, racial microaggressions, and campus racial climate for Latina/o undergraduates. *Harvard Educational Review, 79*(4), 659–690.

3

CREATING A CULTURE OF INQUIRY AROUND EQUITY AND STUDENT SUCCESS

Keith A. Witham and Estela Mara Bensimon

Public postsecondary institutions increasingly find themselves balancing two major sources of external pressure: severe budget constraints at the state level, and a national political climate fixated on accountability, productivity, and increases in college attainment rates. This means institutions not only have to do more with less, but must also demonstrate success within the framework of accountability systems – such as performance funding formulae and other productivity initiatives – that may or may not acknowledge equity among racial and ethnic groups as a primary indicator of success (Bensimon, Rueda, Dowd, & Harris, 2007; Dowd, 2003; Dowd & Tong, 2007). In responding to these external pressures, institutions' cultures become critically important. Those cultures reveal what is most important to the campus community and they provide direction to the strategies that institutions adopt in response to those external pressures (Bergquist & Pawlak, 2008; Dill, 1982; Sporn, 1996; Tierney, 1988).

In this chapter, we argue that institutions can respond to external pressures for accountability and maintain a commitment to equity in outcomes for students of color by fostering a *culture of inquiry*. We prefer the term *culture of inquiry* to *culture of evidence* because the term *evidence* does not fully convey that it is people – not data by themselves – that engage in the social transformation of data into evidence of a particular situation or condition that signals an organizational failure or success. We think it is important to distinguish between a "culture of inquiry" and a "culture of evidence" because the national campaign for a "culture of evidence" promotes data, metrics, and data systems as if they were self-acting (Alford, 1998). Instead, we believe that evidence is shaped by the questions that are asked by individuals who are themselves embedded in institutional, policy, and state cultures, and those cultures in turn are composed of particular assumptions, beliefs, interests, and values that can be informed by evidence and inquiry (Dowd, Bishop, Bensimon, & Witham, in press).

A "culture of inquiry," as we define it, (1) reflects the unique culture of academic institutions by involving faculty and campus practitioners in iterative processes of inquiry, (2) uses data as a jumping-off point for intentional and critical analysis of equity in outcomes, (3) fosters reflection on practices and a process of practitioner self-change, and (4) shifts focus to institutional responsibility, rather than student deficits, when devising solutions. Like other authors in this volume, we define culture more broadly as:

> the collective, mutually shaping patterns of institutional history, mission, physical settings, norms, traditions, values, practices, beliefs, and assumptions that guide the behavior of individuals and groups in an institution of higher education which provide a frame of reference for interpreting the meanings of events and actions on and off campus. (Kuh & Hall, 1993, p. 2)

We extend this definition, however, to reflect Neumann's (1995) understanding of culture as having, "a prominent temporal quality, capturing patterns of knowing (i.e., cognition) constructed over time within a social setting" (p. 253). With this emphasis on socially mediated patterns of constructed cognition, a culture of inquiry is thus a way of describing both organizational learning over time and the elements of organizational culture – artifacts, histories, values, and assumptions (Kuh & Hall, 1993; Schein, 1985) – that inform how individuals within institutions learn about, change, and take responsibility for practices and policies impacting student success.

This chapter begins by suggesting that theories of single- and double-loop learning within organizations (Argyris, 1990, 1993; Argyris & Schön, 1996; Bensimon, 2005), cultural-historical activity theory (Bustillos, Rueda, & Bensimon, 2011; Cole & Engeström, 1993; Cole & Griffin, 1983; Engeström, 1987, 2000, 2001), and participatory action research (Kemmis & McTaggart, 2000) help elucidate the process of building and sustaining an effective culture of inquiry within academic institutions, as well as what the key elements of such a culture might be. We then use these theoretical frameworks to draw a connection between individual actions and the type of organizational learning that characterizes the culture of inquiry. We argue that this emphasis on learning and collective inquiry transcends conventional notions of a culture of evidence as a set of functionalist, "data-driven" practices, in favor of culture as a context for critical meaning-making with an eye toward problematizing the role of structures, policies, and practices in the production of racial inequities in educational outcomes. Finally, we use examples from the Center for Urban Education's (CUE) work that is focused on developing equity-directed data practices within institutions and systems to illustrate one approach to building a culture of inquiry, and we reiterate the key elements of such a culture suggested by the literature and CUE's work with practitioners.

Double-Loop Learning in the Academy

Scenario 1: Confronted with low overall graduation rates, academic leaders in one large state postsecondary system decided to target and address low completion rates in gateway courses for academic majors by changing the processes for imposing prerequisites. Driving this response is the idea that students are failing gateway courses because they lack adequate academic preparation, so additional prerequisite requirements would require students to be more prepared and boost completion rates in these critical early courses and improve graduation rates overall. Without first questioning the institutions' practices for engaging and supporting students in these courses, and without examining differential rates of success in the courses by students of different racial and ethnic groups, however, the new policy risks categorically excluding certain groups of students while doing nothing to address the pedagogic and policy practices that lie at the roots of the low success rates.

Scenario 2: Another large state system acknowledges its low graduation rates and decides to focus on how transfer rates between its 2- and 4-year institutions impact overall system completion rates. The system leadership undertakes a process of system-wide inquiry into its practices and policies, and it examines data on student transfer disaggregated by race and ethnicity. The system's audit reveals that numerous existing practices, such as erroneous course equivalency guidance and admission deadlines that penalize students who do not receive timely advising and guidance, function as significant barriers to transfer. The inquiry also finds that transfer rates differ substantially by race and ethnicity and that, controlling for academic preparation, Latino, African American, and American Indian students who aspire to transfer are significantly less likely to do so than White students. The system leaders respond by convening campus leaders to share in the discussions of the values, histories, and practices informing their respective institutions' approach to transfer admissions. Through this process of inquiry, the system discovers that some 2-year campuses do not have strong transfer support policies in place because of their historical focus on vocational programs. Bringing this history to the surface reveals a contradiction between the values espoused by the system leaders and the policy histories of the campuses. These discussions ultimately result in revisions to practices and policies that improve the ease of transfer between campuses and additional outreach by 4-year institutions to recruit at 2-year campuses with low transfer rates and high concentrations of students of color.

The two narratives above describe real scenarios illustrating some key differences in the way institutional and system leaders diagnose and respond to a crisis of low graduation rates. In the first scenario, administrators identified a problem and implemented a policy to correct it without trying to understand the underlying reasons for the problem and without questioning the assumptions and values at work in the institution that contribute to the problem. Argyris (1990, 1993) and Argyris and Schön (1996) refer to this type of organizational response as "single-loop learning," which they define as "instrumental learning that changes strategies of action or assumptions underlying strategies in ways that leave the values of a theory of action unchanged" (Argyris & Schön, 1996, p. 20). The term *single loop* refers to the process of acquiring feedback and responding to a problem in order to change outcomes through a functional "fix" that does not question the underlying principles that created the problem in the first place. In other words, the organizational learning that takes place is instrumental in nature; it is learning focused on problem-*solving* rather than problem-*questioning* or interrogation of the value systems in which the process or problem is embedded. In the first scenario above, then, without inquiring into the underlying causes of the low completion rates, the problem-solving policy solution implemented may change outcomes, but may do so with significant negative consequences, including erecting a new set of barriers to access and success for already marginalized students of color, first-generation students, and others who are disproportionately unlikely to meet the new prerequisite standards. Moreover, the response does not alter the institution's underlying values around equity in student outcomes and the ways in which those values are manifested in practices and policies surrounding gateway courses.

In the second scenario, administrators questioned the underlying causes of the observed low completion rates. Though they also targeted a specific intervention point, administrators looked at the institutional processes, policies, and values that supported or inhibited transfer before devising a solution. They also used data to get a more fine-grained understanding of the problem, thus empowering campuses to build more nuanced and sustainable interventions. Argyris (1990, 1993) and Argyris and Schön (1996) suggested that, by fostering cultures that reward this type of deliberate questioning of underlying values and causes, or "double-loop learning," the organization gains "the capacity to learn, especially around problems that are embarrassing and threatening" (Argyris, 1990, p. 95). The "double loop" of learning suggests that, beyond the initial problem-solving response (the single loop), the process of questioning underlying mechanisms and values in order to fundamentally change the structures that produced the initial outcomes provides an additional "loop" of learning. In academic institutions, therefore, a culture that supports "double-loop" learning is one that focuses on institutional values and practices, brings invisible issues (e.g., racial inequities) to the surface, and considers how conventional problem-solving approaches may themselves contribute to the problem (Bensimon, 2005; Bensimon et al., 2007). For example, the hundreds of compensatory education programs aimed at increasing access and success among underrepresented students are emblematic of the conventional single-loop learning approach. The purpose of compensatory programs is to assist underprepared or "at-risk" students to learn how to adapt and succeed in academic settings when the institutions' own cultural practices may be producing the inequities that they attempt to eliminate. We equate a culture that recognizes the permanence of racism and encourages inquiry into its own practices with a culture that nurtures and normalizes double-loop learning.

That academic institutions are likely to respond to external accountability pressures with instances of single-loop learning and quick fixes is not surprising. Indeed, accountability systems developed in the policymaking arena are typically not designed to elicit or reward deep inquiry or practitioner involvement (Bensimon et al., 2007; Dowd & Tong, 2007). Rather, metrics focused on efficiency and productivity tend to incentivize institutions to rely on "best practice" and compensatory responses – generalized fixes that have been demonstrated in evaluation research to yield positive outcomes in specific contexts that may or may not match the unique circumstances of individual institutions and almost certainly do not encourage inquiry into the deeply embedded practices that perpetuate racial and ethnic inequities (Bensimon et al., 2007; Dowd & Tong, 2007). Such single-loop learning responses may include the amassing of data without a clear audience, purpose, or process for making them actionable, or the type of top-down policy measures described in the first scenario above (Dowd, 2005; Dowd & Tong, 2007). Without involving practitioners and administrators in intentional processes of double-loop learning to address underlying institutional values and assumptions, "best practice" responses fall short of yielding sustainable changes in practice. In fact, large, expensive, and ambitious initiatives to implement "best practices" often find themselves in the embarrassing position of having to admit failure despite the investment of millions of dollars.

Moreover, the unique cultures of academic institutions themselves may serve as barriers to double-loop learning. In the second scenario above, racial inequities had to be made visible in order to create the conditions for effective response to them. Yet many practices in academic institutions, including admissions and the distribution of financial aid, are firmly anchored in "rationalized myths" that dominate the organizational culture and lead to formal structures and procedures that obfuscate such disparities (Birnbaum, 1988; Meyer & Rowan, 1977). The "myth of meritocracy," for example – that historical racism and stratification of opportunity are irrelevant when effort and ability define success – prevents colleges from addressing underlying inequities in race, ethnicity, and class (Alon & Tienda, 2007; Brint & Karabel, 1989). Harper and Hurtado (2007) found that the true racialized experiences of students of color on college campuses are often hidden or ignored by institutions' commitments to "diversity" and "multiculturalism" – concepts that celebrate difference without recognizing underlying inequities. Indeed, addressing racial inequities as issues of diversity in access or multiculturalism in campus climates preempts a deeper interrogation of underlying values and structures required for double-loop learning.

Moreover, when confronted with external accountability measures, these embedded rationales lead not only to solutions focused on student deficits – such as the prerequisite policy example discussed above – but also to organizational "defensive reasoning." In his work on the tensions of organizational change, Argyris (1990) suggested that individuals within organizations are inclined to react defensively when ingrained assumptions about the validity of processes are contradicted or challenged. In such cases, Argyris argued, individuals have "reach[ed] conclusions that they believe they have tested carefully yet they have not, because the way [the conclusions] have been framed makes them untestable" (Argyris, 1990, p. 10). In other words, practices and decision-making structures are deeply embedded in organizational cultures, making the assumptions and values underlying those structures difficult to question. Similarly, in the first scenario described above, changing the prerequisite policy to address success rates in gateway courses answers the question "what do we do about this bad outcome?" based on the premise that success rates are a function of student deficits to which institutional structures must respond. Framing the question in this way, however, does not allow the question of "what are we doing that might yield this bad outcome?" to emerge or be explored. The defensiveness around status quo patterns of response thus tends to "rationalize" and reify the myths and theories driving those practices, preventing meaningful change (Birnbaum, 1988).

Fostering a culture of inquiry thus requires surfacing rationalized myths by providing intentional processes and norms for inquiry. This process is complicated by the fact that academic institutions are home to a complex web of subcultures into which "evidence," as both new forms of cultural artifacts and new practices and values, must fit (Bensimon, 2005; Bensimon et al., 2007). Sporn (1996) identified several qualities of academic organizations that inform their unique cultures and make the alignment of external accountability measures and internal practices particularly difficult, including (1) the ambiguity of goals and standards for performance, (2) the value placed on autonomy and shared governance by faculty, and (3) the large variety of constituencies to whom universities must be accountable. In addition, because of shared governance and the high value that faculty place on autonomy, academic institutions are driven as much, or more, by the ideological norms of the profession than by bureaucratic rules (Austin, 1990; Birnbaum, 1988; Dill, 1982).

The power of disciplinary and professional values in determining organizational behavior leads Dill (1982) to conclude that, "The celebration of academic values such as honesty, sustained curiosity, the communication of knowledge, and continued intellectual growth should be necessary conditions for any vital academic culture" (p. 315). These values may in themselves be myths that require interrogation. Nonetheless, if we accept Dill's idealized rendering of the academic culture, academic organizations would thus seem ripe for the development of a culture of inquiry built around such values. Accountability systems that encourage single-loop learning policy measures, as well as responses that emerge from rationalized myths within institutions, like the example in the first scenario above, would logically seem to contradict and undermine academia's cultural strengths. Meaningful attempts to alter institutional practice based on evidence must therefore work to lower organizational defenses around dominant ideologies and rationalized myths in order to facilitate a culture in which double-loop learning responses are the norm.

Culture, History, and Contradictions: Opportunities for Learning

How do we go about creating a culture of inquiry compatible with the unique characteristics and ideals of academic culture? As previously mentioned, our definition of culture emphasizes Neumann's (1995) suggestion that culture represents shared patterns of knowing constructed over time. The reference to shared patterns of learning over time is a strategic emphasis that recognizes the strengths of the academic organization and attempts to leverage those ideals in developing a culture of inquiry around equity in academic outcomes for all students. Part of the strategy is, as Neumann's (1995) definition suggests, to recognize academic settings – in particular those settings in which decisions are made that impact student success and equity in outcomes, such as classrooms, admissions offices, faculty senate meetings, and the policy-setting domains of system academic affairs officers – as *cultural activity settings* (Engeström, 1987), a special term used by sociocultural theorists (Engeström, 1987; Engeström, Miettinen, & Punamäki, 1999; Tharp & Gallimore, 1988) to capture the "who, what, when, where, why, and how" of the routines that constitute everyday life (Bustillos, Rueda, & Bensimon, 2011). The specific components of an activity setting include subjects (participants), objects (the goals participants are trying to achieve), tools (the forms of mediation available in the setting, which can be symbolic, such as language or concepts, or more tangible, such as physical artifacts), community, rules, and division of labor. The community refers to the specific community formed by those participating in the setting, but also the connections to the various extended communities with which they are associated (Bustillos, Rueda, & Bensimon, 2011). Such settings become the site of growth – the petri dish, in a way – for nurturing a culture of inquiry.

Cultural-Historical Activity Theory

Cultural-historical activity theory (CHAT) is an evolution of Vygotsky's (1978) activity theory that takes the cultural activity setting as a unit of analysis for understanding collective, socially constructed learning, and is thus helpful for conceptualizing how a process of collective learning over time can be transformative (can, in effect, constitute a culture of evidence). Engeström (1987, 2000, 2001) applied CHAT to workplace settings in order to understand how the elements of social-cultural and cultural-historical theories of individual learning might be elevated to understand collective and organizational forms of learning. In addition to the focus on activity settings – organizations as a whole or departments within organizations, for example – as the unit of analysis, Engeström (2001) outlined several principles of CHAT that help shape our vision of a culture of inquiry:

- *Activity settings must be understood as "multi-voiced"*: Activity settings are communities of "multiple points of view, traditions and interests" in which "the division of labor . . . creates different positions for the participants, the participants carry their own diverse histories, and the activity system itself carries multiple layers and strands of history engraved in its artifacts, rules and conventions" (p. 136).
- *History is a critical factor in shaping activity*: "Activity systems take shape and get transformed over lengthy periods of time. Their problems and potentials can only be understood against their own history. History itself needs to be studied as local history of the activity and its objects, and as history of the theoretical ideas and tools that have shaped the activity" (pp. 136–137).
- *Contradictions are sources of learning that promote innovation*: "Contradictions are historically accumulating structural tensions within and between activity systems . . . Such contradictions generate disturbances and conflicts, but also innovative attempts to change the activity" (p. 137).
- *Expansive transformation – learning – can occur in activity settings*: "An expansive transformation is accomplished when the object and motive of the activity are reconceptualized to embrace a radically wider horizon of possibilities than in the previous mode of the activity" (p. 137).

The applicability of Engeström's first two principles to academia is compelling: academic institutions are certainly home to multiple points of view, each situated within their own historical and cultural traditions. In addition to the dominant culture that characterizes the larger institution, numerous individual groups constitute the academic community – faculty, students, and administrators, to name only the most obvious – and each has a corresponding culture in which its roles are rooted and into which its practitioners are socialized (Bensimon, 2005; Bergquist & Pawlak, 2008; Sporn, 1996). Moreover, beneath these multiple individual cultures exist numerous subcultures. Austin (1990), for example, identified the multiplicity of cultures surrounding the role of faculty members, including the culture of the academic profession and the distinct culture of disciplines. A culture of inquiry cannot be divorced from, or ignorant of, these diverse subcultures and the way they inform individuals' perspectives and behaviors. Rather, Engeström's (2001) principles suggest that this diversity of perspective must be integrated into the process of collective learning.

Our understanding of academic institutions and departments or functions within institutions – such as admissions offices, academic departments, or institutional research departments – as cultural activity settings thus provides a framework for identifying, organizing, and invoking history in efforts to foster transformation of the practices and policies impacting equity, as happened in the second scenario above when the history of 2-year colleges as vocational (non-transfer oriented) institutions was revealed as an underlying cause of the lack of transfer support policies. Historicizing the contexts of inequities in student outcomes can also empower practitioners within the institution; it enables individuals to shift from a role in which they must defend practices or policies (e.g., "state law prohibits us from talking about race") to a role in which they serve as detectives and can begin to understand how the practices that structure their daily work have come about, the cumulative impact of those practices, and the possibilities for changing them (Gutiérrez & Vossoughi, 2010). This historicized view of the policies and practices that have brought about institutional norms thus helps attenuate blame or defensiveness within the activity setting and helps participants understand and reflect upon the historical, cultural, and political origins of the structures that regulate their actions.

Moreover, making the multiplicity of perspectives and viewpoints within the institution visible and central to a process of deliberate inquiry allows contradictions to emerge between the espoused values of the campus or system and the *de facto* practices, as happened in the second scenario above, when the two-year campuses' histories as vocational institutions contradicted the system's value on encouraging transfer and its assumption that institutional policies within the system were aligned around that value. Indeed, Engeström's third principle suggests that such contradictions are a necessary catalyst of organizational learning. Cultural-historical activity theory thus urges that we can open the door for contradictions to become learning opportunities by surfacing and acknowledging the histories of the multiple roles and subcultures within academic organizations.

Within a culture of inquiry, then, contradictions become the catalysts for change when they disrupt the patterns of diagnose-and-react that tend to yield instances of single-loop learning. Indeed, a culture *of inquiry* must be one in which contradictions are valued and interrogated, rather than ignored or avoided. Evidence of racial and ethnic inequities in student outcomes, for example, may contradict the histories and assumptions of "diversity" or the myth of meritocracy in which institutions have rooted their practices and policies (Bensimon, 2005). In this way, the contradictions that are nurtured in a culture of inquiry can help to surface the racial inequities and the experiences of minority students that otherwise remain unaddressed by initiatives focused on diversity and multiculturalism (Harper & Hurtado, 2007).

Finally, in its vision of collective learning and transformation of organizational practices, CHAT centralizes the role of "mediating artifacts" based upon Vygotsky's (1978) emphasis on the objects, tools, and languages that mediate interactions between human beings and between humans and their environment and that embody significant cultural meaning (Engeström, 1987, 2001). From a sociocultural perspective (Cole & Griffin, 1983; Engeström, 1987, 2001; Gutiérrez & Vossoughi, 2010), individuals within an activity setting rely on artifacts, including language, to get things done and to create meaning. Situations that reveal a contradiction between what is espoused or expected call for the interrogation and re-mediation of practices. Racial inequity is an outcome that underscores the contradiction between the espoused values of equal opportunity and the reality of a truncated structure of opportunity. In this vein, organizational learning can be understood not as a linear path leading from data accumulation to action, but rather as the capacity of participants within an activity setting to recognize the emergence of a situation that contradicts espoused values or expected results. In the case of racial inequity, organizational learning can be said to happen when participants are able to recognize it as a contradiction (not as the natural occurrence of underpreparation) that calls for deliberate interrogation and re-mediation – a term that captures the intent to change the very cultural elements that mediate individual and institutional practices and behaviors.

Similarly, in our vision of a culture of inquiry, the concept of *re-mediation* aligns with double-loop learning to suggest a transformation of the mediating means – those tools, language, data, and other "artifacts" (e.g., racially disaggregated data; protocols to assess policy from a critical and equity perspective; the concept of equity-mindedness; for additional examples see Bensimon & Malcolm, forthcoming) – that directly mediate practitioners' engagement with their work. Cultural-historical activity theory helps focus inquiry on the tools used in carrying out activities within organizations, and implicates those tools in the processes of inquiry in order to fundamentally alter an institution's approach to constructing policies and practices to promote equity.

Participatory Action Research: Technical, Practical, and Critical Reasoning

Thus far, we have argued that a culture of inquiry provides the context for deliberate and institutionally sanctioned interrogation of underlying values and assumptions about student outcomes and the policies and practices that impact them. We also argued, drawing from CHAT, that activity settings across campuses and systems must serve as sites of cultural meaning-making by practitioners, and that the individual and collective interpretations and perceptions of those individuals must be re-mediated with new artifacts and languages to facilitate critical inquiry. These points lead us to an important final distinction: the differentiation between a functionalist understanding of culture of evidence, in which institutional researchers or others are called upon to perform the "function" of providing and analyzing evidence about student outcomes and promoting "data-driven" policy and practice, and the critical, process-oriented, and social-constructivist vision of a culture of inquiry for which we argue.

To better clarify the difference between these views of a culture of evidence, we adopt participatory action research theory's concept of a "science of practice" (Kemmis & McTaggart, 2000) – that is, a form of research into one's own (or one's own institution's) practices. In constructing a theoretical framework for participatory action research, Kemmis and McTaggart (2000) argued for education researchers to engage in a "science of practice," which, they claimed, "will be constructed in social relations and will involve elements of technical, practical, and critical reasoning about practice" (pp. 582–583). Moreover, the goal of the research being conducted and the role of the researcher dictate the type of reasoning employed (Kemmis & McTaggart, 2000). Thus, functionalist understandings of a culture of evidence are constrained by limiting the type of "science of practice" they construct to those employing only technical forms of reasoning, while ignoring other forms of reasoning necessary to yield double-loop learning around student success and equity.

Technical reasoning, in particular, aims to solve a predefined problem or improve the efficiency of predetermined means. Technical reason is thus like single-loop learning (Argyris & Schön, 1996); the underlying assumptions and values informing practices are not brought into the scope of interrogation, and only the means by which those outcomes are pursued get considered. For example, in arguing for more extensive use of research in community colleges, Bailey and Alfonso (2005) focus on the role of technical reasoning, suggesting that (1) institutional research would "play a more prominent role" on campus, (2) faculty and administrators would consistently use data on student outcomes to make decisions, and (3) colleges would increase data reporting (pp. 3–4). The emphasis on the functions of data collection, use, and reporting is aimed at the effectiveness and efficiency of community colleges' practices. These functions address the technical reasoning around practices but do not question the underlying outcomes being pursued or assumptions on which they are based.

By contrast, the culture of inquiry for which we argue here maintains an ideological goal – equity – and places the practitioner in the role of researcher, thus necessarily invoking other forms of questioning than those that occur within the problem-solving scope of technical reasoning. This iterative and critical form of inquiry also requires "practical reason," which questions both the ends being sought and the means by which those ends have traditionally been pursued, and "critical reason," which questions how the consequences of existing processes or policies adversely affect those involved (Kemmis & McTaggart, 2000). Practical and critical reason shape practitioners' involvement with evidence; they are the modes of cognitive engagement with data, for example, that allow individuals within institutions to shift the framing of inquiry from questions such as "why are students not able to transfer?" to "how are transfer opportunities structured in a way that disadvantages or neglects certain students?"

Practical reasoning guides practitioners' approach to questioning and decision-making in the context of complex or contradictory value systems and structures, such as those operating within academic culture. Thus, an approach to inquiry employing practical reason is more concerned with helping practitioners be aware of the histories and consequences of existing practices, rather than pointing to an immediate solution or a prescribed set of actions (Kemmis & McTaggart, 2000). As a culture of evidence involves practitioners in the interrogation of the histories and values of their work with an underlying commitment to equity, practical reasoning is the vital metacognitive process in which they engage and which calls into question both the outcomes about which institutions collect data and the uses they make of that evidence. Moreover, without critical reasoning, the amelioration of adverse impacts gets lost, and the functionalist priority on the production and dissemination of evidence – and the technical reasoning that appropriates it – comes to stand in for and preempt deeper, critical inquiry about the equity of the ends we pursue in our institutions.

Defining a Culture of Inquiry

Based on lessons from the theory of double-loop organizational learning, cultural-historical theoretical perspectives of organizational transformation, and the forms of reasoning that support participatory action research, we thus far suggest the following to help define what a culture of inquiry is and how it might work within academic institutions to promote racial equity:

A culture of inquiry must both overcome the challenges and exploit the ideals of the distinct larger culture of academic organizations. To foster sustained and meaningful attention to equity, a culture of inquiry is one in which evidence is used to contradict the myths and assumptions that are firmly entrenched in academic culture. However, a strong culture of inquiry also leverages the ideals of academic culture, including the value academia ascribes to continuous learning, honesty, and intellectual growth (Dill, 1982).

A culture of inquiry makes double-loop learning the norm. A culture of inquiry must facilitate and normalize organizational learning responses that questions institutional values, assumptions, and theories of action rather than encouraging quick-fix practices and policies that seek to change outcomes without fundamentally addressing underlying causes.

A culture of inquiry supports an ideological objective of equity, and uses practical and critical reasoning to transform practices and change outcomes. Functionalist notions of a culture of evidence focus on the collection of data by institutional researchers and the systematic analysis and dissemination of "evidence" about outcomes without calling into question the assumptions underlying those outcomes – in other words, the means (data collection) become the ends. Our vision of a culture of inquiry is one in which practitioners take responsibility for critically examining both the way outcomes have been defined *and* the policies and practices that impact them. Both means and ends are called into question, with a constant eye toward equity.

A culture of inquiry re-mediates the practices of organizations by changing the tools, symbols, and languages that guide individual actions and perceptions. The potential to create new mediating artifacts is a critical component of building a culture of inquiry. As in the example of evidence that reveals inequities in student outcomes and thus contradicts entrenched histories and assumptions about diversity and merit, data and the tools and processes that provide access to them are invaluable for *re-mediating* institutional practices and theories of action.

Mediating artifacts are the most tangible and modifiable elements of a culture of inquiry. Those artifacts help link processes of collective learning to the day-to-day actions of individual practitioners in communities across the institution. In the next section, we elaborate on the link between individuals and the institution within a culture of inquiry, and describe how data and language as mediating artifacts can impact the way individual practitioners both independently carry out their work and collectively transform institutional practices to improve equity.

From Individual Practice to Collective Learning about Equity

As we work through the concept of a culture of inquiry, how it might serve to alter practices and policies impacting racial and ethnic equity in academic institutions, and how we might go about intentionally developing such a culture, we must keep in mind the reciprocal mechanisms of culture generally. Kuh and Hall's (1993) definition of culture emphasized the inherited norms and values that determine behaviors of individuals within groups and groups within the larger society. Neumann (1995) emphasized the temporal quality of culture and the accumulation and construction of shared knowledge over time, and Birnbaum (1988) suggested that, for organizations, culture "establishes an 'envelope' or range of possible behaviors within which the organization usually functions" (p. 73). Each of these understandings of culture implies a degree of reciprocal construction and reinforcement between cultural norms and those who uphold them in their daily practices, wherein the norms are being inherited and reified simultaneously. While individual behaviors are being structured and guided by the norms and values of the culture(s) in which they live and work, they also reproduce and reinforce those norms and values by operationalizing them in their daily actions.

The impact of a culture within an institution thus has largely to do with the way it shapes the perceptions and practices of those individuals working within the institution, but the actions of individuals also sustain – or potentially change – the cultures within institutions. Building on the theoretical foundations of CHAT and the interest in constructing a culture of inquiry in which double-loop learning becomes a default response to contradictions, Figure 3.1 illustrates how individuals, within specific activity settings across the institution (e.g., admissions and financial aid, administration, institutional research) are linked to other key aspects of a culture of inquiry within the larger cultural activity setting of the university. The diagram in Figure 3.1 is adapted from Engeström's (1987, 2001) and Cole and Engeström's (1993) structure of human activity settings and it illustrates various aspects of a culture of inquiry promoting equity in student outcomes.

The process of building a culture of inquiry must therefore acknowledge the role of *individuals* – and the assumptions, perceptions, languages, and tools that determine how they go about their daily actions, how they structure their work, and how they interact with the other elements of the academic institution as a cultural sphere. As Figure 3.1 suggests, the efficacy of a culture of inquiry depends as much on the learning of individuals as those individuals' learning depends on the cultural conditions that encourage it. In their work on action research, Bensimon, Polkinghorne, Bauman, and Vallejo (2004) suggested that "The opportunity for institutional change lies in the possibility that individual participants will transfer their learning to other contexts within the institution, and in doing so, enable others to learn and change" (p. 113). Thus, the processes through which individuals engage in the practices that

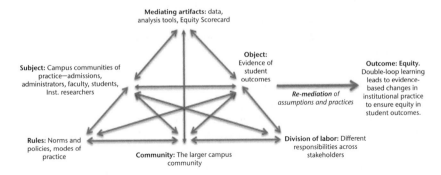

FIGURE 3.1 Aspects of the Culture of Inquiry to Promote Equity in Student Outcomes.

characterize a culture of inquiry are critical, as are the tools that serve to re-mediate existing practices.

Re-mediating Practices with Data

The University of Southern California's Center for Urban Education (CUE) works with campuses and systems to involve practitioners from across departments, divisions, and areas of responsibility in processes of deliberate, iterative inquiry regarding racial and ethnic equity in student outcomes. Experience working with these campuses and systems has shown that public institutions typically produce large quantities of data for a variety of audiences and purposes: institutional researchers submit annual enrollment, graduation, and an abundance of other student and organizational data into the federal Department of Education's Integrated Postsecondary Data Systems (IPEDS); institutions often produce voluminous "accountability reports" that may or may not get posted deep within campus or system websites, and so on (Harris & Bensimon, 2007). However, faculty and other practitioners rarely have access to, or the opportunity to engage with, data on their students' success, and the learning potential of data depends on the determination and willingness of the community to interrogate – not just produce – those data. Because data are only as valuable as the questions asked of them, they are thus a critical but incomplete aspect of a culture of inquiry.

Using data as an entry point to inquiry is a strategy for capitalizing on the value that academic institutions place on learning and inquiry, while also presenting evidence to contradict embedded assumptions and patterns of practice. In this way, the use of data within a culture of inquiry serves as a new form of mediating artifact; disaggregated data on students' success throughout the college pathway must be intentionally presented using tools and processes of inquiry that encourage and reward practitioner engagement. As Harris and Bensimon (2007) argued, allowing practitioners to "take the role of researchers rather than relying on the knowledge produced by outsiders such as consultants or university researchers" (p. 82) allows them to act as detectives, building their own lines of questioning and developing their own hunches about the underlying causes for the patterns they observe in the data.

Involving faculty and other practitioners also achieves broad buy-in to the problem-defining and solution-setting decisions and the ultimate policies or practices that are designed to address those problems and agendas, thus lowering the defensive barriers likely to arise when problems are defined and solutions imposed from outside (Dowd & Tong, 2007; Harris & Bensimon, 2007). Admissions officers, counselors, faculty, and other practitioners are those individuals whose daily work has the most direct impact on student success. Involving those practitioners in the interrogation of their own practices is a way of uncovering their values and assumptions, allowing them to develop and collaboratively test their hunches about causes, and ultimately encouraging them to take ownership over solutions rather than defaulting to "best practices," defensive strategies, or patterns of behavior and action that perpetuate inaction toward inequity (Bensimon, 2005; Harris & Bensimon, 2007). When the day-to-day tasks of campus practitioners can be re-mediated through this form of detective work using deliberate data analysis tools and processes, single-loop learning responses are bypassed in favor of double-loop learning that enables institutions to address the true roots of inequities.

Examples of Data as Mediating Artifact: Vital Signs, Equity Scorecard, and Benchmarking

When the Center for Urban Education (CUE) begins working with campus practitioner teams to inquire into and address racial and ethnic inequities in student outcomes, institutional researchers are asked to populate a data template called the "vital signs," which presents a range of data on student retention and graduation rates disaggregated by race/ethnicity. The vital signs provide key data on equity in student outcomes in a way that is accessible to practitioners whose roles do not typically involve analyzing complex data (Harris & Bensimon, 2007). The vital signs provide a point of entry for practitioners to begin to assess racial/ethnic inequities and gaps in student outcomes and to develop questions about what they observe. As opposed to having problems defined by technical policy measures (e.g., prerequisites limiting access to classes) or by administrative priorities (e.g., being told to improve course completion rates to meet performance funding benchmarks), the vital signs are anchored in evidence and generative – they iteratively nurture curiosity rather than defensiveness and single-loop learning.

As practitioner teams begin defining specific areas for inquiry, such as transfer, developmental education, or student progress in certain majors such as STEM or nursing, CUE uses the Benchmarking Equity and Student Success Tool (BESST) as another form of mediating artifact. The BESST is an interactive data presentation platform that organizes racially disaggregated data on student progress and success into intuitive, institution-defined visual models. Engaging with their own institutional data organized into familiar student experiences (e.g., developmental education course-taking and success, credit accumulation), participants are able to both confront the facts the data present about differences in student outcomes and begin a discussion about the possible causes of racial disparities. The tool thus provides an anchor and context for a shift in the language used to inquire about and address inequities in student outcomes, thereby mediating the relationship between these participants and their institutional histories and structures in new and more productive ways.

Ultimately, practitioners working with CUE use the various data tools and the observations and inquiries they have made to construct an Equity

Scorecard – a collection of indicators, populated with institutional data – that the practitioner team believes reflects critical information about student equity and success on the campus. The specific indicators used in the Scorecard are determined by the participants and may include, for example, retention and persistence, transfer readiness, or intensity of credit accumulation. Importantly, the Equity Scorecard becomes the vehicle through which the team shares its learning with the larger campus; it becomes a tool for re-mediation not only of the individual practitioners' daily practice but also of the ways in which the larger campus approaches and understands student success. The team has thus created a new artifact to mediate the use of evidence within the campus – a tool that facilitates double-loop learning based on intentional and iterative questioning of underlying assumptions about student success and about gaps in success by race and ethnicity.

Re-mediating Practices through New Language

Even when presented with evidence about inequities in student outcomes or gaps in student success, CUE has found that campuses and individual practitioners working in them may not be equipped with the language necessary to address race as a factor in student success. Discussion of race has become taboo on many college campuses, either as the result of superficial initiatives to ensure "diversity" and "multiculturalism" that stifle meaningful discussions about race (Harper & Hurtado, 2007), or as a result of legal action making administrators and practitioners cautious about discussing race, such as affirmative action rulings or Proposition 209 in California (which prohibits state institutions from giving "preferential treatment" to any individual or group based on race, sex, color, ethnicity, or national origin). Harper and Patton (2007) also suggest that college educators and administrators resist talking about race because of the implications it has for their own positions of privilege and the perception of racism as an intractable societal issue on which persistent dialog is tiring and frustrating.

A culture of inquiry must then also provide a new language to re-mediate practitioners' and administrators' engagement with evidence about racial inequity. Although data as a re-mediating tool can provide a foundation for identifying and questioning patterns of inequity in student outcomes, using that evidence constructively requires a new vocabulary through which to engage in dialog and with which to design effective solutions.

Examples of New Language as Mediating Artifact: Equity-Mindedness vs. Deficit-Mindedness

In working with campuses on using data to address inequities in student success, CUE also works to engender a shift in the discourse in which practitioners engage around race. In particular, this shift requires a change in the language and "cognitive frames" through which relationships between academic outcomes and student characteristics are perceived (Bensimon, 2005). Just as Harper and Hurtado (2007) found that the façade of commitment to diversity on campuses tends to obfuscate racial experiences, CUE has found that most campus practitioners tend to think about the relationship between race and academic outcomes in one or both of two ways. The first of these is in terms of *diversity*, in which the focus is on representation of differences and the discourse is structured around terms such as *multiculturalism* and *colorblindness*. The second common approach to addressing racial disparities focuses on student *deficits*, particularly vis-à-vis academic outcomes, in which the focus is on stereotypes associated with economic disadvantage, lack of academic preparation, and other background characteristics attributed to students based on their race or ethnicity.

As practitioners' perceptions of student outcomes are re-mediated by engaging with data and processes of inquiry, CUE also helps to shift the language that practitioners use away from discourses of diversity and deficit-mindedness to focus instead on *equity-mindedness* – an alternative cognitive frame and language that focuses on institutional responsibility for student outcomes and the institutional practices that support or hinder student success (Bensimon, 2005). Practitioners, who are invested in the process of inquiry and their role as detectives, thus begin to shift discourse away from statements such as: "African American students are often unprepared for college-level math because they come from underserved schools" or "Latino students don't want to transfer because they prefer to stay close to home." They instead ask: "What systems do we have in place for our students who need additional academic support?" or "How are we reaching out to our Latino students to support their transfer aspirations?"

Just as data as a mediating artifact help lower defensiveness around observed outcomes, this new language also helps – slowly, but surely – to lower the resistance that individuals feel toward talking about race and ethnicity in relationship to student outcomes. It both provides an entry point for taking responsibility for student success, and moves the dialog away from talking about "preferential treatment" for specific groups based on their perceived deficits. Campus practitioners do not have to feel the same anxiety about discussing race in relation to academic outcomes when they are given a mediating language that places responsibility on, and empowers, the institution to change its own practices.

Conclusion: Practitioners within a Culture of Inquiry

We have argued that a culture of inquiry within academic institutions must overcome the unique challenges, as well as leverage the strengths, of the distinct larger culture of academia. We have also suggested that our notion of a culture of inquiry re-mediates the practices of individuals within organizations by changing the tools and languages that guide individual actions and perceptions, and empowers campus practitioners to make evidence-based decisions that improve equity in student outcomes. Finally, we suggested that a critical, transformative culture of inquiry makes "double-loop learning" the norm as a way of responding to both internal crises (such as inequities in student outcomes) and external accountability pressures, and that such a culture favors critical reasoning and inquiry aimed at the ideological objectives of equity and student success. In conclusion, we turn briefly to implications for practitioners and suggest ways in which practitioners can use evidence to promote meaningful improvements in outcomes for all students as well as equity in outcomes for students from all racial and ethnic groups.

Whereas institutions produce massive quantities of data in response to state and national policy initiatives, or under the guise of a functionalist notion of a culture of evidence, our work has shown that the relationship between the theories driving the collection of data and on-the-ground solutions is often absent. Without building capacity around the use of data, as we have suggested must occur within a culture of inquiry, campuses are limited to using technical reasoning (Kemmis & McTaggart, 2000) and single-loop learning responses that change outcomes without creating sustained changes in institutional values – often with unintended negative consequences. Campuses and systems that have used CUE's tools and processes to build a culture of inquiry around equity have done so, in part, as a way of building this capacity and empowering the practitioners with the most direct influence on student outcomes to alter their underlying beliefs, values, and perceptions – and, therefore, practices. We thus argue that creating a culture of inquiry, as we have described it here, must begin with practitioners using inquiry to change their day-to-day assumptions, decisions, and behaviors.

In particular, the theoretical approaches we have used to understand a culture of inquiry point our attention to the history, language, tools, and data that form the context of our daily work in colleges and universities. As professionals, we can conduct our own inquiry into the processes of our daily work and begin to question the impacts of these taken-for-granted elements on student success and equity in student outcomes. As these inquiries begin to cross departments and accumulate evidence from across communities of practice to more broadly interrogate the institution's values and policies, individual actions are then linked in a culture of inquiry. For practitioners, a culture of inquiry thus begins with questions into our daily routines:

- What evidence do we use to make decisions in our daily activities, where does that evidence come from, and how is it structured? Who provides it, when, and why? Who uses it?

- Are data disaggregated by race/ethnicity and other subgroups and are we asking questions of the data that allow us to determine if there are inequities in student achievement?
- What assumptions and values come into play when we look at data on student outcomes? For example, when we look at data on student outcomes, do we default to assumptions about student deficits or do we question institutional policies and structures?
- What do we know about the histories of the way things are done in our departments or on our campuses? Have policies and processes been reevaluated using evidence to consider outcomes and equity, or are they taken for granted?
- What language is commonly used to talk about accountability and student outcomes? Do we tend to talk about diversity more than equity? "Best practices" more than inquiry into causes? Data reporting more than data inquiry?

A culture of inquiry is more than a buzzword used to suggest "data-driven decision-making" or the production of data in reports that never get read. A culture of inquiry as we have described it here is, in fact, a *culture* – it represents patterns of behaviors motivated by shared norms and values around inquiry and equity, and it is developed over time and across different roles or departments. Within a culture of inquiry in academic institutions, the patterns of perception and practice are mediated by new tools for accessing data, new processes for inquiring about inequities in student outcomes, and new languages for creating generative dialog about racial experiences and inequities in outcomes. Within this re-mediated cultural setting, then, evidence is used to create double-loop learning for individuals and the institution as a whole. A culture of inquiry, finally, is one in which an institution's commitment to equity and success for all students is authentically reflected in transformed practice and policy.

References

Alford, R. R. (1998). *The craft of inquiry*. New York: Oxford University Press.

Alon, S., & Tienda, M. (2007). Diversity, opportunity, and the shifting meritocracy in higher education. *American Sociological Review*, 72(4), 487–511.

Argyris, C. (1990). *Overcoming organizational defenses: Facilitating organizational learning*. Boston, MA: Allyn and Bacon.

Argyris, C. (1993). *Knowledge for action: A guide to overcoming barriers to organizational change*. San Francisco: Jossey-Bass.

Argyris, C., & Schön, D. A. (1996). *Organizational learning II: Theory, method and practice*. Reading, MA: Addison-Wesley.

Austin, A. E. (1990). Faculty cultures, faculty values. In W. G. Tierney (Ed.), *Assessing academic climates and cultures* (New directions for institutional research, no. 68, pp. 61–74). San Francisco: Jossey-Bass.

Bailey, T. R., & Alfonso, M. (2005). *Paths to persistence: An analysis of research on program effectiveness at community colleges.* Report no. 1 in New Agenda Series vol. 6. Indianapolis, IN: Lumina Foundation for Education.

Bensimon, E. M. (2005). Closing the achievement gap in higher education: An organizational learning perspective. *New Directions for Institutional Research, 131,* 99–111.

Bensimon, E. M. & Malcom, L. (forthcoming). *The Equity Scorecard process in theory and practice.* Sterling, VA: Stylus Publishing.

Bensimon, E. M., Polkinghorne, D. E., Bauman, G. L., & Vallejo, E. (2004). Doing research that makes a difference. *Journal of Higher Education, 75*(1), 104–127.

Bensimon, E. M., Rueda, R., Dowd, A. C., & Harris III, F. (2007). Accountability, equity, and practitioner learning and change. *Metropolitan Universities Journal, 18*(3), 28–45.

Bergquist, W. H., & Pawlak, K. (2008). *Engaging the six cultures of the academy: Revised and expanded edition of the four cultures of the academy.* San Francisco: Jossey-Bass.

Birnbaum, R. (1988). *How colleges work: The cybernetics of academic organization and leadership.* San Francisco: Jossey-Bass.

Brint, S., & Karabel, J. (1989). American education, meritocratic ideology, and the legitimation of inequality: The community college and the problem of American exceptionalism. *Higher Education, 18*(6), 725–35.

Bustillos, L. T., Rueda, R., & Bensimon, E. M. (2011). Faculty views of underrepresented students in community college settings: Cultural models and cultural practices. In P. R. Portes & S. Salas (Eds.), *Vygotsky in 21st century society: Advances in cultural historical theory and praxis with non-dominant communities.* New York: Peter Lang.

Cole, M., & Engeström, Y. (1993). A cultural-historical approach to distributed cognition. In G. Salomon (Ed.), *Distributed cognitions: Psychological and educational considerations* (pp. 1–46). New York: Cambridge University Press.

Cole, M., & Griffin, P. (1983). A socio-historical approach to re-mediation. *Quarterly Newsletter of the Laboratory of Comparative Human Cognition, 5*(4), 69–74.

Dill, D. D. (1982). The management of academic culture: Notes on the management of meaning and social integration. *Higher Education, 11*(3), 303–320.

Dowd, A. C. (2003). From access to outcome equity: Revitalizing the democratic mission of the community college. *Annals of the American Academy of Political and Social Science, 586,* 92–119.

Dowd, A. C. (2005). *Data don't drive: Building a practitioner-driven culture of inquiry to assess community college performance.* Indianapolis, IN: Lumina Foundation for Education.

Dowd, A. C., Bishop, R., Bensimon, E. M., & Witham, K. (in press). Re-mediating accountability. In K. Gallagher, R. Goodyear, D. Brewer, & R. Rueda (Eds.), *Urban education: A model for leadership and policy.* New York: Routledge.

Dowd, A. C., & Tong, V. P. (2007). Accountability, assessment, and the scholarship of "best practice." In J.C. Smart (Ed.), *Higher education: Handbook of theory and research, Volume 22* (pp. 57–119). New York: Springer.

Engeström, Y. (1987). *Learning by expanding: An activity-theoretic approach to developmental research.* Helsinki, Finland: Orienta-Konsultit.

Engeström, Y. (2000). Activity theory as a framework for analyzing and redesigning work. *Ergonomics, 43*(7), 960–974.

Engeström, Y. (2001). Expansive learning at work: Toward an activity-theoretical reconceptualization. *Journal of Education and Work, 14*(1), 133–156.

Engeström, Y., Miettinen, R., & Punamäki, R. (1999). *Perspectives on activity theory.* New York: Cambridge University Press.

Gutiérrez, K. D., & Vossoughi, S. (2010). Lifting off the ground to return anew: Mediated praxis, transformative learning, and social design experiments. *Journal of Teacher Education*, *61*(1–2), 100–117.

Harper, S. R., & Hurtado, S. (2007). Nine themes in campus racial climates and implications for institutional transformation. In S. R. Harper & L. D. Patton (Eds.), *Responding to the realities of race on campus* (New directions for student services, no. 120, pp. 7–24). San Francisco: Jossey-Bass.

Harper, S. R., & Patton, L. D. (Eds.) (2007). *Responding to the realities of race on campus* (New directions for student services, no. 120). San Francisco: Jossey-Bass.

Harris III, F., & Bensimon, E. M. (2007). The equity scorecard: A collaborative approach to assess and respond to racial/ethnic disparities in student outcomes. In S. R. Harper & L. D. Patton (Eds.), *Responding to the realities of race on campus* (New directions for student services, no. 120, pp. 77–84). San Francisco: Jossey-Bass.

Kemmis, S., & McTaggart, R. (2000). Participatory action research. In N. K. Denzin & Y. S. Lincoln (Eds.), *Handbook of qualitative research* (2nd edn., pp. 567–605). Thousand Oaks, CA: Sage Publications.

Kuh, G. D., & Hall, J. E. (1993). Using cultural perspectives in student affairs. In G. D. Kuh (Ed.), *Cultural perspectives in student affairs work* (pp. 1–20). Lanham, MD: American College Personnel Association.

Meyer, J. W., & Rowan, B. (1977). Institutionalized organizations: Formal structure as myth and ceremony. *American Journal of Sociology*, *83*(2), 340–363.

Neumann, A. (1995). Context, cognition, and culture: A case analysis of collegiate leadership and cultural change. *American Educational Research Journal*, *32*(2), 251–279.

Schein, E. H. (1985). *Organizational culture and leadership* (1st edn.). San Francisco: Jossey-Bass.

Sporn, B. (1996). Managing university culture: An analysis of the relationship between institutional culture and management approaches. *Higher Education*, *32*(1), 41–61.

Tharp, R. G. and Gallimore, R. (1988). *Rousing minds to life: Teaching, learning, and school in social context.* New York: Cambridge University Press

Tierney, W. G. (1988). Organizational culture in higher education: Defining the essentials. *Journal of Higher Education*, *59*(1), 2–21.

Vygotsky, L. S. (1978). *Mind in society: The development of higher psychological processes.* Cambridge, MA: Harvard University Press.

4

MOVING FROM CULTURES OF INDIVIDUALISM TO CULTURES OF COLLECTIVISM IN SUPPORT OF STUDENTS OF COLOR

Douglas A. Guiffrida, Judy Marquez Kiyama, Stephanie J. Waterman, and Samuel D. Museus

As described in detail by Museus and Harris (2010), a growing body of literature indicates that campus cultures shape college students' experiences. Furthermore, the authors point out that research indicates that many college students of color face additional challenges adjusting to predominantly White institutions (PWIs) because their cultural norms and values vary from those of their campuses. Although many cultural variations have been identified among diverse groups and societies, one of the most promising differences that can aid in understanding disparities in college students' success is the distinction between individualism and collectivism. Individualist societies tend to value independence, competition among members, emotional detachment from family and parents, individual attitudes and perspectives over group norms, and personal goals over the goals of the collective (Triandis, Chen, & Chan, 1998). Alternatively, collectivist societies value interdependence, group synchronization, emotional attachment to families or parents, societal norms over individuality, and the subordination of individual aspirations to the aspirations of the collective (Fox, Lowe, & McClellan, 2005; Triandis, Chen, & Chan, 1998).

It has long been observed that Western cultures tend to be more individualistic, and many non-Western cultures (e.g., African, Asian and Pacific Islander, Latin American, and Native American) tend to be more collectivist in orientation (Beattie, 1980; Coon & Kemmelmeier, 2001; Hetts, Sakuma, & Pelham, 1999; Kirkness & Barnhardt, 1991; Mead, 1967; Triandis, McCuster & Hui, 1990; Yamaguchi, Kuhlman, & Sugimori, 1995). Moreover, cross-cultural psychologists assert that collectivist values positively influence African American, Asian American and Pacific Islander (AAPI), Latin American, and

Native American communities and help these groups deal with experienced racial and class oppression (e.g., Marin & Marin, 1991; Phinney, 1996; Staples & Mirandé, 1980).

Guiffrida (2006) argued that cultural orientations toward individualism and collectivism contribute to the disparities that exist in college student achievement and persistence between White students and students of color. Specifically, he asserted that students who have internalized collectivist cultural orientations face particular challenges adapting to the more Eurocentric, individualist cultures inherent in many institutions of higher education. Whereas students with collectivist orientations arrive at college with a wealth of interpersonal strengths, these strengths often go unrecognized and are inconsistent with the Western, individualist values and norms of the institution. One can imagine, for example, the incongruence between an aggressively competitive environment and a student who places more value on cooperation, a fast-paced institutional environment and a student who is slower and more contemplative or reflective, or a campus culture based on consumerism and a student who values sustainability, as is found in many Native American and Pacific Islander cultures. Additionally, Western-based systems often ignore collectivist-based, non-European curricula, including the rich languages and histories of non-European groups. Although it is impossible and unethical to essentialize all students of color as collectivist and all White students as individualist, existing research does suggest that students of color may be more likely than White students to maintain collectivist values (Gaines, Marelich, Bledsoe, Steers, Henderson, & Granrose, 1997; Triandis, 1989). Addressing the needs of collectivist-oriented students, therefore, is one important means of fostering success among many college students of color.

In this chapter, we share a brief overview of research that (1) supports the assertion that students with collectivist orientations face challenges when transitioning to higher education and (2) highlights the strengths of collectivist cultural orientations, particularly as these strengths are drawn upon when navigating individualist cultures at higher education institutions. We conclude with suggestions for adapting campus cultures in ways that embrace collectivist norms as a necessary component of the academic curriculum and social support structure.

Research on Collectivism and Individualism in Higher Education

Although few studies have investigated correlations between cultural orientation and college student achievement and persistence, results of two studies suggest that students from collectivist cultures may face additional challenges adapting to the Eurocentric norms that predominate in many PWIs (Dennis, Phinney, & Chuateco, 2005; Thompson & Fretz, 1991). Thompson and Fretz, for example, examined whether bicultural adaptive variables predicted levels of academic and social integration among African American students at a PWI. The researchers found that academically well-adjusted African American students had more positive attitudes toward individualist and competitive learning environments than African Americans who were less academically adjusted. They also found that more positive attitudes toward competitive learning situations were associated with greater social adjustment to college. Thompson and Fretz concluded that successful African American students either enter college with more individualist norms or learn to quickly adapt to individualist environments that characterize academia.

Dennis et al. (2005) conducted a study of college students using an assessment of cultural norms related to collectivism and individualism. The researchers surveyed 100 first-generation Latino students attending an urban commuter university and assessed the extent to which students were motivated to attend college based on *career/personal motivation* (i.e., personal interest, intellectual curiosity, and desire to attain fulfilling careers) or *family expectation motivation* (to meet the expectations of the family). The authors hypothesized that, because students of color are heavily influenced by collectivist values, both *career/personal* and *family expectation* motivation would be important predictors of their college adjustment. Consistent with their hypothesis, they found that *career/personal motivation* was a predictor of college adjustment and a slight predictor of college commitment when controlling for other variables such as high school GPA. However, contrary to their expectations, *family expectation motivation* was not significantly related to college adjustment and commitment when controlling for other variables. The authors concluded that, although many students of color are motivated by both individually oriented and family-based forms of motivation, the individual-based motivations were more closely related to college adjustment and commitment. Additionally, whereas many of these students of color lived in families and communities that valued collectivist norms, their abilities to integrate those collectivist norms with the individualist norms that are valued by PWIs were most predictive of their success.

The results from Dennis et al. (2005) and Thompson and Fretz (1991) suggest that students of color who espouse collectivist cultural orientations may be at risk for academic underachievement or attrition if they are not able to assimilate to individualist norms. These findings indicate that PWIs continue to be dominated by Western, assimilation-based norms that are insensitive and even oppressive to people with collectivist orientations. Rather than valuing the diverse traditions and strengths of collectivist students, the findings from these studies suggest that collectivist students may be required to abandon salient elements of their cultural identities and traditions if they wish to become successful at PWIs. This assimilationist perspective is particularly a problem given research that has highlighted the strengths that collectivist values can provide students of color when navigating PWIs (see Delgado, 2002; González, 2002; Guillory, 2008; Rosas & Hamrick, 2002).

To understand how the inconsistencies between individualist and collectivist cultural norms can impact undergraduate student achievement and success, it is useful to examine two areas of research on college students: (1) the impact of student relationships with families and friends from home on academic success and (2) the relationship between involvement in culturally based campus activities and academic success.

Impact of Families and Friends from Home on College Success

According to Tinto (1993), successful college students need to *break away* from their home communities in order to become *integrated* into the academic and social life of the university or college that they attend. Indeed, there have been several studies that have supported the notion that higher levels of *social integration* correlate with academic success in college (see Braxton & Lee, 2005). The applicability of this proposition to students of color, however, has been challenged – both conceptually (see Hurtado, 1997; Kuh & Love, 2000; Museus & Quaye, 2009; Nora, 2001; Rendón, Jaloma, & Nora, 2000; Tierney, 1992, 1999; Waterman, 2007) and by findings from numerous studies that have concluded that those students can gain tremendous support from families, friends, and other members of their home communities (Cabrera, Nora, Terenzini, Pascarella, & Hagedorn, 1999; Delgado, 2002; Gloria, Robinson Kurpius, Hamilton, & Wilson, 1999; González, 2002; Guiffrida, 2004a, 2005; Hendricks, Smith, Caplow, & Donaldson, 1996; Hurtado, Carter, & Spuler, 1996; Museus, 2008; Museus, Maramba, Palmer, Reyes, & Bresonis, 2011; Museus & Quaye, 2009; Nora & Cabrera, 1996; Rosas & Hamrick, 2002).

Qualitative studies investigating the experiences of students of color indicate that some students perceive members of their families as among their most important assets in college because they provide them with cultural connections, strategies for dealing with oppression, and strong encouragement and inspiration to succeed (Delgado, 2002; González, 2002; Rosas & Hamrick, 2002). Waterman (2004), for example, found that Native American college students glean enormous support from their family and communities. In a qualitative study of 54 Haudenosaunee (Iroquois) college graduates, Waterman found that "family" was their greatest source of support in college. Participants indicated that family offered money, rides, words of encouragement, and emotional support. Communities provided a place of comfort from the non-Native institutions that participants attended. These findings are consistent with other research on Native American college students (see Guillory, 2008; Lindley, 2009). Similarly, Museus and his colleagues (2011) interviewed 30 Southeast Asian American students (Cambodian, Hmong, Laotian, and

Vietnamese) and found that family expectations and support was the most important facilitator of their success. Although there is a dearth of literature on this population at the higher education level, these findings are consistent with research underscoring the importance of family and culture on Southeast Asian American students in K–12 education (Ngo & Lee, 2007).

Qualitative research conducted with students of color indicates, therefore, that families can be very supportive of undergraduates from collectivist cultures and that not *all* students need to *break away* from their families and communities to succeed in college in the way delineated by Tinto (1993). Cultural orientation provides one explanation about why breaking away from relationships from home may be a necessary prerequisite to college success for some students and harmful to the success of others. Students from collectivist cultures are more likely to desire, or be expected, to maintain relationships with families and friends from home while in college than students from individualist cultures. Moreover, whereas students from individualist cultures may more easily break away to become integrated into the academic and social realms of their colleges, students from collectivist cultures find value in establishing connections in college while maintaining strong connections with those who are supportive at home. In fact, attempts by well-intentioned faculty and staff to *integrate* students with collective orientations into the culture of the university not only may be met with resistance by students and families, but could potentially be harmful to students by robbing them of strong cultural support networks at home.

It is important to note, however, that relationships between connections to home and college success are complex. This complex relationship was illustrated in the results of a qualitative study conducted by Guiffrida (2005) with African American college students to understand the conditions under which families were perceived as supporting or hindering student academic achievement and persistence. Many of the lowest-achieving students in his study, including the ones who dropped out, indicated that they felt their parents were not supportive of them going to college and offered little financial or emotional support. Instead, these students described how their obligations to their families, which included providing the family with financial support, emotional support, and other head-of-household duties, distracted them from their academics. High-achieving students, on the other hand, perceived their families, irrespective of their incomes or levels of education, as among their most important assets in college. Rather than requiring them to lend support at home, these students' families encouraged them to focus on school, regardless of the needs of the family. In fact, families of high achievers often encouraged students to view their college success as their most important obligation to their family and to the Black community. Guiffrida concluded that, to succeed at PWIs, it is important for African American college students to strengthen relationships with family members who provide emotional, academic, and financial support and encourage their students to make healthy connections at their college campuses.

Museus et al. (2011) provide another example of the complexity of the relationships between connections to home and success. As mentioned, they found that Southeast Asian Americans' parental expectations and support, and the resulting pressure to succeed, facilitated the success of those students. However, they also noted that, in a few cases, that pressure became excessive, led to students feeling that they could not do anything right, and eradicated their motivation. Museus et al.'s study underscores the fact that, although expectations are important, they can have a detrimental effect if they are excessive or not coupled with support, and their findings are consistent with research suggesting that Asian American and Latin American students' obligations to family positively influence academic motivation to a certain point, but that those with the highest levels of family obligation exhibit levels of academic achievement as low as those with the lowest levels of family obligation (Fuligni, Tseng, & Lam, 1999).

The extent to which families understand and value Western, assimilation-based systems of higher education is an indicator of whether their students benefit from strong connections to home or become distracted from academics by these connections, but the responsibility of the institutions and the actors within them must also be examined. For example, the issue of how much *value* is placed on education is something that can be complex. First, what types of education are we, as actors within institutions of higher education, asking families to value? It is possible that Western, individualist expectations of *valuing* education may not align with those of certain collectivist communities? In Latino communities, for example, education may be expressed in a number of ways that are inconsistent with Western forms of education, including using *consejos*, which are advice-giving narratives (Delgado-Gaitan, 1994; Lopez, 2001); counternarratives intended to resist problematic school practices (Villenas, 2001); or drawing upon funds of knowledge (Moll, Amanti, Neff, & González, 1992; Valenzuela, 1999). Second, we acknowledge that, although many families with collectivist values may, in fact, support Western-based systems of higher education, their life circumstances or cultural values may make it necessary for all family members, even those attending college, to contribute to the immediate needs of the family. Because our society has historically engaged in actions to force Indigenous communities to assimilate and eradicate their ethnic heritage (Adams, 1995), the maintenance and revitalization of those communities and traditional culture therefore go beyond a sense of obligation – it is an issue of survival. The only ways to continue, maintain, and revitalize those Indigenous communities and cultures are to remain connected to family and community.

In a discussion of the college transition experiences of Latina/o students, Rios-Aguilar and Kiyama (in press) offer the *funds of knowledge* framework

(Moll et al., 1992) as one way to understand the assets that students acquire and bring from their home communities to help in navigating in and through college. Funds of knowledge refer to the diverse knowledge and resources found in Latina/o households (Moll et al., 1992). Specifically, funds of knowledge are conceptualized as the "historically accumulated and culturally developed bodies of knowledge and skills essential for household or individual functioning and well-being" (Moll et al., 1992, p. 133). McIntyre, Rosebery, and Gonzalez (2001) note that funds of knowledge can include language, social practices, and various other forms of knowledge influenced by life experiences and found in homes and communities. Rios-Aguilar and Kiyama suggest that, by understanding students' experiences through an asset-based framework such as funds of knowledge, researchers can better understand the values that influence, inform, and assist students in navigating educational processes in and through college and in the development of professional aspirations. Rios-Aguilar and Kiyama point to specific examples of how funds of knowledge can prove useful in the navigation of K–12 education for Latina/o students and suggest that those same resources and values could also be applied to higher education processes. Such a framework embraces the collectivist orientation of students' home communities and can be a useful tool in combating deficit ideologies often espoused by higher education institutions.

Although funds of knowledge have been applied mostly in K–12 classrooms, there are a few examples of how the framework has been incorporated into systems of higher education (see, for example, Van Neil, 2010). Research suggests that curricula and programs developed in the funds of knowledge tradition for K–12 students can embrace collectivist communities in ways that support college-going behaviors among the collective. One example is the College Knowledge Academy (a pseudonym), which represents a partnership between a state university and a local school district consisting of approximately 85% Hispanic/Latino families. The program provided families with information about the courses that their children were required to take in high school to be eligible to apply for state institutions, connected them with faculty members from the university who shared similar racial/ethnic backgrounds, and exposed them to the university through tours, performances, and classroom experiences. In what follows, we highlight findings from three studies that have examined the program and demonstrate how a program that is rooted in collectivist values can facilitate college-going cultures.

Kiyama (2010, 2011) conducted pre- and post-program interviews and oral history interviews with six families who participated in the College Knowledge Academy to understand the impact of the program from the perspectives of the participants. Results indicated that access to social capital provided the families with the resources and knowledge necessary to understand and navigate the K–12 schooling system. For example, one family that had long been associated with the school district as volunteers, and had one family member who was a school bus driver, described how these associations allowed the family to network and connect with teachers and administrators at the school to learn about courses, classrooms, and involvement opportunities. Kiyama (2011) argued that, because of their extensive social networks, families have opportunities to access the same social capital around the college knowledge they are receiving as participants in the College Knowledge Academy. Moreover, college knowledge gained in the Academy was not only shared with those who were formally enrolled in the program but, because of their collectivist orientation, affected college opportunity in the larger community.

Findings from Kiyama's (2010, 2011) studies parallel those of Lew (2009), who suggested that, for Korean American families who were involved in collectivist settings (e.g., a community church), the networks developed in those settings were instrumental in providing social capital to community members and perpetuating norms and values such as attending college within the community. These norms and values influenced the college-going opportunities for Korean American high school students. Lew's (2009) findings underscore the fact that the collectivist orientations and opportunities resulting from such groups were not limited to Latina/o, African American, or Native American communities.

In a separate study of the same college outreach program, Kiyama, Lee, and Rhoades (in press) interviewed the faculty, staff, and administrators who were involved in the program to understand how they came to be involved, their specific roles and functions, and their views of the program. What emerged was an example of a *critical agency network* of faculty, staff, and administrators coming together in an effort to build and deliver college knowledge to the local Latina/o community. Kiyama et al. offer this critical agency network as a way to understand how a network of siloed professionals came together to form a subculture around a common cause. Those involved with the outreach program shared "a critique of the academy's role in reproducing social inequalities and a commitment to changing that through their service" (p. 31), and "this subculture was rooted not in academic disciplines, but in a commitment to social justice" (p. 30). In essence, the outreach program is based upon a collectivist orientation and aimed at changing the college opportunity structure for Latina/o students. The outreach program was created for a community that functions on collectivist ideals. Thus, the program itself and the ideals it embodied represented the community it aims to serve. Such programs are able to connect with Latina/o students at home, in the community, and on campus.

The Impact of Campus Involvement on College Success

A second way in which differences among collectivist and individualist cultural orientations can impact college student achievement relates to the ways in which students become involved in college. One powerful form of campus involvement for students of color is participation in culture-based student organizations. Several studies indicate that cultural student organizations assist students of color in bridging the cultural gap that exists between their home environments and the environments at PWIs (e.g., Mallinckrodt & Sedlacek, 1987; Murguia, Padilla, & Pavel, 1991; Museus, 2008; Padilla, Trevino, Gonzalez, & Trevino, 1997). Indeed, these organizations can facilitate what Museus (in press) refers to as cultural integration – the integration of the academic, social, and cultural spheres of student life. Researchers have also found that cultural student organizations provide students with supportive mentoring relationships with people of color, opportunities to give back through community service projects and by advocating for systemic changes on campus, and a "respite" from the White world in which they can feel comfortable dressing, talking, and socializing in ways that are comfortable and familiar (Guiffrida, 2003, p. 9).

Despite the well-documented benefits of participation in cultural student organizations, there have been studies that have indicated that involvement in these organizations can be problematic to students of color, if they distract those students from their academics (Flemming, 1984; Fries-Britt &Turner, 2002; Hines, 1997) or isolate students from the larger campus environment (Pascarella & Terenzini, 1991). Guiffrida (2004b) interviewed academically high- and low-achieving African American students to examine the conditions under which participation in African American student organizations supports and hinders their academic achievement and persistence. Findings suggest that cultural orientation may play a role in whether this involvement supports or hinders academic achievement. Although most of the students in the study were very active in cultural student organizations, low-achieving students were more likely to describe themselves as *over-involved* with African American student organizations to the point that their involvement interfered with their academic achievement. High-achieving students, on the other hand, tended to describe themselves as *actively involved* and detailed the benefits of their participation in these groups on their academic achievement and persistence.

In exploring the differences between self-described *over-involved* low achievers and *actively involved* high achievers, Guiffrida (2004b) uncovered salient differences between the students' definitions of success. Over-involved low achievers tended to hold definitions of success that valued service and giving back to the Black community over academic success, several even going as far as labeling academically high-achieving students who were less active in these groups as "selfish" (p. 9). Actively involved high achievers valued academic success above all else in defining a successful African American student and perceived self-proclaimed *over-involved* students as using their involvement as a poor excuse for their academic lapses.

Viewing these two perspectives from a cultural orientation lens, the values of the over-involved low achievers tended to align with the collectivist orientation. Seeking to make changes on campus and give back to the Black community, they viewed their involvement in these culturally based organizations as central in defining themselves as successful African American students. Conversely, the actively involved high-achieving students tended to align with individualist values. Whereas many of the high achievers in the study indicated that they felt that they had strong support from their home communities, they viewed their own academic success as most important in defining a successful African American student and viewed their peers' involvement in systemic change efforts as distractions from the main purpose of college (to get good grades, graduate, get a good job, etc.). This research suggests, therefore, that cultural orientations may shape the reasons that students become involved in student organizations and the ways in which they engage in these organizations. Students socialized in individualist cultures may seek to join organizations that support their individual academic and social needs in college, whereas students socialized in collectivist cultures might seek involvement with organizations that allow them to focus their efforts on societal change.

Similarly, Kiyama and Luca (2010) have documented the social and academic benefits gained by students of color during their employment as peer mentors in a university retention initiative. Among the most salient elements of their peer mentor experience was the sense of belonging and collectivism that was formed among other peer mentors and professional staff. Similar to the benefits of participating in culturally based student organizations, the relationships that students formed as part of their participation in this program with other students of color provided participants with access to extensive social networks, professional and academic opportunities, and new campus resources. The shared value of giving back to their communities of color, or reciprocity (Coleman, 1988; Newton, 1997), was evident in their reasons for deciding to work as peer mentors and in articulating their future professional goals. As indicated in social capital literature (Coleman, 1988; Stanton-Salazar, 2001), the reciprocal nature of these relationships illustrates the sense of obligation, trust, and accomplishment that is developed among a collectivist community. Kiyama and Luca concluded that, the more connections students of color felt with other peer mentors, professional staff, the college community, and extended networks with people of color, the more a "sense of obligation and reciprocity developed" (Kiyama & Luca, 2010, p. 21). This sense of obligation and reciprocity was important as students recognized the value of giving back to a community that had invested in them and helped them succeed. Research on Native Americans also finds reciprocity to be valued and, sometimes, the very reason for attending college (Guillory, 2008; Lindley, 2009; Waterman, 2007).

Changing Campus Cultures to Foster Success among Students of Color

Research reviewed in this chapter indicates that there are differences in the ways in which students from collectivist and individualist orientations may seek to engage in campus academic and social systems. In the following sections, we provide suggestions for addressing the needs of collectivist college students. We begin by providing suggestions for adapting college cultures and support structures in ways that allow these cultures to capitalize on the strengths of students' who espouse collectivist orientations. We also provide several suggestions for the ways in which institutions of higher education can assist in preparing collectivist students and their families for adaptations that can increase their success in college.

One important way in which colleges and universities can begin to shift their cultures to make them more accessible and welcoming to students from collectivist cultural orientations is by educating college faculty, staff, and students about collectivist traditions. This is particularly important given research that has found that college personnel often do not understand these rich traditions. For example, Guillory and Wolverton (2008) studied the administrators at three PWIs to assess their understanding of Native American college students' needs and found that "institutions did not fully understand the Native American student mindset, and, as a consequence, they failed to adequately meet their specific needs" (p. 84).

Some ways in which university communities can become knowledgeable about collectivist cultures is through learning from campus subcultures that reflect students' home communities (e.g., campus cultural centers and ethnic studies programs) and collaborations with ethnic communities external to the institution. Indeed, many institutions have learned and can learn much from African American, AAPI, Latino/a, and Native American cultural centers and ethnic studies programs that house individuals who are knowledgeable about collectivist communities of color. Experts in those cultural centers and ethnic studies programs can consult and provide professional faculty and staff development about the cultures of those communities. Such consultation and professional development could, for example, include (1) helping inform colleges about cultural, religious, or spiritual events that may conflict with the university calendar, (2) providing alerts about other potential cultural conflicts that might arise, such as events or policies that would infringe on Native American treaty rights, and (3) assisting colleges in providing academic advising, counseling, and university recruitment and retention initiatives in ways that are culturally sensitive and appropriate for each student.

Several examples of the aforementioned collaborations exist. On example is evident in Chicago, where the American Indian Center works collaboratively with Northwestern University in developing and providing comprehensive services to Native Americans. Most notable is that the partnership that they have created allows the college to work together with Native Americans in conducting research rather than the Native Americans being merely the subject of the research conducted by members of the university. Another salient example of such collaboration is the Asian American Studies Program at the University of Massachusetts Boston, where faculty work collaboratively with Asian American community members to teach courses, host extracurricular activities, and organize field trips for Asian American Studies courses. It is important to note that both of these examples are based on asset-minded perspectives that engage ethnic minority campus subcultures and communities as entities that have something meaningful and valuable to contribute to the educational experience.

A growing number of colleges have parent relations programs that are specifically designed to facilitate connections with parents and provide resources for them. Representatives from this office can serve as a resource to parents by welcoming them to campus, keeping them informed about upcoming events, and providing advocacy for parents. However, colleges that are serious about changing cultures to foster success among students of color from collectivist orientations must also learn about the communities from which students come and maintain broad and inclusive definitions of what constitutes a family. Western, individualist definitions of family tend to include only biological parents and siblings, whereas collectivists often include extended family members (aunts, cousins, grandparents, etc.), close friends and neighbors, and other influential members of the community (e.g., tribal and religious or spiritual leaders) in their definitions of family (Heilman, 2008). Additionally, colleges need to hire and retain a diverse staff with individuals who espouse collectivist values so that family members, friends, and students will feel comfortable seeking and receiving assistance from them.

Another way that colleges can embrace collectivist values is by offering a wide range of cultural activities for students, while also taking steps to prevent overinvolvement. Faculty members, academic advisors, college counselors, and student organization advisors must become proficient in identifying students with potential for becoming over-involved in these organizations and to provide them with leadership and time management strategies. Such strategies will help students effectively balance academic and organizational responsibilities to prevent their involvement from negatively affecting their academic achievement. Additionally, colleges seeking to capitalize on the strengths of collectivist students, including the potential they have for leading groups that foster positive systemic change on campus and in society, should recognize service to these organizations as part of the college curriculum. Institutions can do this, for example, by allowing students in these organizations to gain academic credit for their leadership and service to the community.

Along the same lines, college career services also must adapt their perspectives in ways that accommodate the needs of students from collectivist orientations. According to Waterman (2004), career counselors often assume a Western, individualist perspective regarding student mobility during job searches, which manifests in the assumption that all students are willing to move away from their home communities in pursuit of employment opportunities. Waterman points out that students from collectivist orientations may not hold the same values about mobility and may choose, instead, to return to their home communities to live, work, and contribute in meaningful ways after their college graduation, even if that means forgoing a range of career opportunities. Colleges that are committed to embracing collectivist values need to ensure that career counselors are sensitive to the needs of collectivist students when assisting them in career opportunities and potential moves without making judgments about students who choose to return home after graduation.

Colleges also need to focus on hiring and retaining faculty of color who share collectivist orientations in order to provide students with mentors who understand them and who can assist them in capitalizing on the strengths of their collectivist values. Just as important is the need for colleges to train faculty with more individualist values about the needs of collectivist students so they can adopt pedagogical practices that embrace collectivist norms and values. Faculty must be sensitive, for example, to collectivist students' desires or needs to return home for cultural nourishment and to support their families. It is important that these students be afforded opportunities to make up assignments when they need to go home to attend to the needs of their community, even if the reasons for going home are not consistent with individualist values.

Faculty can also adapt classroom environments to make them less competitive and more communal by encouraging collaborations among students in the form of group projects. Such collective work, such as study groups, has been identified as a critical factor in facilitating academic success among students of color (Fullilove & Treisman, 1990; Treisman, 1992). It is especially important for faculty to prepare students for these group experiences by affirming the various styles of group engagement, including differences that may emerge in the interpersonal styles of collectivist and individualist students. When presented properly, group projects allow students not only to learn to work effectively together, but also to appreciate the diverse interpersonal strengths that each student brings to the group. Additionally, by structuring a communal environment within group work and the classroom itself, space is created for students to share their home and community experiences and resources as important forms of knowledge (i.e., funds of knowledge) in the classroom. Incorporating students' diverse forms of knowledge into learning activities can lead to greater engagement, sense of community, and learning.

Changing campus cultures should also involve sustained efforts by colleges to engage local communities of color, specifically parents and families of elementary school-aged students of color. Research by Kiyama and colleagues suggests that outreach with local communities and families can affirm collectivist cultures and build a holistic college-going culture starting at the early elementary grade levels. Research on these outreach programs suggests that, to sustain meaningful connections with students of color, colleges must integrate families' home knowledge and assets into outreach initiatives, validate families' preexisting college knowledge, embrace families' extensive social networks, and understand families' unique educational ideologies. Meaningful college outreach programs must create opportunities for participants to share their college knowledge, educational practices, and strategies used in their homes with one another. For example, Kiyama (2010) found that families would often share educational tips during program breaks, such as creating designated homework space for kids. Colleges seeking to embrace collectivist orientations need to formally incorporate that sharing into their outreach programming to validate families' home educational practices and connect them with program curricula. By doing so, they can build on the knowledge that families already possess.

Additionally, college outreach programs must acknowledge and validate the collectivist values that some communities of color espouse. With respect to the strong social networks that families possess, Kiyama (2010) argued that outreach programs can help parents highlight how they have activated these networks in acquiring K–12 educational information and assist families in recognizing they have the same tools available to them when navigating postsecondary education. Building on the example of the family who was involved with the school district as volunteers and a bus driver, we see that these same social networks could be useful when addressing higher education questions and concerns. For example, because of the families' multiple connections to the school, they built engaging and ongoing relationships with school administration. Such relationships differ from a more traditional line of communication through which one typically makes an appointment to speak with a school administrator. The relationships with administrators can be valuable assets when making decisions about higher education as lines of communication are already established and open.

Assisting Collectivist Students in Navigating Individualist Campus Cultures

Although the emphasis of this chapter is on changing college cultures in ways that make them more amenable to collectivist students, there are also a number of steps that colleges can take to assist collectivist students and their families in understanding and adjusting to the individualist aspects of the college environment. Such efforts should begin during new student orientations. This process will probably be enhanced by including upperclassmen and their

parents who identify with collectivist values and who have successfully negoti-
ated their initial transitions to the more individualist culture at their respective
colleges, as well as faculty and staff from the college who also identify with
collective orientations.

One issue of particular relevance to students and family members with
collectivist orientations is how to negotiate the challenges that arise as the students form new social connections in college. This can be a particular problem
if parents, siblings, and other community members are dependent upon the
college-going students to provide support at home. Helping transitioning
students to anticipate interpersonal conflicts that may arise as a result of their
college transitions and providing them with coping strategies for dealing with
these issues may effectively circumvent crises that could impact their academic
performance.

At the same time, orientation staff should also educate families about their
children's upcoming experiences at college and assist those families in exploring the ways in which they can support their children during the transition
to higher education. These efforts could include actively helping families
strategize ways of finding sources of support that will partially replace that
which has been provided by the child about to enter college. Orientation
can also be an opportunity to help parents and other members of the home
community understand that subtle changes in thinking and behaving on
the part of the college-going student are normal and can indicate positive
growth and development rather than an abandonment of family/commu-
nity values. Likewise, orientation programs can also assist family members
from collectivist orientations to understand how important the emotional
and financial support they provide their children is to college success, even
small contributions (e.g., money for laundry) if that is all the family is able to
provide. Orientation leaders can encourage families to provide this support
in ways that motivate students and avoid inducing guilt for taking away from
family resources.

Another topic that should be addressed at new student orientation is the
role that involvement in culturally based student organizations and college
retention programs can have in supporting the success of students of color,
particularly those from collectivist orientations. Research suggests that participation in these culturally based activities can provide opportunities to fulfill
a number of essential needs that many collectivist students share, including
the need to connect with other collectivist students, faculty, and staff, and to
give back and make meaningful changes at college and in the larger community. At the same time, students and their families should be informed about
the negative consequences of students from collectivist orientations becoming overly involved in these activities. Therefore, in addition to encouraging
them to become involved in these organizations, orientation staff should also
provide cautions about overinvolvement and strategies to prevent collectivist

students from allowing their participation to negatively impact their academic achievement.

Conclusion

Research suggests that students of color who espouse collectivist orientations experience a number of challenges in college because their cultural orientations are inconsistent with the Western, individualist cultures that predominate at many institutions of higher education. In this chapter, we present several salient steps in which colleges can begin to shift their cultures to accommodate and embrace collectivist orientations. Such initiatives include collaborating with local cultural centers; educating parent relations staff and strengthening their services; expanding and lending greater support to culturally based student organizations, cultural centers, and student support programs; engaging local communities of color through extensive outreach programming with youth and families; and educating college faculty, advisors, and career counselors about the needs and strengths of collectivist students. Colleges that are able to adapt their cultures in ways that embrace collectivist orientations will not only allow collectivist students to flourish at college without abandoning their cultural traditions, but also provide a more communal, welcoming environment for all students.

References

Adams, D. W. (1995). *Education for extinction: American Indians and the boarding school experience: 1875–1928*. Lawrence: University of Press of Kansas.

Beattie, J. (1980). Representations of the self in traditional Africa. *Africa, 50*, 313–320.

Braxton, J. M., & Lee, S. D. (2005). Toward reliable knowledge about college student departure. In A. Seidman (Ed.), *College student retention: Formula for student success* (pp. 107–128). Westport, CT: Praeger Publications.

Cabrera, A. F., Nora, A., Terenzini, P. T., Pascarella, E. T., & Hagedorn, L. S. (1999). Campus racial climate and the adjustment of students to college: A comparison between White students and African-American students. *Journal of Higher Education, 70*(2), 134–160.

Coleman, J. S. (1988). Social capital in the creation of human capital. *American Journal of Sociology, 94*, S95–S120.

Coon, H. M., & Kemmelmeier, M. (2001). Cultural orientations in the United States: (Re)examining differences among ethnic groups. *Journal of Cross-Cultural Psychology, 32*(3), 348–364.

Delgado, D. B. (2002). Learning and living pedagogies of the home. *International Journal of Qualitative Studies in Education, 14*(5), 623–639.

Delgado-Gaitan, C. (1994). Consejos: The power of cultural narratives. *Anthropology & Education Quarterly, 25*(3), 298–316.

Dennis, J. M., Phinney, J. S., & Chuateco, L. I. (2005). The role of motivation, parental support, and peer support in the academic success of ethnic minority first-generation college students. *Journal of College Student Development, 46*(3), 223–236.

Flemming, J. (1984). *Blacks in college.* San Francisco: Jossey-Bass.

Fox, M. J. T., Lowe, S. C., & McClellan, G. S. (Eds.). (2005). *Serving Native American students* (New directions for student services, no. 109). San Francisco: Jossey-Bass.

Fries-Britt, S. L., & Turner, B. (2002). Uneven stories: The experiences of successful black collegians at a historically black and a traditionally white campus. *Review of Higher Education, 25*(3), 315–330.

Fuligni, A., Tseng, V., & Lam, M. (1999). Attitudes toward family obligations among American adolescents with Asian, Latin American, and European backgrounds. *Child Development, 70*(4), 1030–1044.

Fullilove, R. E., & Treisman, E. M. (1990). Mathematics achievement among African American undergraduates at the University of California, Berkeley: An evaluation of the mathematics workshop program. *Journal of Negro Education, 59*(3), 463–478.

Gaines, S. O., Jr., Marelich, W. D., Bledsoe, K. L., Steers, W. N., Henderson, M. C., Granrose, C. S., et al. (1997). Links between race/ethnicity and cultural values as mediated by racial/ethnic identity and moderated by gender. *Journal of Personality and Social Psychology, 72*(6), 1460–1476.

Gloria, A. M., Robinson Kurpius, S. E., Hamilton, K. D., & Wilson, M. S. (1999). African American students' persistence at a predominantly white university: Influences of social support, university comfort, and self-beliefs. *Journal of College Student Development, 40*(3), 257–268.

González, K. P. (2002). Campus culture and the experiences of Chicano students in a predominantly white university. *Urban Education, 37*(2) 193–218.

Guiffrida, D. A. (2003). African American student organizations as agents of social integration. *Journal of College Student Development, 44*(3), 304–320.

Guiffrida, D. A. (2004a). Friends from home: Asset and liability to African American students attending a predominantly White institution. *NASPA Journal, 24*(3), 693–708.

Guiffrida, D. A. (2004b). How involvement in African American student organizations supports and hinders academic achievement. *NACADA Journal, 24*(1/2), 88–98.

Guiffrida, D. A. (2005). To break away or strengthen ties to home: A complex question for African American students attending a predominantly white institution. *Equity and Excellence in Education, 38*(1), 49–60.

Guiffrida, D. A. (2006). Toward a cultural advancement of Tinto's theory. *Review of Higher Education, 29*(4), 451–472.

Guillory, J. (2008). *Diverse pathways of "giving back" to tribal community: Perceptions of Native American College Graduates.* Unpublished doctoral dissertation, Washington State University, Pullman, Washington.

Guillory, R. M., & Wolverton, M. (2008). It's about family: Native American student persistence in higher education. *Journal of Higher Education, 79*(1), 59–87.

Heilman, E. (2008). Hegemonies and "transgressions" of family: Tales of pride and prejudice. In T. Turner-Vorbeck & M. M. Marsh (Eds.), *Other Kinds of Families: Embracing Diversity in Schools* (pp. 7–27). New York: Teachers College Press.

Hendricks, A. D., Smith, K., Caplow, J. H., & Donaldson, J. F. (1996). A grounded theory approach to determining the factors related to the persistence of minority students in professional programs. *Innovative Higher Education, 21*(2), 113–126.

Hetts, J. J., Sakuma, M., & Pelham, B. W. (1999). Two roads to positive regard: Implicit and explicit self-evaluation and culture. *Journal of Experimental Social Psychology, 35*, 512–559.

Hines, S.M. (1997). *Factors influencing persistence among African American upperclassmen in natural sciences and science related majors.* Paper presented at the annual meeting of the AERA, Chicago.

Hurtado, A. (1997). Understanding multiple group identities: Inserting women into cultural transformations. *Journal of Social Issues, 53*(2), 299–328.

Hurtado, S., Carter, P. F., & Spuler, A. (1996). Latino student transition to college: Assessing difficulties and factors in successful college adjustment. *Research in Higher Education, 37*(2), 135–158.

Kirkness, V. J., & Barnhardt, R. (1991). First Nations and higher education: The four Rs – respect, relevance, reciprocity, responsibility. *Journal of American Indian Education, 30*(3), 1–15.

Kiyama, J. M. (2010). College aspirations and limitations: The role of educational ideologies and funds of knowledge in Mexican American families. *American Educational Research Journal, 47*(2), 330–356.

Kiyama, J. M. (2011). Family lessons and funds of knowledge: College-going paths in Mexican American families. *Journal of Latinos and Education, 10*(1), 23–42.

Kiyama, J. M., Lee, J. J., & Rhoades, G. (in press). A critical agency network model for building an integrated outreach program. *Journal of Higher Education.*

Kiyama, J. M., & Luca, S. G. (2010). The invisible web of opportunity: Exploring the social benefits of peer mentors in retention programs. Unpublished manuscript.

Kuh, G. D., & Love, P. G. (2000). A cultural perspective on student departure. In J. M. Braxton (Ed.), *Reworking the student departure puzzle* (pp. 196–212). Nashville, TN: Vanderbilt University Press.

Lew, J. (2009). A structural analysis of success and failure of Asian Americans: A case of Korean Americans in urban schools. *Teachers College Record, 109*(2), 369–390.

Lindley, L. S. (2009). *A tribal critical race theory analysis of academic attainment: A qualitative study of sixteen Northern Arapaho women who earned degrees at the University of Wyoming.* Unpublished doctoral dissertation, University of Wyoming, Laramie.

Lopez, G. (2001). The value of hard work: Lessons on parent involvement from an (im)migrant household. *Harvard Educational Review. 71*(3), 416–437.

Mallinckrodt, B., & Sedlacek, W. E. (1987). Student retention and the use of campus facilities by race. *National Association of Student Personnel Administrators (NASPA) Journal, 24*(3), 28–32.

Marin, G., & Marin, B. (1991). *Research with Hispanic populations.* Newbury Park, CA: Sage.

McIntyre, E., Rosebery, A., & Gonzalez, N. (2001). *Classroom diversity: Connecting curriculum to students' lives.* Portsmouth, NH: Heinemann Publishers.

Mead, M. (1967). *Cooperation and competition among primitive people.* Boston, MA: Beacon Press.

Moll, L., Amanti, C., Neff, D., & González, N. (1992). Funds of knowledge for teaching: Using a qualitative approach to connect homes and classrooms. *Theory into Practice, 31*, 132–141.

Murguia, E., Padilla, R. V., & Pavel, M. (1991). Ethnicity and the concept of social integration in Tinto's model of institutional departure. *Journal of College Student Development, 32*, 433–439.

Museus, S. D. (2008). The role of ethnic student organizations in fostering African American and Asian American students' cultural adjustment and membership at predominantly White institutions. *Journal of College Student Development, 49*(6), 568–586.

Museus, S. D. (in press). Using cultural perspectives to understand the role of ethnic student organizations in Black students' progress to the end of the pipeline. In D. E. Evensen & C. D. Pratt (Eds.), *The end of the pipeline: A journey of recognition for African Americans entering the legal profession.* Durham, NC: Carolina Academic Press.

Museus, S. D., & Harris, F. (2010). The elements of institutional culture and minority college student success. In T. E. Dancy II (Ed.), *Managing diversity: (Re)visioning equity on college campuses* (pp. 25–44). New York: Peter Lang Publishing.

Museus, S. D., & Quaye, S. J. (2009). Toward an intercultural perspective of racial and ethnic minority college student persistence. *Review of Higher Education, 33*(1), 67–94.

Museus, S. D., Maramba, D. C., Palmer, R. T., Reyes, A., & Bresonis, K. (2011). *An explanatory model of Southeast Asian American college student success: A grounded theory analysis.* Paper presented at the 2011 Annual Meeting of the American Educational Research Association, New Orleans, LA.

Newton, K. (1997). Social capital and democracy. *American Behavioral Scientist, 40*(5), 575–586.

Ngo, B., & Lee, S. (2007). Complicating the image of model minority success: A review of Southeast Asian American education. *Review of Educational Research, 77*(4), 415–453.

Nora, A. (2001). The depiction of significant others in Tinto's "rites of passage": A reconceptualization of the influence of family and community in the persistence process. *Journal of College Student Retention, 3*(1), 41–56.

Nora, A., & Cabrera, A. F. (1996). The role of perceptions of prejudice and discrimination on the adjustment of Minority students to college. *Journal of Higher Education, 67*(2), 119–148.

Padilla, R. V., Trevino, J., Gonzalez, K., & Trevino, J. (1997). Developing local models of minority student success. *Journal of College Student Development, 38*(2), 125–138.

Pascarella, E. T. & Terenzini, P. T. (1991). *How college affects students: Findings and insights from twenty years of research.* San Francisco: Jossey-Bass.

Phinney, J. S. (1996). When we talk about American ethnic groups, what do we mean? *American Psychologist, 51*, 918–927.

Rendón, L. I., Jaloma, R. E., & Nora, A. (2000). Theoretical considerations in the study of minority student retention in higher education. In J. M. Braxton (Ed.), *Reworking the student departure puzzle* (pp. 127–156). Nashville, TN: Vanderbilt University Press.

Rios-Aguilar, C. & Kiyama, J. M. (in press). Funds of knowledge: A proposed approach to study Latina/o students' transition to college. *Journal of Latinos and Education.*

Rosas, M., & Hamrick, F. A. (2002). Postsecondary enrollment and academic decision making: Family influences on women college students of Mexican descent. *Equity and Excellence in Education, 35*(1), 59–69.

Stanton-Salazar, R. D. (2001). *Manufacturing hope and despair: The school and kin networks of U.S. Mexican youth.* New York: Teachers College Press.

Staples, R., & Mirandé, A. (1980). Racial and cultural variations among American families: A decennial review of the literature on minority families. *Journal of Marriage and the Family, 42*, 887–903.

Thompson, C. E., & Fretz, B. R. (1991). Predicting the adjustment of black students at predominantly white institutions. *Journal of Higher Education, 62*(4), 437–450.

Tierney, W. G. (1992). An anthropological analysis of student participation in college. *Journal of Higher Education, 63*(6), 603–618.

Tierney, W. G. (1999). Models of minority college-going and retention: Cultural integrity versus cultural suicide. *Journal of Negro Education, 68*(1), 80–91.

Tinto, V. (1993). *Leaving college: Rethinking the causes and cures of student attrition* (2nd edn.). Chicago: University of Chicago Press.

Treisman, U. (1992). Studying students studying calculus: A look at the lives of minority mathematics students in college. *College Mathematics Journal, 23*(5), 362–372.

Triandis, H. C. (1989). The self and social behavior in differing cultural contexts. *Psychological Review, 96,* 506–520.

Triandis, H. C., Chen, X. P., & Chan, D. K. (1998). Scenarios for the measurement of collectivism and individualism. *Journal of Cross-Cultural Psychology, 54*(2), 323–338.

Triandis, H. C., McCusker, C., & Hui, C. H. (1990). Multicultural probes of individualism and collectivism. *Journal of Personality and Social Psychology, 59*(5), 1006–1020.

Valenzuela, A. (1999). *Subtractive schooling: U.S.-Mexican youth and the politics of caring.* Albany: State University of New York Press.

Van Neil, J. (2010). *Eliciting and activating funds of knowledge in an environmental science community college classroom: An action research study.* Unpublished doctoral dissertation, University of Rochester, Rochester, NY.

Villenas, S. (2001). Latina mothers and small-town racisms: Creating narratives of dignity and moral education in North Carolina. *Anthropology & Education Quarterly. 32*(1), 3–28.

Waterman, S. J. (2004). *The Haudenosaunee college experience: A complex path to degree completion.* Unpublished dissertation, Syracuse University, Syracuse, NY.

Waterman, S. J. (2007). A complex path to Haudenosaunee degree completion. *Journal of American Indian Education, 46*(1), 20–40

Yamaguchi, S., Kuhlman, D. M., & Sugimori, S. (1995). Personality correlates of allocentric tendencies in individualist and collectivist cultures. *Journal of Cross-Cultural Psychology, 26,* 658–672.

5

FOSTERING CULTURES OF INCLUSION IN THE CLASSROOM

From Marginality to Mattering

Stephen John Quaye and Stephanie H. Chang

Within postsecondary institutions, classrooms are places in which faculty and students create subcultures where learning is supposed to happen. However, many students of color find these spaces exclusive and marginalizing, which impedes their ability to learn (Terenzini, Cabrera, Colbeck, Bjorklund, & Parente, 2001). One approach to fostering inclusive classroom cultures is to address racial diversity directly and engage students in dialogues about racial issues. In this chapter, we discuss strategies for moving the culture of classrooms from marginalizing and silent on racial matters to classroom cultures of inclusiveness. We begin with a review of literature on campus and classroom cultures and preparedness among faculty to facilitate racial dialogues. Next, we discuss the theoretical framework that guides our arguments. We then discuss the methodology and methods that guided a study of faculty who facilitate racial dialogues within their classrooms, and we utilize data from participants in that inquiry to reveal the ways they endeavored to foster cultures of inclusion within the classroom. Finally, we conclude this chapter with a discussion and implications for practice.

Representation in the Campus Culture

Based on the experiences of two Chicano students, González (2002) explored the relationship between campus culture and those undergraduates' persistence and described campus culture in relation to social, physical, and epistemological characteristics. The structural diversity (Hurtado, Milem, Clayton-Pederson, & Allen, 1998) in racial and ethnic demographics is part of González's social component of campus culture. The "social world" (p. 202) is the "lack of Chicano representation" (p. 202) in the population, political power, and language spoken on campus. The physical aspect of campus culture includes buildings, sculptures, and "other physical symbols, such as posters, banners, or flyers" (González, 2002, p. 205) that also relate to a lack of Chicano representation on campus. Additionally, González identified an epistemological component of campus culture that refers to the "knowledge existing and being exchanged on campus" (p. 207). For the two Chicano students in González's qualitative study, the combination of a missing Chicano academic program and Chicano courses on campus did not demonstrate an inclusive or welcoming campus culture for Chicano students. The thread throughout defining campus culture, in terms of González's study, is representation; a lack of representation within the dominant campus culture excludes certain populations.

A Black student in Feagin, Vera, and Imani's (1996) study described perusing the college yearbook and finding little representation of students of color among the hundreds of photos. Researchers have illuminated the power of symbols and the subtle messages that portraits – such as those found in yearbooks – send to students from different racial/ethnic groups (Hebdige, 1979; Magolda, 1999, 2000; Quantz, 1999; Salzman, 2001), and the lack of Black student representation in the yearbook signals a campus culture of exclusion. The lack of attention to representation of students of color means that those students will continue to experience marginalization because institutions do not include their experiences, stories, or histories. Furthermore, by excluding students of color, the dominant narrative is one that primarily includes and values White students. This reality is a function of the fact that the dominant campus culture is founded on values, beliefs, and assumptions of the White majority.

White culture, in this regard, perpetuates a dominant social identity, belief system, and mode of teaching (Adams, 1992; Dessel, 2010). In terms of race, sexuality, and gender, the dominant identities on most college campuses include White heterosexual men who likely believe in the religious traditions of Christianity and value teaching and learning under a "banking concept of education" (Freire, 1970, p. 72). Freire's metaphor of banking education places faculty in positions of power and the beholders of all knowledge, whereas students passively receive and accept knowledge. This manner of teaching and learning maintains a social order or hierarchy of power on college campuses and in society (Adams, 1992; Dessel, 2010; Freire, 1970). Adams (1992) noted the following: "How confusing it must be, then, for students whose historical and cultural experience has not reflected the belief of the dominant culture" (p. 7). For students of color attending predominantly White institutions (PWIs), the campus culture presents a challenge of locating subcultures that understand the difficulty of fitting in on campus.

To transform classroom cultures, Adams (1992) named faculty as the key constituent at postsecondary institutions to deconstruct and analyze the exclusive nature of campus culture:

> The role of college faculty in consciously or unconsciously transmitting a dominant cultural system is especially important in addressing present challenges since, in higher education, all roads lead back to the faculty who have control in matters of teaching, evaluation, and curriculum. (p. 7)

Tsui (2000), in a study on the effects of campus culture on students' critical thinking, found that, when faculty took active measures to help students define knowledge for themselves, the classroom culture became more inclusive and advanced students' critical thinking abilities. When the classroom culture was not attuned to the differential experiences that students bring as a result of their racial or ethnic backgrounds, then students of color had the burden of working within classroom cultures that did not include their "stories, icons, and rituals" (Dessel, 2010, p. 413). This unfairly placed students of color in the position of representing their entire racial and ethnic communities (hooks, 1994; Tatum, 1997). Therefore, a clear consequence of dominant classroom cultures is the adverse influence on students of color. To address exclusive campus cultures, Dessel (2010) presented measures to improve intergroup relationships between students on campus; one approach for doing so was fostering meaningful dialogues (Tsui, 2000) between faculty and students since research demonstrates that faculty and student interaction influences campus culture (e.g., Lambert, 1993). In a review of faculty and student interaction literature, Lambert found that the informal nature or out-of-classroom interaction between faculty and students contributed to the socialization of "students' values, attitudes, and beliefs" or culture (p. 971). Lambert also found that it was the responsibility of faculty to create a culture in the classroom that invited students to interact. The next section of the literature review addresses faculty's preparedness to facilitate a particular type of interaction: racial dialogues.

Faculty Preparedness to Engage in Racial Dialogues

Garcia and Van Soest (2000) studied faculty members' responses to racial interactions during their courses and found that some – mostly White – faculty attempted to deflect racial tension through humor, whereas others – mostly faculty members of color – addressed racial issues directly and displayed cultural competence in their responses. Thus, the findings suggest that faculty members' backgrounds may shape their ability to respond to race in the classroom. For instance, Garcia and Van Soest noted: "faculty who have experienced oppression in their own lives (e.g., women, people of color) were significantly more responsive" (p. 32) to the classroom scenarios addressing issues of diversity. The notion that faculty members of color were more likely to empathize with scenarios based on race in the classroom does not discount the experiences of White faculty members, but suggests that a faculty member's social identity and response to racial interactions can influence the classroom culture.

In a study of White faculty facilitating difficult dialogues on race, Sue, Torino, Capodilupo, Rivera, and Lin (2010) found that eight participants lacked the training or education to facilitate these dialogues. Participants mentioned not having good strategies for facilitating difficult dialogues. They also asserted that the disciplines in which White faculty taught did not seem ready for difficult dialogues, describing their academic fields as "conservative" and "very behind other conversations around race" (p. 1101). Overall, participants seemed unsure of how to proceed during racial dialogues, for their graduate and faculty training did not prepare them to engage in racial discourse within the classroom context. Thus, there appears to be a lack of preparation among faculty to facilitate racial dialogues, particularly White faculty, which can then contribute to cultures within the classroom that are marginalizing for students of color. Nevertheless, faculty members have a responsibility to shape the culture of classrooms that is inclusive, encouraging, and inviting of students' experiences.

Mattering, Marginality, Race, and Learning Partnerships

In the preceding discussion, we reviewed literature on the culture of campuses, as well as the inadequate preparation of many faculty members to facilitate racial dialogues. Our theoretical framework builds on that literature by underscoring theories that relate to creating a culture of inclusion in the classroom. We highlight three theories and frameworks in this section: Mattering and Marginality, Critical Race Theory (CRT), and the Learning Partnerships Model. Rather than discussing these theories in isolation, we discuss them together to draw connections between the three theories and the focus of our chapter.

The classroom is a space where students expect to engage in learning, but when students experience marginality from the culture of the classroom (Schlossberg, 1989) it presents barriers to learning. Students can experience marginality and feel out-of-place or a lack of belonging to the classroom culture. Feeling out-of-place is common when students begin their transition into new cultures (i.e., the transition into postsecondary institutions) and that exclusion is enhanced for students of color because of their race and ethnicity. For instance, in Villalpando's (2003) examination of the self-segregation of Latina/o students, he quoted one Latina student who stated, "I hate this . . . we are the only Chicana/os in this entire [dining hall] . . . the White fraternity boys are in that corner, the sorority girls are right next to them, and the jocks are across the way" (p. 627). The student provided expression of marginality, and such feelings can permeate both out-of-class and classroom experiences.

Schlossberg (1989) positioned mattering as the concept that intersects marginality, meaning that students who felt isolated needed to know that they were "significant" (p. 13). In the classroom, experiencing significance means that faculty members pay close attention to the students who experience marginality. For the student in Villalpando's (2003) study, mattering can mean that faculty members are open to hearing and listening to Chicana/o students' experiences. The theoretical framework that Villalpando used in support of facilitating students' sense of mattering is CRT. Critical Race Theory can be used in the classroom to situate students' learning about race in their own experiences (Ladson-Billings, 1998), which is one of the principles of Baxter Magolda's (2004) Learning Partnerships Model (LPM). The traditional classroom environment perceives students as objective learners, where faculty members are the beholders of knowledge and students are passive actors who only receive knowledge (Freire, 1970). As we discuss in the following paragraphs, CRT and the LPM challenge the notion that students are objective learners and advocate that faculty and students co-construct knowledge in the classroom based on individual experiences with race and racism.

Critical Race Theory evolved from Critical Legal Studies (CLS) (Ladson-Billings, 1999), which investigates the social and political implications of race and racism in society (e.g., Civil Rights Movement) (Ladson-Billings & Tate, 1995). This investigation of race and racism attracted scholars in disciplines beyond Legal Studies and into academic disciplines such as Education, African American Studies, Sociology, and Women's Studies. As an interdisciplinary theory, the focus of CRT is always to center knowledge that is related to race and racism (Delgado & Stefancic, 2001; Ladson-Billings, 1998). Critical Race Theory scholars (Delgado & Stefancic, 2001; Ladson-Billings, 1999; Ladson-Billings & Tate, 1995; Solórzano, 1997; Villalpando, 2003) frequently cite that CRT (1) is interdisciplinary in nature, (2) centers on race and racism, (3) recognizes the social construction of race, (4) uses counterstories and experiential knowledge, and (5) promotes theory to practice, or praxis. Critical Race Theory provides a useful framework for understanding how to create inclusive classroom cultures.

Regarding the first tenet, CRT is a non-traditional theoretical framework in education because it considers multiple disciplinary perspectives. Second, CRT "seeks to transform the relationship among race, racism, and power" (Delgado & Stefancic, 2001, p. 144). To make race, racism, and power focal points, CRT defines race and racism as social constructions, whereby "race [as a] socially constructed category, created differential racial groups" (Solórzano, Ceja, & Yosso, 2000, p. 60). Race and racism are "normal and natural to people in this culture [and] the strategy becomes one of unmasking and exposing race and racism in its various permutations" (Ladson-Billings, 1998, p. 12).

As the third tenet of CRT, race and racism as social constructions reveal that White people are privileged and people of color (i.e., marginalized racial identities) experience racial oppression (Ladson-Billings, 1999; Wise, 2008). Therefore, CRT can emphasize a specific focus on the experience of students of color. The experiences of these students are what CRT scholars would describe as experiential knowledge (Delgado & Stefancic, 2001; Ladson-Billings, 1999; Ladson-Billings & Tate, 1995; Solórzano, 1997; Solórzano et al., 2000; Villalpando, 2003).

As the fourth tenet of CRT, the use of counterstories and experiential knowledge (Delgado & Stefancic, 2001; Ladson-Billings, 1999; Ladson-Billings & Tate, 1995; Solórzano, 1997; Solórzano et al., 2000; Villalpando, 2003) personalizes and values students of color as students who experience marginalization. Counterstories are "formalized storytelling" (Ladson-Billings, 1999, p. 14) that emphasize the voices and experiences of those with marginalized racial and ethnic identities. As Delgado and Stefancic (2001) noted, "critical storytellers believe that stories also have valid destructive function [since] society constructs the social world through a series of tacit agreements mediated by images, pictures, tales, and scripts" (p. 42).

The act of including voices and experiences from those who are marginalized can constitute an act of liberation and integration of CRT into practice or praxis (Ladson-Billings, 1999). This leads into the fifth tenet of CRT, bringing CRT from theory to practice. Using CRT as a methodology is an intentional process of highlighting the racial experiences of students of color and advocating for issues of social justice (Solórzano, 1997). Solórzano wrote, "[the] theory has an overall commitment to social justice and the elimination of racism" (p. 7). Although all the characteristics of CRT are important and relevant, for an inclusive classroom culture to support students in mattering, strong emphasis is placed on the use of counterstories and experiential knowledge (Delgado & Stefancic, 2001; Ladson-Billings, 1999; Ladson-Billings & Tate, 1995; Solórzano, 1997; Solórzano et al., 2000; Villalpando, 2003). Recognizing students' counterstories and experiential knowledge validates students as knowers and situates learning in their experiences with race and racism, two LPM principles (Baxter Magolda, 2004). Using theories that center students' identity, experiences, and engagement with knowledge addresses the need to shift or change norms, values, and assumptions in classroom culture.

Faculty members and students collaboratively create classroom culture but do so in connection with the culture of their campus, as González (2002) noted in his study of two Chicano students. Schein (1996) wrote: "culture can be understood historically if we think about how we get concepts in the first place" (p. 231), which aligns with the use of CRT, LPM, and the Theory of Mattering and Marginality since these theoretical frameworks take into account the social-historical past that contributes to the emergence and perpetuation of race and racism in the United States. Schein defined culture as "shared norms, values, and assumptions" (p. 221), and thus the culture of race and racism is in part about ensuring that stories of students of color become normally shared, culturally valued, and assumed to be assets in the classroom.

Delgado Bernal (2002) stated: "students of color are holders and creators of knowledge, they often feel as if their histories, experiences, cultures, and languages are devalued, misinterpreted, or omitted within formal educational settings" (p. 106). To value and make known that students' "histories, experience, culture, and language" (p. 106) matter (Schlossberg, 1989) is an act of challenging dominate narratives. Challenging dominate narratives means to "shatter complacency, challenge dominate discourse on race, and further the struggle for racial reform" (Solórzano & Yosso, 2002, p. 32). Solórzano et al. (2000) used CRT to highlight the experience of African Americans. This study illustrated that African American students, similar to the Chicana/o students in Villalpando's (2003) study, experience a sense of invisibility on campus. To demonstrate students' experience, researchers used interviews and focus groups to bring forward storytelling, voice, and the experiental knowledge (Solórzano, 1997; Solórzano et al., 2000). For instance, an African American student in Solórzano et al.'s (2000) study stated, "I've had times when a guy in the class . . . [said], 'Well, I don't want to work with you because you're Black' . . . and it was upsetting cause . . . I came here thinking that it wouldn't be like this, and that was naïve" (p. 67). Understanding the experience of this student is a source of knowledge; the African American student is sharing and telling her story in her voice about the marginalization she experiences in the classroom. By focusing on personal narratives and experiential knowledge in CRT, marginalized students are "naming one's own reality" (Ladson-Billings & Tate, 1995, p. 57). Providing space and time to name and speak about the experience of marginalization (Ladson-Billings & Tate, 1995) is valuing students as whole learners in the classroom environment.

Students enter classrooms as subjective learners with personal experiences according to their social identities. In CRT, the focus is on their experiences with race and racism. Seeing students as subjective learners who have valuable experiences to share in the classroom demonstrates that the experience of marginalization matters (Schlossberg, 1989). Baxter Magolda's (2004) LPM defines learning "as a partnership among teachers and learners" (p. 214). When learning is a partnership, the power dynamics among teachers and learners are lessened to welcome and situate students as having experiential knowledge that matters. Both CRT and LPM center learning within students' experiences. Critical Race Theory and LPM work to change the traditional classroom culture that Freire (1970) termed the banking model of education, whereby teachers deposit knowledge into students. Critical Race Theory focuses on the experience of marginalization with race and racism for students of color, and LPM encourages the co-construction of knowledge between teachers and students. Shifting the culture of the classroom from one in which students may feel out-of-place to one in which students matter and construct knowledge fosters new possibilities for academic and social success among diverse populations.

Situating the Study

The data for this study come from a critical race case study that was conducted by the first author of this chapter. Therefore, in this section, instances of first-person refer to Quaye. I was interested in hearing directly from participants about the strategies they employed to facilitate dialogues about racial issues. Given my interest in the meanings that participants made of their facilitation, I utilized qualitative data-gathering methods and talked directly with participants. The study was based in constructivism, meaning I believed in the importance of the varied meanings people make about their experiences and the importance of hearing the multiple realities of participants (Phillips & Soltis, 2004). Constructivists assert that, given the varied ways that human beings interpret the world, it is important to listen to these different interpretations and work to make meaning of their different realities. Critical Race Theory also guided the study given the inquiry's explicit attention to race and racism (Ladson-Billings, 1999). I listened to how participants challenged dominant ideologies, two of which are colorblindness and ignoring issues of race (Delgado Bernal, 2002). Participants engaged racial realities directly in a classroom setting. Critical Race Theory helped me focus on the racialized meanings from participants and examine how race and racism were central topics in their courses.

Site

The site for this study was the 2007 meeting of the National Conference on Race and Ethnicity in American Higher Education (NCORE) that was held in San Francisco, California. I chose NCORE as a space in which to examine this topic given the central focus on race at this conference. I determined that people who attended this conference would likely have useful information and experience about facilitating dialogues of this nature. Thus, I performed a comprehensive review of past program booklets from the 2004, 2005, 2006, and 2007 NCORE meetings and identified those persons who had presented on a topic that was my research focus of understanding how faculty facilitate racial dialogues. I contacted these individuals and asked if they would be at the 2007 conference and willing to be interviewed about their experiences. One hundred and fifty-three participants met my criteria, but only a small segment attended the 2007 meeting and I did not have the time or space to interview that many people. Thus, based on availability at the 2007 conference and available resources, I ultimately included 22 participants in my study.

Data Collection and Analysis Procedures

Semi-structured interviews were the primary data collection procedure used for this study. I created a list of questions to enable participants to discuss their facilitation approaches for racial dialogues with me (Patton, 2002). However, I also probed further into participants' comments and allowed the interview to go in the direction that made sense given the person's remarks. In addition to interviews, I also reviewed some documents for this study (Hodder, 2000), including the faculty member's syllabi, to take note of readings, engagement activities, course expectations, and the design of the course. I also looked at campus newspapers at the participants' institutions to see if there were relevant campus culture issues related to race that might have affected students' abilities or willingness to engage in these dialogues. Since I did not interview participants on their home campuses, I wanted to be able to include these campus culture issues if they were necessary. I analyzed the data by looking across the different cases to examine patterns and differences in participants' approaches (Yin, 2003) (for a detailed discussion of methods, see Quaye, 2008).

Making the Classroom Culture More Inclusive

The findings presented in this section are those that most aligned with the focus of this chapter – efforts at facilitating dialogues in ways that made the classroom culture more inclusive. Thus, we report data on the following three themes: the notion of a safe space, inviting students to share their stories, and co-constructing knowledge with students. These elements are similar to aligned with the social, physical, and epistemological aspects of campus discussed by González (2002).

Creating a Safe Space

Participants in the present study wrestled with the notion of safe space. Classroom spaces are often seen as places in which students can candidly discuss topics that generate many uncomfortable feelings (e.g., racism, sexism, oppression). The goal of creating safe spaces is to cultivate a culture within that space where mistakes are acceptable with the hope of learning more about these topics and engaging openly with others. Paige,[1] a White woman, described the culture of her classroom as such:

> I don't believe that you can learn anything if you don't trust the person. The climate of your class has to be trustworthy; it has to be the kind of

place that people feel safe. It is important to establish and meet the needs of students in terms of their trust level – to ask questions, to inquire, to learn, and a trust level that I am going to do my best to provide the kinds of experiences and information that they need to do well.

Trust and safety were essential components of the culture that Paige aimed to cultivate within her classrooms; she endeavored to foster a classroom space that perpetuated a culture in which students could trust each other and feel safe. Laurel, an African American woman, further described the importance of creating classroom cultures that are based on trust and safety:

> You don't start off, "So, let's talk about race." It's a gradation. I have to create a safe space first. I start from a place of non-judgment, and I will do some exercises first to make people easy in talking. I tend to talk in a way that people can be somewhat detached and not have to necessarily feel that they're going to be the guilty White person, the angry Black person, the quiet Asian person, or all of the stereotypes that we struggle with. I want to protect students, not from what they hear, but from being hurt unnecessarily. I try to create safe spaces, where people can leave class going, "Hmm," as opposed to, "I'm never going to go back to that class again. I'm done. I'm dropping this class." We might go to a lecture on Ann Coulter, or somebody who is on the opposite side of me, so they can see that I'm not this "one conversation Laurel."

Rather than immediately beginning discussions with addressing race directly and immediately, Laurel mentioned the importance of gradually getting to the point of discussing race by starting with lower-risk activities to help students feel at ease with engaging with their peers. Doing so, she suggested, helped counter stereotypes among students and unnecessary hurt. She wanted to ensure that students continued to progress in the dialogues, which moved into discussions with progressively more depth and difficulty. Additionally, by starting at "a place of non-judgment," Laurel's assumption was that suspending judgment would invite more dialogue.

Not all participants agreed on the importance of creating a safe space. Some preferred to use the term "safer space" instead. As shared by Teva, a White woman:

> I don't believe in "safe space." I believe in a "safer space," and safety includes discomfort. Part of a safer space is, how do we move through discomfort? How do we deal with anger? How do we deal with sadness? Part of safety is not "no one ever makes me angry." That is not safe because that is not real. If it is real, it is like, "Okay, when I feel that, how do I work with it in a class?"

Recognizing some of the connotations from the word *safe*, Teva instead used the term *safer space* to acknowledge that discomfort was a natural and expected emotion during these difficult dialogues. She endeavored to help students manage the emotions they experienced rather than ignoring them. Emotions, according to Teva, were necessary elements of these dialogues that warranted attention and discussion.

Inviting Students to Share Stories

Given their efforts to foster a classroom culture that was inclusive and reflected a sense of mattering, participants believed in the importance of students sharing their personal narratives and voices alongside academic content during racial dialogues. Thus, they invited students to share their stories about race and racism, as a means to help them personalize these issues. For example, Sabrina, a White woman, noted the following:

> I used to do the traditional, "Here's the content, let me lecture, let's have a discussion." I realized that students would learn better though concrete experience, reflection, and application than they do necessarily though abstract thinking. It's important for students to bring their whole selves to the classroom – there's room for emotion and personal storytelling. I make sure [their experience] is as valued as the expert content that comes in the readings or the lectures. I try to be flexible in that if there's something that they want to know or a place they want to go, I'm willing to change the syllabus or pursue something different. I want them to own their own learning.

Rather than lecturing to students about racial issues, Sabrina believed in the importance of grounding students' learning in their own experiences and did so through reflection and asking them to use their personal experiences (i.e., emotions and stories) to connect them with the "expert content" from readings. She engaged students' stories so that their peers could hear the varied and similar ways in which students made sense of racial issues. Wanting students to own their learning, she also used their preferences to pursue topics that were of interest to them. Another participant, Keely, a White woman, noted a similar point in teaching "Diversity 101":

> The most productive way to teach [about racial realities] is to engage students about first their personal experiences, beliefs, advice, and biases, instead of just going in and presenting all this data and lecture materials and the history. It won't mean quite as much to them unless they first think about their own experiences and what they've learned in their lives from their parents, school, and society. I would engage them in an activity

first around the topic and then process and follow-up with data to create as safe of an environment in the classroom as possible, so that students feel comfortable being honest and open about what they've learned and what they think.

As conveyed by Keely, facilitating dialogues about racial realities necessitated starting with students' personal experiences rather than first lecturing and using data. In order to help students feel comfortable in engaging race, Keely invited learners to speak about their experiences in school and society and what they learned from parents about racial issues. She invited students to co-construct the culture within the classroom rather than socializing students to the dominant culture of academia by treating them as empty vessels needing to be filled with knowledge. Doing so made students more willing to participate in the dialogues.

When asked to describe their facilitation approach, most participants did not mention specific theories upon which their practices are based. However, Kaela's (a Lebanese American woman) facilitation approach was grounded in the work of Baxter Magolda (2004):

> My philosophy is rooted in Baxter Magolda's theories of teaching and learning – to ground material in students' experiences. I try to create an environment that's going to facilitate students moving into more complex, critical, and conceptual ways of knowing. According to Baxter Magolda, that's related to students feeling like the material really applies to them personally and has something to do with their lives, giving them an opportunity for voice. I encourage them to do some writing where they're using first person, and they're relating to the material not just intellectually, but in other ways, too, especially teaching about gender and race because it is personal.

She believed that, in order to best facilitate these dialogues, she needed to connect the material to students' experiences, which created a culture in the classroom where students felt that they mattered. Again, using personal stories was one approach to doing so because these narratives enabled students to see how they could use their own stories as valid material during the dialogues. Relating the racial and gendered material to their personal experiences, Kaela noted, provided students with more opportunities to make sense of these issues in their lives.

Co-constructing Knowledge with Students

Creating a classroom culture of inclusion during racial dialogues meant participants co-constructed knowledge with students by seeing students and themselves as both teachers and learners. This approach fostered an environment where students discussed racial issues. Kaela shared the following:

> I give them [learners] opportunities to create knowledge together to understand that knowledge is socially constructed. For some students, that's really hard because they think, "You mean, you're not just going to tell me the answer, and I give it back to you on a test?" It's really important for students to understand that what we're going to be doing in the classroom is a creation of knowledge, that what they're learning is not just what they're going to find in the textbook. They're going to learn from each other, and they're going to learn from their own selves and their reflections.

Students were surprised when they were expected to co-create knowledge in the classroom because they did not experience this in other courses, so having this kind of ownership often required that participants help students understand the socially constructed nature of knowledge and begin to see their peers as valuable contributors to the learning process. When students created knowledge, they co-constructed the epistemological element of the classroom culture.

As Laurel noted, these dialogues allowed students to see themselves as scholars:

> My work is to make people curious and help them to know that I'm not all-knowing. The work for you [learners] is to be curious and to know more – to help you see yourself as a scholar, instead of just taking this class because it's "check-off as you move through." Particularly for students of color, I need to help you see yourself as a scholar.

Rather than simply checking off this course, Laurel wanted to help students shift their understanding of a faculty member by disclosing to students that she was not all-knowing. Thus, she wanted to share knowledge with students so that they would also see how they could contribute meaningful knowledge to these dialogues.

In another portion of her interview, Laurel mentioned that she espoused Freire's (1970) principles in her facilitation style, as she strove to help students see themselves as teachers and learners during these dialogues:

> [I espouse] a Freireian sense of participation in education. I have maybe a broader knowledge, but I don't have all the knowledge, so I encourage sharing of that knowledge by students with me and others. I enter the classroom as a teacher and a learner. I try to equalize the power dynamics in the room. We're in a circle in the classroom. I try to create an atmosphere

that we're all here in a lifelong learning process. This isn't going to be the definitive class on race or ethnicity. It's a lot of self-exploration, reflection, learning about one's own self and be[ing] willing to listen and understand the perspectives of others. [We try to] understand society, structures, systems of oppression, and how they play out for one individually, depending on their identity and how that affects others. We're not just teaching about the oppressed group. We're teaching about the oppressor as well.

Realizing that she did not hold all relevant knowledge, Laurel used specific measures to exemplify her Freireian philosophy. She and students sat together in a circle to remove her from the front of the room. In addition to reflection activities that prompted students to explore the sources of their own and peers' knowledge, she asked students to consider the cultural systems involved in maintaining oppression. Thus, she worked to jointly construct knowledge with students so that they could also take ownership over their learning during these racial dialogues.

Recommendations for Fostering Inclusive Classroom Cultures

The participants in this study wrestled with the notion of a safe or safer space where students struggled with how to create a trusting classroom environment where mistakes were allowed. In addition, they invited students to use their personal stories during dialogues to make sense of the academic content as well as co-constructed knowledge with students so that students could see themselves as both teachers and learners during dialogues and value their cultural assumptions, norms, and values. The strategies used by participants and the theoretical framework in this chapter help better understand how to foster inclusive classroom cultures.

These practices were emblematic of Baxter Magolda's (2004) LPM principles, wherein she advocates that educators situate learning in students' experiences, validate students as knowers, and mutually construct knowledge with students. Although Kaela was the only participant who mentioned Baxter Magolda's principles explicitly, others utilized facilitation approaches that were consistent with her LPM. The creation of a safe or safer space that was built on trust and openness embodied their belief that, for learners to discuss racial issues, they needed to be in a culture that included and affirmed their experiences, values, and voices. In addition, by inviting students to speak from their personal experiences, they realized that they needed to situate learning about racial issues in participants' direct experiences and cultural beliefs. Furthermore, co-constructing knowledge with students reflected an interest in mutually constructing knowledge (i.e., the epistemological cultural dimension) with them and seeing them as teachers in the classroom. These practices created a culture in which students were willing to engage racial issues directly because their cultural values, stories, and beliefs were included in the process. Participants did not only lecture to students but provided them with numerous, sustained opportunities to speak from their vantage points and share their personal narratives about race and racism in their lives. Thus, educators who wish to engage these dialogues in their own courses should provide opportunities for students to see themselves as knowledgeable and listen to the cultural beliefs and values of students.

Asking students of color, in particular, to see themselves as scholars in the classroom is consistent with a central tenet from CRT, the recognition of experiential knowledge and counternarratives (Delgado & Stefancic, 2001; Ladson-Billings, 1998). Since students of color are regularly socialized not to see themselves as scholars and are marginalized within higher education settings, participants wanted to challenge this customary belief among students. They did so by using counternarratives from students of color in the classroom where they shared their racial experiences and began to see themselves as scholars.

Consistent with the principles of mattering and marginality by Schlossberg (1989), participants in the present study worked to shift the classroom from a space that was silent on racial matters to a space where racial issues were discussed directly and consistently. Thus, they wanted to make students of color feel that they mattered in the classroom setting by engaging racial issues. Participants challenged the colorblind ideology that one should not talk about race and instead facilitated racial dialogues by asking students to share racial memories and stories and engage with their peers during these dialogues. These practices enabled students to feel like they mattered and moved the voices of students of color to the center during these dialogues.

As mentioned in the literature review, exclusive campus cultures have negative effects on students' sense of belonging, mattering, and persistence (González, 2002). Thus, it is important that faculty who facilitate these dialogues strive to foster campus and classroom cultures that are inclusive. One approach for doing so, as seen throughout the aforementioned data, is addressing racial issues directly and developing the means to facilitate these dialogues. When race was treated with care, students learned that they can and should discuss racial matters. This practice also demonstrated to learners that their faculty members cared about discussing these issues rather than ignoring race. Consequently, to counteract the exclusive classroom cultures that pervade many PWIs, faculty can develop their skills in facilitating racial dialogues and work to address race directly during their courses. Faculty should also pay attention to the culture of their classrooms by asking students to name what assumptions, norms, and values are being perpetuated within it. In addition, faculty should find avenues for enabling students to take ownership over aspects of their learning by specifying the ways in which they want the classroom structured to facilitate racial dialogues. Doing so demonstrates to students their own authority and expertise – critical factors in the LPM (Baxter Magolda, 2004).

Conclusion

In this chapter, we made a case for strategies faculty might employ to facilitate racial dialogues and structure the classroom culture in inclusive ways. Using theories of Critical Race Theory, Mattering and Marginality, and the Learning Partnerships Model, we discussed how these three theories are helpful for designing classroom contexts that are attuned to learners' racial/ethnic identities and privilege the narratives and experiences of students. Considerations for implementing inclusive classroom cultures include:

- acknowledging the sociohistorical relevance of a culture that perpetuates race and racism and other systemic issues and identities that influence the classroom;
- creating "safe" or "safer spaces" by building trust, acknowledging assumptions, and inviting students to share their personal experiences;
- asking students to personalize content by identifying how they can relate content to their own experiences;
- encouraging students to see themselves as educators and scholars by implementing activities through which they come to their own conclusions based on their own cultural values, norms, and practices;
- explicitly stating one's own cultural biases, assumptions, and values about teaching about issues of race and racism.

As seen throughout the findings, fostering a classroom culture of inclusion necessitates thinking through what a safe space means and looks like, inviting students to share their stories about race, and co-constructing knowledge with students. Participants in the current study confirmed that these practices can help facilitate racial dialogues effectively and enable students of color to no longer feel excluded or marginalized in the classroom.

Note

1 All names are pseudonyms.

References

Adams, M. (1992). Cultural inclusion in American college classroom. *New Directions for Teaching and Learning: Teaching for Diversity, 49*(1), 5–17.

Baxter Magolda, M. B. (2004). Learning partnerships model: A framework for promoting self-authorship. In M. B. Baxter Magolda & P. M. King (Eds.), *Learning partnerships: Theory and models of practice to educate for self-authorship* (pp. 37–62). Sterling, VA: Stylus Publishing.

Delgado Bernal, D. (2002). Critical race theory, Latino critical theory, and critical raced-gendered epistemologies: Recognizing students of color as holders and creators of knowledge. *Qualitative Inquiry, 8*(1), 105–126.

Delgado, R., & Stefancic, J. (2001). *Critical race theory: An introduction*. New York: New York University Press.

Dessel, A. (2010). Prejudice in schools: Promotion of an inclusive culture and climate. *Education and Urban Society, 42*(4), 407–429.

Feagin, J. R., Vera, H., & Imani, N. (1996). *The agony of education: Black students at White colleges and universities*. New York: Routledge.

Freire, P. (1970). *Pedagogy of the oppressed*. New York: Continuum.

Garcia, B., & Van Soest, D. (2000). Facilitating learning on diversity: Challenges to the professor. *Journal of Ethnic & Cultural Diversity in Social Work, 9*(1/2), 21–39.

González, K. P. (2002). Campus culture and the experiences of Chicano students in a predominantly White university. *Urban Education, 37*(2), 193–218.

Hebdige, D. (1979). *Subculture: The meaning of style*. London: Routledge.

Hodder, I. (2000). The interpretation of documents and material culture. In N. K. Denzin & Y. S. Lincoln (Eds.), *Handbook of qualitative research* (2nd edn., pp. 703–716). Thousand Oaks, CA: Sage.

hooks, b. (1994). *Teaching to transgress: Education as the practice of freedom*. New York: Routledge.

Hurtado, S., Milem, J. F., Clayton-Pederson, A. R., & Allen, W. R. (1998). Enhancing campus climates for racial/ethnic diversity: Educational policy and practice. *The Review of Higher Education, 21*(3), 279–302.

Ladson-Billings, G. (1998). Just what is critical race theory and what's it doing in a nice field like education? *International Journal of Qualitative Studies in Education, 11*(1), 7–24.

Ladson-Billings, G. (1999) Preparing teachers for diverse student populations: A Critical Race Theory perspective. *Review of Research in Education. 24*, 211–247.

Ladson-Billings, G., & Tate, B. (1995). Toward critical race theory of education. *Teachers College Record, 97*(1), 47–67.

Lambert, M. A. (1993). Student–faculty informal interaction and the effect on college student outcomes: A review of literature. *Adolescence, 28*(112), 971–977.

Magolda, P. M. (1999). Using ethnographic fieldwork and case studies to guide student affairs practice. *Journal of College Student Development, 40*(1), 10–21.

Magolda, P. M. (2000). The campus tour ritual: Exploring community discourses in higher education. *Anthropology and Education Quarterly, 31*(1), 24–36.

Patton, M. Q. (2002). *Qualitative research & evaluation methods* (3rd edn.). Thousand Oaks, CA: Sage.

Phillips, D. C., & Soltis, J. F. (2004). *Perspectives on learning* (4th edn.). New York: Teachers College Press.

Quantz, R. A. (1999). School ritual as performance: A reconstruction of Durkheim's and Turner's use of ritual. *Educational Theory, 49*(4), 493–513.

Quaye, S. J. (2008). *Pedagogy and racialized ways of knowing: Students and faculty engage racial realities in postsecondary classrooms*. Unpublished doctoral dissertation, The Pennsylvania State University, University Park, PA.

Salzman, P. C. (2001). *Understanding culture: An introduction to anthropological theory*. Long Grove, IL: Waveland Press.

Schein, E. H. (1996). Culture: The missing concept in organization studies. *Administrative Science Quarterly, 41*(2), 229–240

Schlossberg, N. K. (1989). Marginality and mattering: Key issues in building community. *New Directions for Student Services, 48*, 5–15. doi: 10.1002/ss.37119894803

Solórzano, D. (1997). Images of words that wound: Critical race theory, racial stereotyping and teacher education. *Teacher Education Quarterly, 69*(1/2), 60–73.

Solórzano, D., & Yosso, T. (2002). Race methodology: Counter-storytelling as an analytical framework for education research. *Qualitative Inquiry, 8*, 23–44.

Solórzano, D., Ceja, M., & Yosso, T. (2000). Critical race theory, racial microaggression, and campus racial climate: The Experiences of African American college students. *Journal of Negro Education, 69*(1/2), 60–73.

Sue, D. W., Torino, G. C., Capodilupo, C. M., Rivera, D. P., & Lin, A. I. (2010). How White faculty perceive and react to difficult dialogues on race: Implications for education and training. *Counseling Psychologist, 37*(8), 1090–1115.

Tatum, B. D. (1997). *"Why are all the Black kids sitting together in the cafeteria?": And other conversations about race.* New York: Basic Books.

Terenzini, P. T., Cabrera, A. F., Colbeck, C. L., Bjorklund, S. A., & Parente, J. M. (2001). Racial and ethnic diversity in the classroom: Does it promote student learning? *The Journal of Higher Education, 72*(5), 509–531.

Tsui, L. (2000). Effects of campus culture on students' critical thinking. *The Review of Higher Education, 23*(4), 421–441.

Villalpando, O. (2003). Self-segregation or self-preservation? A critical race theory and Latina/o critical theory analysis of a study of Chicano college students. *International Journal of Qualitative Studies in Education, 16*(5), 619–646.

Wise, T. (2008). *White like me: Reflections on race from a privileged son.* Brooklyn, NY: Soft Skull Press.

Yin, R. K. (2003). *Case study research: Design and methods* (3rd edn.). Thousand Oaks, CA: Sage.

6

CULTURAL INTEGRATION IN CAMPUS SUBCULTURES

Where the Cultural, Academic, and Social Spheres of College Life Collide

Samuel D. Museus, Sơn Ca Lâm, ChuYu Huang, Pratna Kem, and Kevin Tan

I was not an active student. I did not consider myself American – I am not Black or White. Then, the summer before tenth grade, I joined the Coalition for Asian Pacific American Youth (CAPAY) at UMass Boston. The first field trip I went on with CAPAY was to Mount Hope Cemetery. There was a stark difference between a majority of the cemetery and the back section, where we were going. In the back, there was trash everywhere. Headstones were broken, crooked, and covered by unmowed grass. It looked like an abandoned field. We gathered around a man in shorts and a t-shirt, who I later discovered was the Director of the Asian American Studies Program at UMass Boston. He told us the story of Mount Hope cemetery. The back section was the Chinese burial ground, dating back to the 1930s. Those buried there were the first Chinese to settle in Boston. Now they lay forgotten and neglected.

We picked up trash around the graves and pulled up weeds where we could. We burned incense and prayed to show our respect for these men who lay forgotten there. As we were working, a truck came up. Several men came out with clippers and mowers to cut the grass. I was told that the cemetery had sent people to clean the back sections today because they were informed that we'd be coming. When the men finished, one guy stepped on the face of a headstone while walking back to his truck. Shocked, I told the coordinator of CAPAY that this had happened. She asked me, "And, how does that make you feel?" This trip made no sense to me up until that moment. I stood there unable to answer her as the blood rushed to my face, "I don't know. . ."

This was my first of many lessons in Asian American Studies. My family is refugees from the Vietnam War, and I was born in the refugee camps in the

Philippines. In Asian American Studies, I learned about the historical contexts of my family's stories. They were too painful for my family to tell me and too insignificant for the public school system to teach me about. The lessons that I learned through the Asian American Studies Program at UMass Boston were not always in the classroom, but I carry them with me wherever I go. It is these connections that are made between education and students' lives, communities, and histories that leave lasting marks on us. – Son Ca Lâm

This opening narrative illustrates how ethnic subcultures within our educational institutions can and do validate the lives of students of color. In the story, Son-Ca experiences an awakening as a result of an extracurricular fieldtrip that was organized by two ethnic subcultures at UMass Boston: the CAPAY youth organization and Asian American Studies programs. She develops a bond with these programs that leads to greater connections to the historical and social contexts in which she exists. Also, those bonds engage Asian American history and communities, thereby stimulating her identification as an Asian American and validating that identity.

In the following section, we synthesize literature on campus subcultures in higher education and success among diverse student populations. Specifically, we highlight the power of ethnic subcultures in fostering *cultural integration* – the integration of students' cultural backgrounds and identities with the academic and social spheres of students' lives – and the role of such integration in validating students' cultural backgrounds and identities (Museus, in press). Then we illustrate how such cultural integration and validation shapes students' experiences through the voices of three students affiliated with Asian American Studies. We conclude the chapter with implications of this discussion for college and university leaders who are interested in fostering success among racially diverse college student populations.

Campus Subcultures and Cultural Integration

There is a substantial body of scholarly literature that underscores the reality that students of color often encounter unwelcoming or hostile environments at predominantly White institutions (PWIs) (e.g., Feagin, 1992; Feagin, Vera, & Imani, 1996; González, 2003; Harper & Hurtado, 2007; Hurtado, 1992; Lewis, Chesler, & Forman, 2000). Extant research also highlights the fact that campus subcultures can provide safe environments for students of color at PWIs (Guiffrida, 2003; Harper & Quaye, 2007; Kiang, 2002, 2009; Murguía, Padilla, & Pavel, 1991; Museus, 2008, 2010, 2011, in press; Museus & Quaye, 2009). Building on the work of Bolton and Kammeyer (1972), we argue that a *campus subculture* is a distinct system that is developed by a subset of members of an institution and consists of specific norms, values, beliefs, and assumptions that differ from the dominant culture of the campus and guide the thought and behavior of its group members. Group members transmit those norms, values, beliefs, and assumptions to newcomers to facilitate conformity to and perpetuation of them.

Many racial and ethnic minority students seek out and get involved in campus subcultures and those subcultures serve several purposes for students of color. First, evidence indicates that targeted support programs, ethnic studies programs, and ethnic student organizations can provide safe havens for students (González, 2003; Guiffrida, 2003; Harper & Quaye, 2007; Kiang, 2002, 2009; Museus, 2008, 2010). Second, those subcultures can foster important connections between students and their institutions that facilitate those undergraduates' success (González, 2003; Kiang, 2002, 2009; Museus, 2008, 2010, in press; Museus & Quaye, 2009). Museus (2010), for example, found that programs that offer targeted support for students of color can facilitate their success by creating three types of connections: early connections between students and their institutions, continuous connections between undergraduates and their campuses, and integrated connections that lead to a multiplicity of linkages between students and various departments, programs, and institutional agents across their campuses.

A third critical function that campus subcultures serve for students of color at PWIs is that they integrate what are often fragmented aspects of those students' lives (Museus, in press). Indeed, scholars have highlighted the importance of integrating the academic and social aspects of students' college experiences. Higher education researchers, for example, have underscored the importance of learning communities, which function to build connections between students' academic and social lives (Astin, 1993; Braxton, Milem, & Sullivan, 2000; Johnson, Johnson, & Smith, 1998; Stassen, 2003; Tinto, 1998). Scholars have also demonstrated how the integration of the academic and social spheres of life in college can contribute to higher levels of success among students of color specifically (Fullilove & Treisman, 1990; Treisman, 1992).

Equally important as the integration of the academic and social spheres of students' experiences is the building of connections between these two components and the cultural sphere of their lives (i.e., their cultural backgrounds and identities). Indeed, several studies illustrate the positive outcomes associated with merging the academic sphere of students' experiences with their cultural background and integrating the social sphere with their cultural heritages (e.g., González, 2003; Harper & Hurtado, 2007; Kiang, 2002, 2009; Guiffrida, 2003; Museus, 2008). When postsecondary institutions engage the cultural backgrounds and identities of students in an academic or social sphere of college life, they create environments characterized by greater inclusivity than when those cultural backgrounds and identities are not engaged.

The potential power of many campus subcultures is, in part, a result of their ability to foster cultural integration (see Figure 6.1). As mentioned, we use the

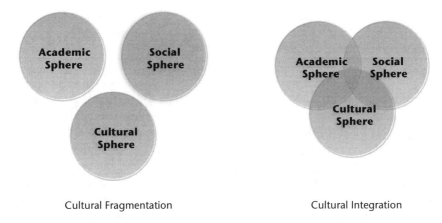

Cultural Fragmentation   Cultural Integration

FIGURE 6.1 Cultural Fragmentation and Cultural Integration.

term *cultural integration* to refer to the integration of all three critical aspects – the academic, social, and cultural components – of racial and ethnic minority students' experiences (Museus, in press). Specifically, campus subcultures can create spaces, academic courses, workshops, projects, and activities that facilitate cultural integration. Such integration is critical when college students of color must navigate larger institutional environments that do not typically facilitate such integration. In the second half of this chapter, we illustrate how campus subcultures can foster cultural integration and how such integration leads to the validation of students' cultural backgrounds and identities. Before we move forward with that discussion, however, it is important to clarify what we mean by integrating students' cultural backgrounds and identities.

It has been decades since Tinto (1987, 1993) discussed the role of academic and social integration in facilitating success among college students. Tinto developed his theory of student integration, which is based on the notion that undergraduates must separate from their home cultures, transition to the cultures of their campuses, and assimilate into those campus cultures to succeed. The assumption is that completing those three stages can lead to academic and social integration – students' integration into the academic and social subsystems of their campuses. Several scholars, however, have questioned the underlying assumptions of Tinto's theory for their cultural bias and inadequacy in explaining the success of students of color (e.g., Attinasi, 1989; Hurtado & Carter, 1997; Kuh & Love, 2000; Nora & Cabrera, 1996; Rendón, Jalomo, & Nora, 2000; Tierney, 1992, 1999). They argue that expecting students of color to detach from their home communities in order to succeed places an unfair burden on those undergraduates to sever meaningful and fruitful ties with their home communities. Consequently, to some extent, the terms *academic integration* and *social integration* themselves have been associated with cultural bias and inadequacy (Hurtado & Carter, 1997; Museus, Nichols, & Lambert, 2008). Thus, it is important to distinguish these terms from our concept of cultural integration.

Although we use the term *integration* in our discussion, our concept of cultural integration differs from Tinto's (1987, 1993) concepts of academic and social integration in multiple substantial ways. First and perhaps most obvious is the fact that, unlike academic and social integration, the concept of cultural integration includes the critical component of engaging students' cultural backgrounds and identities in the academic environment. Second, rather than focusing on the extent to which students assimilate into the academic and social subsystems of their respective campuses, cultural integration refers to the extent to which academic, social, and cultural components of students' lives are meaningfully reflected in spaces, courses, projects, activities, or set of activities. Third, because the focus of the concept of cultural integration is primarily on the educational environment and activities rather than students, any members of an institution can be involved in facilitating this integration, but the primary burden should be assumed by the faculty, administrators, and staff because they are the ones who are responsible for designing and structuring most learning environments.

It is also important to clarify what we mean by engagement of students' cultural backgrounds and identities. The literature on the role of culture in racial and ethnic minority college students' success has underscored the importance of precollege cultures in shaping students' dispositions with which they come to college, in determining the extent to which students' have to adjust to the cultures on their respective campuses, and ultimately the likelihood that students will succeed (Kuh & Love, 2000; Museus & Quaye, 2009; Museus & Truong, 2009; Rendón et al., 2000; Tierney, 1999; Torres, 2003). Specifically, that literature suggests that the level of incongruence between racial and ethnic minority students' respective home cultures and the cultures found on their campuses is positively related to cultural dissonance, or tension due to the incongruence between students' cultural meaning-making systems and the new cultural knowledge that they encounter, and such dissonance is inversely related to the likelihood of success (Museus & Quaye, 2009). A limitation of this literature, however, is that it does not reflect the complexity of the cultures from which students come.

Framing Students of Color as Cultural Assets

Students of color navigate many different cultures before college, including the cultures that exist within their families, ethnic communities, neighborhoods, and schools. Thus, when researchers speak of racial and ethnic minority students' *precollege cultures* or *cultural backgrounds* (e.g., Kuh & Love, 2000; Museus

& Quaye, 2009; Tierney, 1999), the former can be used to refer to a range of cultures in which students were previously engaged to varying degrees and the latter can be conceptualized as the experiences that students of color have accumulated navigating several different cultural milieus. It is important for educators to be aware of the multiplicity of those students' precollege cultures and cultural backgrounds.

Of particular importance in our discussion of cultural integration are students' families and ethnic communities. To make sense of how we can understand the ways that the variety of family and ethnic community cultures shape students' dispositions and experiences, we build on the work of Bourdieu (1986) and Yosso (2006). Bourdieu coined the term *cultural capital* to refer to a set of linguistic and cultural competencies that individuals inherit or learn. He delineated three forms of cultural capital: the institutionalized, objectified, and embodied states. The institutionalized state has to do with licenses that are conferred by institutions or governing bodies to individuals and represent sanctioned statuses, whereas objectified cultural capital refers to cultural goods and the ability to enjoy those goods. However, most relevant to the current discussion is embodied cultural capital, which is a set of dispositions that develop over time, in part as a result of the cultures that an individual navigates. In other words, embodied capital is cultural capital that is encountered in the environment and internalized by the individual. In Bourdieu's work, he underscored the fact that individuals from affluent families and communities are more likely to inherit and accumulate cultural capital, which, in turn, increases their likelihood of success in society because society values the capital that they inherit.

It has been noted that the assumption in Bourdieu's (1986) theory is that students of color come into the education system bearing disadvantages that hinder their success due to their racial and ethnic backgrounds (Valenzuela, 1999; Yosso, 2006). Yosso argues that it is important to avoid such deficit perspectives and refrain from viewing some communities as having cultural value and others as not. Building on the work of Yosso (2006) and other education scholars (e.g., Bourdieu, 1986; Kuh & Hall, 1993; Kuh & Whitt, 1988; Stanton-Salazar, 1997), we argue that students of color can serve as cultural assets because they have internalized valuable resources from the cultures from which they come and can therefore function as assets that reflect the values, knowledge, skills, and networks of their diverse racial and ethnic communities.

First, students of color bring *cultural values* that can enrich the learning environment on college campuses. The work of Fullilove and Treisman (1990) provides a salient example of this reality. Consistent with research finding that non-Western communities are more likely to espouse collectivist values than Western societies (Beattie, 1980; Coon & Kemmelmeier, 2001; Hetts,

Sakuma, & Pelham, 1999; Kirkness & Barnhardt, 1991; Mead, 1967; Triandis, McCusker, & Hui, 1990; Yamaguchi, Kuhlman, & Sugimori, 1995), Fullilove and Treisman discovered that Chinese Americans espoused more collectivist orientations toward their math homework than other racial and ethnic groups, which led them to work collaboratively and do better than other populations as a result of their collective efforts. Educators have subsequently utilized these findings to develop effective support programs for Black and Latino students in Science, Technology, Engineering, and Mathematics (for review of literature in this area, see Museus, Palmer, Davis, & Maramba, 2011), providing a compelling example of how one group's cultural values and corresponding working styles can contribute to enriching the academic environment for diverse student populations (Museus & Chang, 2009; Museus et al., 2011).

Second, racial and ethnic minority students enter college with rich *cultural knowledge* of their ethnic communities, which includes understandings of those communities' histories, traditions, geographies, and social and political issues. Several scholars have written about the value of students' knowledge (for discussion, see Chapter 2). Perhaps the most important form of student knowledge is their personal experiences and diverse perspectives that are so fundamental to creating robust learning environments in higher education. If postsecondary educators engage and validate this knowledge, students can play a central role in enriching the learning environment on their respective campuses.

Third, students of color bring important *cultural skills* to college. Examples of such skill are linguistic proficiencies and abilities navigating oppressive institutional environments (Yosso, 2006). These skills can serve to enrich the college environment for all students as well. If given the opportunity, racial and ethnic minority undergraduates can utilize those skills to inform institutional decision-making, communicate with diverse communities in service-learning projects and other community engagement activities, or mentor younger students of color around the navigation of institutional barriers that function to oppress their communities.

Finally, students' come from communities with *cultural networks* that are rich with human and other resources (Stanton-Salazar, 1997; Yosso, 2006). Indeed, students enter college with connections to religious communities, ethnic community organizations, business establishments, philanthropic organizations, and educational institutions – all of which can serve as valuable resources that can enhance learning opportunities in curricular and co-curricular activities. In sum, it is important for educators to recognize that students possess important cultural values, knowledge, skills, and networks that can contribute to efforts to improve the undergraduate experience for all students on their campuses. By recognizing these ways in which students of color can function as cultural assets, educators can better cultivate learning environments that are robust with rich and diverse resources.

Cultural Integration of Cultural Assets

Thus far, we have underscored the importance of cultural integration and discussed how students of color can serve as assets to college educators and their respective campuses. In this section, we provide an example of one campus subculture – an Asian American Studies Program at UMass Boston – that fosters cultural integration by engaging students as cultural assets and integrating their cultural backgrounds and identities into their academic and social experiences. First, we discuss the role of physical and epistemological space in the Asian American Studies Program. Next, we discuss how Asian American Studies faculty, staff, and students use those spaces to cultivate cultural integration through (1) culturally validating curricula, (2) support and motivation for campus and community activism, and (3) cultural community engagement. It should be noted that, in a way, separating these three methods of cultural integration into categories oversimplifies the fluidity and interconnectedness among them. In reality, a singular activity can include all three components. Nevertheless, we provide the typology as a heuristic for readers to understand the different ways in which Asian American Studies cultivates cultural integration.

Describing the Program

The Asian American Studies Program has approximately 20 faculty members who have primary appointments in other departments. The program offers more Asian American Studies courses than any other Asian American Studies Program or Department in New England, totaling approximately between 25 and 30 courses per year. It is founded on the core values of space, voice, and rights for Asian American people and communities and it places special emphasis on underresourced Asian American communities, including Southeast Asian American, refugee, and low-income populations (Kiang, 1997, 2008; Lin, Suyemoto & Kiang, 2009; Tang & Kiang, 2011). The program has an office that includes one large and two small rooms. The large room provides a space where faculty, staff, and students gather daily to both work and socialize. In it are a large table, several chairs, and five computers for student use. One of the small rooms houses the program's library, and both small rooms have computers and are where faculty members hold office hours and other meetings.

Asian American Studies faculty and staff provide a substantial amount of support for students in this program, both inside and outside the classroom. Critical is the fact that the nature of this support ranges from academic advising, through personal and professional development, to support for student-initiated projects within the school and across local communities (Kiang, 2000; Kiang et al., 2008). Most importantly, the faculty and staff in the program provide ample opportunities for cultural integration to occur. In the remainder of this section, we discuss how Asian American Studies fosters cultural integration in space through culturally validating curricula, support for co-curricular activism, and cultural community engagement. We utilize the reflections of undergraduate student-authors – ChuYu Huang (a Chinese American female senior), Pratna Kem (a Cambodian American male senior), and Kevin Tan (a Cambodian American male junior) – and, through their experiences, describe the ways in which Asian American Studies engages the academic, social, and cultural spheres of their lives.

The Physical and Epistemological Space: "For the First Time . . . I Found a Community . . . to Pursue the Answers"

There are two types of space that play a critical role in the experiences of students in the Asian American Studies Program. First, within Asian American Studies, *physical spaces* are designated for courses, meetings, campus projects, and community activities. One key physical space is the Asian American Studies office, where faculty, staff, and students regularly engage in both formal and informal academic and social interactions. Kevin explained this in the following:

> In the program office, students can go to meet with professors, seek help with their ongoing work, or just interact with others. This office is also open for anyone to walk in and ask questions, get information on events or scholarship type opportunities. Most people who go there are very familiar with each other and relationships are built and grow from daily interaction.

As Kevin describes, the Asian American Studies office is a physical space that houses the program and where faculty and students can convene and interact around both academic and social issues. Other physical spaces created and utilized by Asian American Studies include classrooms and auditoriums that are used as venues reserved for co-curricular events. However, these physical spaces also serve as spaces where academic and social interactions are connected to an Asian American group identity or a subculture within the larger cultural landscape of the campus. Indeed, Kinzie and Mulholland (2007) discuss how physical spaces are meaningfully linked to group identities on campus when they assert that subcultures "demarcate [physical] space to affirm their presence" and that the "identification of territory contributes to group identity formation as well as enabling others to identify them" (p. 109). Consistent with that assertion is the fact that the Asian American Studies Program's physical spaces are demarcated areas where group identity is recreated and reaffirmed, faculty and students build community around that identity, those affiliated with Asian American Studies can be found, and those seeking connections to the program know where to go to make these associations.

Within and beyond the physical spaces in which Asian American Studies faculty, staff, and students interact, those individuals construct *epistemological spaces* – the second type of critical space utilized within Asian American Studies. Epistemological space refers to metaphysical places that can exist in and transcend the physical space of the Asian American Studies office and sometimes the campus, but they are metaphysical places in which Asian American Studies faculty and students explore the creation, exchange, exploration, and validation of knowledge. Pratna offered these comments about his realization that he was being denied such epistemological spaces during his K–12 education:

> I had always known that I was a Cambodian American and I was proud of that, but aside from knowing where my parents were from, I knew very little about my roots. That all changed for me in the eighth grade. My English teacher that year had assigned the class to read the diary of Anne Frank, while my history teacher was going through the unit on the Holocaust and World War II. One day while doing my reading, I asked my mother if she had ever heard of the Holocaust. Her response was "no." I explained to her about the concentrations camps and the genocide that took place under the reign of Hitler. She then replied that she had never heard of the Holocaust, but that she had survived a Cambodian holocaust. I looked at her with confusion, disbelief, and wonder. What she told me next was unbelievable. She told me about her life in Cambodia, the rise of the communist party, the Khmer Rouge, and how she came to the United States. For the first time, I was hearing a story of my family's past, my people's past, a past that I had never learned about in school. I realized that, to find out more about my history, I had to take the initiative and learn on my own time. I became curious and began to ask questions. I wanted to know everything. I wanted to feel connected to some piece of history just as my classmates felt connected their history.

Pratna's comments highlight the problematic denial of epistemological spaces where Cambodian American and other Asian American students can learn about their histories and communities (Lin, Suyemoto & Kiang, 2009; Tang, 2008b). He went on to reflect on how, in college, Asian American Studies finally provided him with the epistemological space to ask questions, seek answers, and co-construct knowledge around the meaning of being Cambodian American in his life:

> I knew I was an American, but why didn't I feel like a part of anything American? What did it mean to be a Cambodian living in America? What did it mean to be Cambodian American? I did not feel like there was a space for me to nurture that curiosity and desire to learn more. Fortunately for me, that changed. I was finally able to find that space in my freshman

year of college when I discovered the Asian American Studies Program at the University of Massachusetts Boston. It was there that, for the first time, I found a community of support from peers and mentors to pursue the answers to the question I had asked myself for so long.

In Pratna's reflection, he refers to an epistemological space that provides room for his "curiosity and desire to learn more." The epistemological space is where students' personal academic questions and concerns, which are often trivialized or ignored in the dominant discourse, are voiced and explored. Pratna alludes to the fact that this voice and exploration is connected to social interactions as he discusses the community of support that consists of faculty and students who helped him pursue the answers to his questions. Finally, those academic and social components of the epistemological space revolve around questions about and exploration of his cultural background and identity (Lin et al., 2009). In the remainder of this section, we discuss how physical spaces and epistemological spaces are utilized to cultivate cultural integration through culturally validating curricula, support for campus and community activism, and cultural community engagement.

Culturally Validating Curricula: "That Was the Moment Where I Felt the Power in Sharing Personal Narratives with Others"

One way that the faculty members in the Asian American Studies Program cultivate cultural integration is by the intentional design of culturally validating curricula. We use the term *validating* rather than *relevant* – as in culturally relevant teaching – because the curricula does not just relate to students' lives but *engages* their identities and stories. And we use the term *curricula*, rather than *pedagogy*, to highlight the fact that, in this program, the subject is central to the classroom community and not the teacher. The instructors and students all significantly contribute to defining what is taught and what is considered valuable and valid knowledge.

One example of culturally validating curricula in effect is the Asian American Media Literacy course. While the course trains students to be critical in analyzing mainstream portrayal of stereotypical Asian Americans in the media, it also equips them with skills to become more than consumers. Students in the course become producers of media that tell stories of their lived experiences, challenging dominant stereotypical images of Asian Americans. Through these stories, students are encouraged to find the *political in the personal*, and the *universal in the individual*. Students are encouraged to appreciate and share their stories, and their experiences are validated in a school-wide showcase of their final projects, which consist of personal narrative digital stories (Hanisch,

1970; Horne, 1904). Coming from marginalized backgrounds, many students feel that their voices and experiences are not significant or worthy of being heard. However, through the course, they come to realize that their personal voices related to a collective story of the complexities, commonalities, and diversity within Asian America. Kevin shared the following:

> Creating these digital stories provides authentic examples of personal narratives of the issues that Asian Americans deal with. Some of these stories have cultural ties like languages being spoken, ideas focused around home, or even a personal immigration or migration story. Due to the nature of our stories, each student learned a lot about each other and the struggles they may have endured, and they became closer as a result.

Kevin's statement underscores the cultural integration that takes place in this course. He discusses how the academic curriculum engages students' cultural and linguistic backgrounds, but he also underscores the social component, as he notes that, through students sharing and learning about each other's stories and struggles, members of the classroom community build strong social bonds and "become closer as a result."

There is an annual exhibition of digital stories from this course in an auditorium located on the university's campus. It is not uncommon to have hundreds of faculty, staff, and students attend the class exhibitions. Over the years, the Media Literacy course has garnered a returning audience of viewers, participants, and alumni support – a group that has built a community of their own that was created and is sustained through the space created in the curricular domain. In this way, the epistemological space that is created within the course transcends the physical spaces of the classroom and, in some cases, even the campus.

Through the cultural integration that takes place within it, the Media Literacy course functions to validate the cultural backgrounds and identities of students who enroll in it. ChuYu illustrated this validation in the following statement:

> I remember attending the annual campus wide event where the students from the course presented their digital stories. I was very moved and inspired by the digital stories that I had seen, so I decided to enroll into the course . . . I was able to share some experiences I would never share with anyone because it was so personal and I did not want to be judged . . . For the event, it was an open invitation to invite family, friends, and the community to listen to our stories. My friend came to support me and watched my digital story. That was the moment where I felt the power in sharing personal narratives with others.

She went on to underscore the social component of the course as well as she stated that "The close-knit community in the classroom has led to friendships that will last forever."

The sharing and showcasing of students' personal stories not only validates their voices, but it also empowers them as they inspire other students to tell their stories. ChuYu provides an example of this when she mentions her motivation to take the course after being moved by the student productions she witness, and feeling "the power in sharing personal narratives with others." Thus, students not only learn from professors, but also learn from each other (Tang, 2011; Tang & Kiang, 2011). The valuing of students' voices and learning from each other is a theme throughout the courses offered by the Asian American Studies Program.

Motivation and Support for Campus and Community Activism: "There Was a Desire to Do More . . . to Contribute to the School Environment Now"

In the Asian American Studies Program, student engagement and learning in the classroom leads to activism outside of coursework on campus and in the community surrounding the university. Faculty motivate and support students' organizing to advocate for positive social change on campus and in the community. Kevin discussed how Asian American Studies motivated him to start an ethnic organization on campus and the role of his student organization in his experience:

> After my first year of coursework, there was a desire to do more. I wanted to contribute to the school environment somehow. There have been a number of student organizations that you could join but there wasn't a Cambodian cultural group. After speaking with a bunch of people, it started to become more of a realistic idea to start a student club. With the support of my peers and Asian American Studies faculty, the Khmer Culture Association would be a university recognized student club as of the fall 2009 semester.

Through his Asian American Studies courses, Kevin was inspired to "do more" in the co-curricular domain. He found motivation and support from Asian American Studies to establish the Khmer Culture Association. Kevin also noted the motivation for starting the organization, which revolved around his responsibility to educate others about Cambodian American issues:

> Cambodian Americans, like other Southeast Asians, are not model minorities. Throughout the years, Cambodians have had trouble overcoming

issues like racism and achieving the "American Dream." Although there has been progress throughout the years, there are several issues that exist in our communities and our homes. Part of our responsibility is to explain this to others.

Many of the students are involved in student-led programs – including the Khmer Culture Association, Asian American Student Organization, Asian Student Union, and Pacific Asian American Students and Studies Association in Graduate Education – that advocate for social awareness and positive social change. Students in these programs find support from faculty and staff in Asian American Studies and, through the organizations, promote progress in their racial, ethnic, and cultural communities on and off campus. Like Kevin, ChuYu was inspired by the Asian American Studies Program to get involved in an organization:

> Inspired by the Asian American Studies Program, I applied to be a part of the Sticky Rice Project. The Project trains facilitators to teach anti-racism workshops that focus on the Asian American experience. The project raises social awareness and gives back to the community by educating community members about racism. It bridges people together and concentrates on the Asian American experience.

Both Kevin's and ChuYu's comments emphasize how the organizations in which they are involved focus on addressing problems that exist within their racial, ethnic, and cultural communities. Those organizations, however, function to cultivate strong social bonds that affect those students' experiences. Faculty and staff also engage students in campus and community activism in other ways. They accompany them to conferences, collaboratively plan campus events that revolve around important social and political issues that are relevant to Asian America, and expose them to opportunities that allow them to develop better understandings of problems in Asian American communities and the skills to address those issues.

Of course, this organizing has a social component as well. Students build strong bonds with both faculty and peers through their involvement in various organizations. Pratna expressed this in the following comment:

> Being involved with the Asian American Student Organization helped me meet faculty and other students who supported me through all my undergraduate years and I have a feeling that they will continue to do so long after I've left the university . . . I think that working closely with my peers in those organizations brought us closer together. We bonded, and I think we will stay good friends.

Pratna's comment illuminates the strong connections and friendships that develop, in part, as a result of the collaborative efforts that take place in campus organizations.

Cultural Community Engagement: "It Was Especially Empowering to All of Us . . . Because These Are the Communities We Come From"

The third way that members of Asian American Studies foster cultural integration is through cultural community engagement – that is, engagement of Asian American communities external to the campus. Asian American Studies faculty members engage the surrounding cultural communities in numerous ways (Kiang et al., 2008; Tang, 2011). First, the faculty have developed and maintain a complex reciprocal relationship with the community, by which the Asian American Studies students learn from community members and Asian American students advocate to improve Asian American communities external to the campus (Tang, 2008a). ChuYu explained how faculty members tap into the knowledge and expertise within the external cultural community with the following comments:

> Not only is there a community setting in the classroom, but professors also encourage and bring opportunities to students from communities outside of the classroom. They will bring in speakers, like community organizers, who discuss the current issues that local communities are struggling with or introduce alumnae and what they have been involved in after graduating.

The Asian American Studies faculty also bring students out into the community to hold course-related activities, go on field trips, and attend community events. This branching out into the community enables students to connect the curriculum to the communities from which they come and to which they still belong. Son-Ca's opening story about Mount Hope Cemetery was a salient example of the impact that such a field trip can have on the growth of a student. Kevin remembers another field trip that had a powerful impact on his experience:

> When I took the course on Southeast Asians, my first Asian American Studies course, we went on a field trip to Revere, Massachusetts. I recall walking up and down Shirley Avenue observing the different businesses as we learned about the history of the town. When I was younger I remember visiting the same area with my family every once in a while, but never really knew anything about the community there. Like my hometown, Revere also had a very large Cambodian community. During the field trip,

I started to realize that there were very common issues that Southeast Asian communities have to deal with. Gang violence and high drop-out rates led me to wonder what contributed to these instances being so high. I find that in my own experience, I could have just as easily been in that situation had my parents not sent me to a different school system.

Kevin recalls how this trip stimulated his recognition of important social issues and the connections and common struggles among Southeast Asian American communities, but is also able to readily see how his own life is connected to those struggles and communities – making his educational experience relevant.

Asian American Studies faculty bringing students from their courses out into the community comes in the form of required field trips, but also manifests in voluntary community events that students are eager to attend. Pratna describes one such event that a faculty member held in a local Cambodian restaurant:

> The Floating Rock Restaurant event was held in honor of the restaurant moving to a bigger space in Cambridge. After students performed their poems, the floor was opened up to provide a space for community members to share their experiences in the restaurant and the Cambodian community in Revere . . . What was important about the events was that it brought the community together to share their stories about the importance of having a space where they felt safe to share their voices and be together. It was especially empowering to all of us in the class because these are the communities we come from. And it is meaningful to know that these are the communities we are going back to.

Whereas Asian American Studies faculty engage the knowledge and expertise of community members, they also give back to the local Asian American communities in several ways. For example, the program encourages and supports students to become active and engage in the local community. As a result, many alumni of the program become leaders in various Asian American community organizations surrounding the campus, advocating for underresourced and oppressed groups within those communities (Tang, 2008a; Kiang, 2008).

Asian American Studies faculty, staff, and students also help organize events for local youth and other members of the cultural community. One example of this organizing are the activities organized by CAPAY – the youth organization to which Son-Ca referred in the opening story, which is housed in the Asian American Studies Program. CAPAY organized several events for youth in the local community, including an annual conference, which includes workshops that are facilitated by Asian American Studies faculty, staff, and students (Kiang, 2001, 2004).

In many ways, because of the plethora of connections that have been created and are maintained, the lines between the Asian American Studies Program, CAPAY, and the cultural community are blurred (Kiang, 2004). Many of the Asian American Studies faculty and staff were and are community leaders. Some youth that go through CAPAY become UMass Boston students later on. Many Asian American Studies alumni go back to work in and serve in the local communities and become community leaders themselves. In sum, members of the Asian American Studies program are members of the community and vice versa.

Recommendations for College Educators

The discussion above has several implications for institutions that seek to cultivate cultures that maximize success among diverse student populations. We offer four recommendations below. Although not exhaustive, the list can help college educators think about how they can utilize campus subcultures, such as the one discussed in this chapter, to transform their institutions.

Learn from and Leverage Subcultures

It is important for institutional leaders to both be sensitive to subcultures and promote models of effective practice on their campuses (Schein, 1992). Thus, campus leaders should pay particular attention to those subcultures that effectively connect, engage, motivate, and empower students from racial and ethnic minority populations. At institutions where high-impact subcultures, such as the one described in this chapter, that facilitate the success of racial and ethnic minority student populations exist, campus leaders should learn from those subcultures and promote them as effective models for increasing success among particular student populations.

Although the example that we use in this chapter is an Asian American Studies Program, the concepts apply to any group that can form an identity and has a community – including Black, Latino, Native American, Pacific Islander, multiracial, urban, low-income, and lesbian, gay, bisexual, and transgendered communities. Of course, there are examples of programs at institutions all over the country that do some of the things discussed in this chapter, but there are also many institutions that do not have subcultures that achieve the same kind of cultural integration and validation as the program described above.

Promote and Reward for Cultural Integration Initiatives

Cultural integration leads to cultural validation, and that validation has a positive influence on the experiences of students of color because it facilitates undergraduates' connections to their institutions and maximizes those students' learning and success (Rendón, 1994, 2002; Rendón et al., 2000; Museus & Quaye, 2009). Faculty and staff, therefore, should consider the concept of cultural integration and how that integration can apply to various environments across their campuses. Cultural integration is not something that can only transpire in an Ethnic Studies Program or ethnic student organizations. Rather, all faculty can engage in cultural integration as they develop their courses, construct classroom environments, and interact with students outside the classroom – as demonstrated by faculty in the examples above. Similarly, staff can make efforts to employ this concept of cultural integration into projects, activities, and events that they plan. In reality, cultural integration is something that should take place to some extent across all departments, programs, and offices on college campuses.

Institutional leaders should also consider rewarding innovative efforts and activities that fall into the category of cultural integration. Reward structures are a critical component of the cultures of college campuses because they send signals to members of the institution about what is valued by the campus (Kuh & Whitt, 1988). Rewards can also be an important mechanism for institutional leaders to embed particular values, beliefs, and assumptions into the culture of an organization (Schein, 1992). Therefore, institutional decision-makers should consider identifying cultural integration as one criterion in evaluating faculty and staff for annual teaching and research awards, staff achievement awards, and promotion and tenure processes.

Make Engaging Diverse Voices within the 3 Cs a (Classroom, Campus, and Community) Core Value and Norm

It is critical that educators engage the voices of students from racial and ethnic minority populations (see Chapter 2). In the program described above, educators do so in the classroom. They also acknowledge the importance of and make room for minority students' stories, as well as other community members' voices, in campus events outside of the classroom and in community events outside the walls of the campus. College educators should make efforts to similarly engage the voices and stories of students and community members in the curricula and other activities in which they are involved.

Moreover, postsecondary educators should make efforts to embed this voice engagement as a core value in their institutions and a norm throughout the cultures of their campuses. Across the country, faculty, staff, and students gather at co-curricular events during which professors and professional experts share their opinions about historical, economic, social, and political issues. These events are fundamental components of the culture of higher education and they create a vibrant academic community that is based on the exchange of ideas. However, students are often included in these activities only as receptors of knowledge. College educators should normalize events that simultaneously engage faculty and staff but acknowledge and incorporate the voices and stories of students of color. They can do this by promoting such events that are already taking place on campus or allocate resources to academic programs that are willing to work collaboratively with student organizations to plan and execute such events.

Utilize Cultural Community Connections

Sometimes, when the term *community engagement* is used, it is conceptualized as community service and service learning. In our example above, individuals and organizations within the community are more than receivers of service from faculty, staff, and students. Rather, they engage community members as resources that possess valuable knowledge. They bring community members into academic spaces and students into cultural community spaces. They co-construct epistemological spaces with community members both on and off campus. In a sense, community members *are* a part of this subculture, whereas faculty, staff, and students in the program are members of the surrounding cultural communities.

Faculty should seek to strengthen bonds with community members and the linkages between their classrooms and the communities from which their students come. They can do this by incorporating field trips into their courses, inviting guest speakers from the community, and organizing co-curricular events in the community. For such practices to be adopted campus-wide, however, institutional leaders must commit to valuing cultural community engagement, and they must make intentional efforts to enact that value. This means that institutional leaders should consider incorporating the engagement of diverse communities into their missions, defining what they mean by *community engagement* in institutional documents, clarifying that this entails more than community service and service learning, and promoting models of engagement that integrate members of the community into the cultures of the campus.

Conclusion

Leading an institution effectively is a matter of integrating elements of the institution and cultivating common goals, language, and behaviors among institutional members (Schein, 1992). This is not an easy task because many colleges and universities have become so large and consist of so many subcultures that the identification of goals, language, and behaviors that are common across environments within those institutions can be challenging. One useful strategy for institutional leaders is to scale up subcultures that consist of important values, beliefs, and assumptions that effectively foster success among students of color so that those subcultures have a larger presence at the institution and can influence other groups and individuals on their campuses. To do this, campus leaders must identify high-impact subcultures, promote them as models, and support their growth. If institutional leaders can identify subcultures in which cultural integration is valued and normalized, they can learn from and leverage those subcultures to foster more pervasive positive institutional transformation.

References

Astin, A. W. (1993). *What matters in college? Four critical years revisited.* San Francisco, CA: Jossey-Bass.

Attinasi, L. C., Jr. (1989). Getting in: Mexican Americans' perceptions of university attendance and the implications for freshman year persistence. *Journal of Higher Education, 60*(3), 247–277.

Beattie, J. (1980). Representations of the self in traditional Africa. *Africa, 50,* 313–320.

Bolton, C. D., & Kammeyer, K. C. W. (1972). Campus cultures, roles orientations, and social type. In K. Feldman (Ed.), *College and student: Selected readings in the social psychology of higher education* (pp. 377–381). New York: Pergamon Press.

Bourdieu, P. (1986). The forms of capital. In J. Richardson (Ed.), *Handbook of theory and research for the sociology of education.* Westport, CT: Greenwood Press.

Braxton, J., Milem, J., & Sullivan, A. (2000). The influence of active learning on the college student departure process. *Journal of Higher Education, 71,* 569–590.

Coon, H. M., & Kemmelmeier, M. (2001). Cultural orientations in the United States: (Re-)examining differences among ethnic/racial groups. *Journal of Cross-Cultural Psychology, 32,* 348–364.

Feagin, J. R. (1992). The continuing significance of racism: Discrimination against Black students in White colleges. *Journal of Black Studies, 22,* 546–578.

Feagin, J. R., Vera, H., & Imani, N. (1996). *The agony of education: Black students at White colleges and universities.* New York: Routledge.

Fullilove, R. E., & Treisman, P. U. (1990). Mathematics achievement among African American undergraduates at the University of California, Berkeley: An evaluation of the mathematics workshop program. *Journal of Negro Education, 59*(3), 463–478.

González, K. P. (2003). Campus culture and the experiences of Chicano students in a predominantly White university. *Urban Education, 37*(2), 193–218.

Guiffrida, D. A. (2003). African American student organizations as agents of social integration. *Journal of College Student Development, 44*(3), 304–319.

Hanisch, C. (1970). The personal is political. In S. Firestone and A. Koedt (Eds.), *Notes from the second year: Women's liberation: Major writings of the radical feminists.* New York: Radical Feminism.

Harper, S. R., & Hurtado, S. (2007). Nine themes in campus racial climates and implications for institutional transformation. In S. R. Harper, & L. D. Patton (Eds.), *Responding to the realities of race on campus* (New directions for student services, no. 120, pp. 7–24). San Francisco: Jossey-Bass.

Harper, S. R., & Quaye, S. J. (2007). Student organizations as venues for Black identity expression and development among African American male student leaders. *Journal of College Student Development, 48,* 127–144.

Hetts, J. J., Sakuma, M., & Pelham, B. W. (1999). Two roads to positive regard: Implicit and explicit self-evaluation and culture. *Journal of Experimental Social Psychology, 35,* 512–559.

Horne, H. H. (1904). *The philosophy of education: Being the foundation of education in the related natural and mental sciences.* New York: Cornell University.

Hurtado, S. (1992). The campus racial climate: Contexts and conflict. *Journal of Higher Education, 63*(5), 539–69.

Hurtado, S., & Carter, D. (1997). Effects of college transition and perceptions of the campus racial climate on Latino college students' sense of belonging. *Sociology of Education, 70*(4), 324–345.

Johnson, D. W., Johnson, R. T., and Smith, K. A. (1998, July/August). Cooperative learning returns to college: What evidence is there that it works? *Change.*

Kiang, P. N. (1997). Pedagogies of life and death: Transforming immigrant/refugee students and Asian American Studies. *Positions, Duke University Press, 5*(2), 529–555.

Kiang, P. N. (2000) Long-term effects of diversity in the curriculum: Analyzing the impact of Asian American Studies in the lives of alumni from an urban commuter university. In *Diversity on campus: Reports from the field* (pp. 23–25). Washington, DC: National Association of Student Personnel Administrators.

Kiang, P. N. (2001). Pathways for Asian Pacific American youth political participation. In G. H. Chang (Ed.), *Asian Americans and politics: Perspectives, experiences, prospects* (pp. 320–257). Stanford, CA: Stanford University Press.

Kiang, P. N. (2002). Stories and structures of persistence: Ethnographic learning through research and practice in Asian American Studies. In Y. Zou & H. T. Trueba (Eds.), *Advances in ethnographic research: From our theoretical and methodological roots to post-modern critical ethnography* (pp. 223–255). Lanham, MD: Rowman & Littlefield.

Kiang, P. N. (2004) Linking strategies and interventions in Asian American Studies to K–12 classrooms and teacher preparation. *International Journal of Qualitative Studies in Education, 17*(2), 199–225.

Kiang, P. N. (2008). Crouching activists, hidden scholars: Reflections on research and development with students and communities in Asian American Studies. In C. R. Hale (Ed.), *Engaging contradictions: Theory, politics, and methods of activist scholarship* (pp. 299–318). Berkeley: CA. University of California Press.

Kiang, P. N. (2009). A thematic analysis of persistence and long-term educational engagement with Southeast Asian American college students. In L. Zhan (Ed.), *Asian American voices: Engaging, empowering, enabling* (pp. 59–76). New York: NLN Press.

Kiang, P. N., Suyemoto, K. L., & Tang, S. S. L. (2008). Developing and sustaining community research methods and meanings in Asian American Studies coursework at an urban public university. In T. P. Fong (Ed.), *Handbook of ethnic studies research: Approaches and perspectives* (pp. 367–398). Lanham, MD: Rowman & Littlefield.

Kinzie, J. and Mulholland, S. (2007). Transforming physical spaces into inclusive learning environments. In S. Harper (Ed.), *Creating inclusive college environments for cross-cultural learning and student engagement* (pp. 103–120). Washington, DC: National Association of Student Personnel Administrators.

Kirkness, V. J., & Barnhardt, R. (1991). First nations and higher education: The four R's – respect, relevance, reciprocity and responsibility. *Journal of American Indian Education, 30*(3), 1–15.

Kuh, G. D., & Hall, J. E. (1993). Using cultural perspectives in student affairs. In G. D. Kuh (Ed.), *Cultural perspectives in student affairs work* (pp. 1–20). Lanham, MD: American College Personnel Association.

Kuh, G. D., & Love, P. G. (2000). A cultural perspective on student departure. In J. M. Braxton (Ed.), *Reworking the student departure puzzle* (pp. 196–212). Nashville, TN: Vanderbilt University Press.

Kuh, G. D., & Whitt, E. J. (1988). *The invisible tapestry: Culture in American colleges and universities.* Washington, DC: Association for the Study of Higher Education. ASHE-ERIC Higher Education Report Series, 1.

Lewis, A. E., Chesler, M., & Forman, T. A. (2000). The impact of "colorblind" ideologies on students of color: Intergroup relations at a predominantly White university. *Journal of Negro Education, 69*(1/2), 74–91.

Lin, N. J., Suyemoto, K. L., and Kiang, P. N. (2009). Education as catalyst for intergenerational refugee family communication about war and trauma. *Communication Disorders Quarterly, 30*, 195–207.

Mead, G. H. (1967) *Mind, self, & society: From the standpoint of a social behaviorist* (Charles W. Morris, Ed.). Chicago: University of Chicago Press.

Murguía, E., Padilla, R. V., & Pavel, M. (1991). Ethnicity and the concept of social integration in Tinto's model of institutional departure. *Journal of College Student Development, 32*, 433–54.

Museus, S. D. (2008). The role of ethnic student organizations in fostering African American and Asian American students' cultural adjustment and membership at predominantly White institutions. *Journal of College Student Development, 49*(6), 568–586.

Museus, S. D. (2010). Delineating the ways that targeted support programs facilitate minority students' access to social networks and development of social capital in college. *Enrollment Management Journal, 4*(3), 10–41.

Museus, S. D. (2011). Generating Ethnic Minority Success (GEMS): A collective-cross case analysis of high-performing colleges. *Journal of Diversity in Higher Education.* Retrieved May 25, 2011, from http://psycnet.apa.org/index.cfm?fa=buy.optionToBuy&id=2011-05316-001.

Museus, S. D. (in press). Using cultural perspectives to understand the role of ethnic student organizations in Black students' progress to the end of the pipeline. In D. H. Evensen & C. D. Pratt (Eds.), *The end of the pipeline: A journey of recognition for African Americans entering the legal profession.* Durham, NC: Carolina Academic Press.

Museus, S. D., & Chang, M. J. (2009). Rising to the challenge of conducting research on Asian Americans in higher education. In S. D. Museus (Ed.), *Conducting research on Asian Americans in higher education* (New directions for institutional research, no. 142, pp. 95–105). San Francisco: Jossey-Bass.

Museus, S. D., Nichols, A. H., & Lambert, A. (2008). Racial differences in the effects of campus racial climate on degree completion: A structural model. *Review of Higher Education, 32*(1), 107–134.

Museus, S. D., Palmer, R., Davis, R. J., & Maramba, D. C. (2011). *Racial and ethnic minority student success in STEM education.* San Francisco: Jossey-Bass. *ASHE-ERIC Monograph Series, 36*(6).

Museus, S. D., & Quaye, S. J. (2009). Toward an intercultural perspective of racial and ethnic minority college student persistence. *Review of Higher Education, 33*(1), 67–94.

Museus, S. D., & Truong, K. A. (2009). Disaggregating qualitative data on Asian Americans in campus climate research and assessment. In S. D. Museus (Ed.), *Conducting research on Asian Americans in higher education* (New directions for institutional research, no. 142, pp. 17–26). San Francisco: Jossey-Bass.

Nora, A., & Cabrera, A. (1996). The role of perceptions of prejudice and discrimination on the adjustment of minority students to college. *Journal of Higher Education, 67*(2), 119–148.

Rendón, L. I. (1994). Validating culturally diverse students: Toward a new model of learning and student development. *Innovative Higher Education, 19*(1), 33–51.

Rendón, L. I. (2002). Community College Puente: A validating model of education. *Educational Policy, 16*(4), 642–667.

Rendón, L. I., Jalomo, R. E., & Nora, A. (2000). Theoretical considerations in the study of minority student retention in higher education. In J. M. Braxton (Ed.), *Reworking the student departure puzzle* (pp. 127–156). Nashville, TN: Vanderbilt University Press.

Schein, E. H. (1992). *Organizational culture and leadership* (2nd edn.). San Francisco: Jossey-Bass.

Stanton-Salazar, R. D. (1997). A social capital framework for understanding the socialization of racial minority children and youths. *Harvard Educational Review, 67*(1), 1–40.

Stassen, M. L. A. (2003). Student outcomes: The impact of varying living–learning community models. *Research in Higher Education, 44*, 581–613.

Tang, S. S. L. (2008a) Community-centered research as knowledge/capacity-building in immigrant and refugee communities. In C. R. Hale (Ed.), *Engaging contradictions: Theory, politics and methods of activist scholarship* (pp. 237–263). Berkeley, CA: University of California Press.

Tang, S. S. L. (2008b). Challenges of policy and practice in under-resourced Asian American communities: Analyzing public education, health, development issues with Cambodian American women. *Asian American Law Journal, 15*, 153–175.

Tang, S. S. L. (2011). Developing media literacy for feminist advocacy in Asian American communities. *On Campus with Women, 38*(3), 1. Retrieved June 1, 2011, from http://www.aacu.org/ocww/volume38_3/national.cfm.

Tang, S. S. L. & Kiang, P. N. (2011). Refugees, veterans, and continuing pedagogies of PTSD in Asian American Studies. In M. Ouellet (Ed.), *An integrative analysis approach to diversity in the classroom* (New directions for teaching and learning, no. 125, pp. 77–87). San Francisco: Jossey–Bass.

Tierney, W. G. (1992). An anthropological analysis of student participation in college. *Journal of Higher Education, 63*(6), 603–618.

Tierney, W. G. (1999). Models of minority college-going and retention: Cultural integrity versus cultural suicide. *Journal of Negro Education, 68*(1), 80–91.

Tinto, V. (1987). *Leaving college: Rethinking the causes and cures of student attrition.* Chicago: University of Chicago Press.

Tinto, V. (1993). *Leaving college: Rethinking the causes and cures of student attrition* (2nd edn.). Chicago: University of Chicago Press.

Tinto, V. (1998). College as communities: Taking the research on student persistence seriously. *Review of Higher Education, 21*, 167–178.

Torres, V. (2003). Mi casa is not exactly like your house. *About Campus, 8*(2), 2–7.

Treisman, U. (1992). Studying students studying calculus: A look at the lives of minority mathematics students in college. *College Mathematics Journal, 23*(5), 362–372.

Triandis, H. C., McCusker, C., & Hui, C. H. (1990). Multimethod probes of individualism and collectivism. *Journal of Personality and Social Psychology, 59*, 1006–1020.

Valenzuela, A. (1999) *Subtractive schooling: US-Mexican youth and the politics of caring.* New York: SUNY Press.

Yamaguchi, S., Kuhlman, D. M., & Sugimori, S. (1995). Universality of personality correlates and dimensionality of person's collectivistic tendencies. *Journal of Cross-Cultural Psychology, 26*, 658–672.

Yosso, T. J. (2006). *Critical race: Counterstories along the Chicana/Chicano educational pipeline.* New York: Routledge.

7

THE ROLE OF STUDENT AGENCY, STUDENT EMPOWERMENT, AND SOCIAL PRAXIS IN SHAPING SUPPORTIVE CULTURES AT TRADITIONALLY WHITE INSTITUTIONS

Uma M. Jayakumar

> If there is no struggle, there is no progress . . . Power concedes nothing without a demand. It never did and it never will.
>
> Frederick Douglass (1988)

In the higher education literature, organizational culture is largely conceived of as an institutionally constructed phenomenon defined by artifacts (e.g., written documents, physical spaces, celebrated figures, rituals, campus events and activities), institutional values, and assumptions (e.g., expressed through mission statements and allocation of funding, and guiding campus practices, policies, and decisions) (Kuh & Whitt, 1988; Manning, 1993; Museus, 2007; Schein, 1992); it is also a means through which institutions socialize new members and communicate behavioral expectations (Geertz, 1973; Masland, 1985). Although organizational culture is a set of norms, expectations, and values deeply embedded within institutional practices and structures (Masland, 1985), it exists only to the extent that institutional actors "perform" the culture of an institution (Giroux, 1983). As Giroux (1983) explains, organizational culture is "constituted by the relations between different classes and groups bounded by structural forces and material conditions and informed by a range of experiences mediated, in part, by the power exercised by the dominant society" (p. 309). Furthermore, although the power to shape the organizational culture is more accessible to the dominant group, power is effervescent and can be tapped into and exercised with equal force by all parties involved (Foucault, 1980; Giroux, 1983). In terms of creating organizational cultures that support underrepresented and low-income students of color, what this means is that students of color and their allies have agency in shaping the culture and ensuring it is one that is aligned with their values, beliefs, and needs.

Most research on organizational culture, as it relates to the success of students of color, focuses on a top-down approach. It is important to place the onus on institutions for the environments and educational experiences they make available and existing racial disparities in student outcomes. Nonetheless, as Maldonado, Rhoads and Buenavista (2005) suggest, "it has probably been too much to expect that predominantly White universities, guided by predominantly White administrative staffs and faculty, would institute in significant ways a multicultural framework" (p. 608) and, likewise, genuinely transform traditionally existing monolithic institutional cultures. On the unlikelihood of people in positions of power relinquishing that power, Freire (1970) states:

> It is only the oppressed who, by freeing themselves, can free their oppressors. The latter, as an oppressive class, can free neither others nor themselves. It is therefore essential that the oppressed wage the struggle to resolve the contradiction in which they are caught. (p. 56)

Even well-intentioned and racially conscious administrators and faculty of color, and White allies with a commitment to organizational actions and values inclusive of communities of color, often proceed with caution in outspokenly challenging upper-level administrators higher in the chain of command in the university power structure. According to Chesler and Crowfoot (2000), "their role generally is limited to advice and debate on administrative decisions, and passive (and covert) resistance to dicta with which they disagree individually or collectively" (p. 453). Students, on the other hand, are not clouded by the real or perceived risk of losing their subordinate positions in the power structure of higher education organizations, nor do they operate within institutional channels of debate and discussion; "the experience of marginality in turn, often gives students an impetus and opportunity (even a freedom) to organize and exert influence through extraordinary and even illegitimate channels" (p. 453). This is evidenced throughout the history of higher education in which students of color have most outspokenly challenged exclusionary actions on college campuses, naming them as manifestations of institutional racism, and have been at the forefront of demanding change through public protest, disruption, and demonstration (Chesler & Crowfoot, 2000; Rhoads, 2000; Yamane, 2001).

In the Critical Race Theory (CRT) tradition of counterstorytelling, this chapter shares the experiences of two graduate students who felt empowered to push back on organizational behavior they perceived as a retreat from racial justice, from the values they viewed as integral to a supportive culture for students of color, and from the stated institutional values that drew them to the university. The culmination of the student movement led by two Black female graduate students facilitated a decisive shift in the university leadership's original position and a reversal of a previous decision, finally bringing forth a new commitment from the institution to keep a program designed to increase access to college for poor and underrepresented students of color. Through this institutional example of change this chapter demonstrates how dominant narratives and concerns that guide institutional behavior often do not account for the concerns of students of color and how certain institutional practices or decisions can trigger prior experiences of oppression and a desire for social praxis. I present the narratives that were written by two graduate students for a course final assignment that called for reflecting on their experiences and reactions to the university's decision to discontinue Upward Bound. The chapter concludes by suggesting that, when institutions embrace the transformative potential of students of color, they can foster a more inclusive campus culture. In the following section, I describe the circumstances that prompted the student movement.

The Case of Upward Bound at University West[1]

Upward Bound is a federally funded program of national recognition and one of very few college outreach programs that focuses on students who are the least resourced and face the greatest barriers to making it to a 4-year institution. The program was the first of the TRIO initiatives born out of President Lyndon B. Johnson's 1964 Economic Opportunity Act (McElroy & Armesto, 1998).[2] The students in the program come from low-income families (150% of national poverty level, which in 2010 was $33,075 for a family of four), have both parents that have not gone to college (making it more difficult for those parents to aid them with the college application process), and themselves attend some of the most underresourced high schools in the nation (U.S. Department of Education, 2011).

For 45 years standing – since obtaining the first grant in 1966 – University West (UW) has proudly hosted the Upward Bound (UB) program. University West Upward Bound is one of the oldest and largest of the 953 federally funded UB programs. University West's program has served 627 students from diverse racial backgrounds over the past 12 years with 2009–10 students reflecting the following racial breakdown: 31% Asian American/Pacific Islander, 37% African American/Black, 21% Latino/a, 2% White, and 8% multiracial. The program has consistently exceeded the 90% national UB average success rate for sending participants to college. The program also facilitates the development of UW undergraduate and graduate students through employment as resident advisors, tutors, or instructors, and by providing campus service-learning opportunities. The latter function earned the program various awards over the years; most recently the program director received UW's highest merit award for University and Community Service. In addition, the program serves as a training ground for preparing social justice oriented educators and contributes to building a trusting relationship between UW and poor communities of San Francisco.

Unfortunately, despite their value, programs such as Upward Bound are experiencing budget cuts and retrenchment across the country (Burd, 2011). For example, in the 2011 budget year, TRIO programs received a $45-million cut (Burd, 2011). Reflecting this national trend, UW made a decision to discontinue its UB program on account of projected enrollment increases, space limitations and compelling constraints facing the university, and possibly other considerations. The Upward Bound Director was informed in November 2010 of the decision and told it was based on campus construction and resource constraints. The news reached faculty, staff, students, and the community several months later when UW administrators announced in February 2011 that the decision to not renew the Upward Bound contract was based on space issues. This led to protest on various levels in the form of demonstrations, letters, petitions, and outreach to the university leadership team, the university board of trustees, media, the NAACP, and public officials. Various constituents were moved to action; nonetheless, most would agree that it was the students who created the consolidated movement that would eventually lead to overturning a seemingly fated decision. The students took the lead and did the hard work of organizing large-scale demonstration and protest; they called upon faculty and staff again and again to participate in various forms of protest that they had orchestrated (e.g., contacting public officials and media, attending demonstration, raising awareness). Although an extensive list of the actions and efforts made by various constituents, as well as an organizational analysis of the decision-making or change process, is beyond the scope of this chapter, I share one of the few university-wide public announcements of the leadership's position to further illustrate the concerns and rationale for the initial decision expressed through the dominant institutional narrative. The following excerpt is from an email that went out to the university community two days before the first of three student-organized acts of demonstration and protest, one community-organized protest, one collective faculty response, and numerous individual letters and pleas to the University leadership for dialogue and reconsideration.

> Today, UW leaders and I met with representatives from the community to discuss the future of the Upward Bound program. UW has announced that it will not renew the program's contract when it expires in August 2012 . . . UW believes strongly in Upward Bound. However, there is no easy solution to our severe space limitations on campus; we have already moved entire programs off campus. We are now conducting a comprehensive space review that will likely lead us to relocate other programs as well. We have also been forced to dramatically reduce the number of outside

organizations that we can accommodate on campus, many of which have long-time relationships with UW. The University West is proud to have hosted Upward Bound on our campus and the role it has played in helping at-risk students prepare for college. We can no longer accommodate any program, no matter how worthy, at the expense of denying space and support to our own students. (university-wide communication, March 1, 2011)

In response to student protesters who marched up to the leadership offices to deliver a petition claiming that the decision to discontinue Upward Bound went against the social justice mission of UW, the President explained:

I want to be clear about the mission of the University. If you take the document, it says vision, mission, values. The mission of the university is to promote learning in a Jesuit catholic tradition for graduate, undergraduate and professional students. So it's not an unlimited commitment to everybody. It's a commitment to our undergraduate, graduate and professional students. So my responsibility is to ensure that our resources serve the mission.[3]

As mentioned earlier, although an analysis or understanding of the decision-making process or factors involved is beyond the scope of this chapter, what can be gleaned from these public statements are the dominant narratives that students were presented with, which led to their dissent. The decision was framed as rational, neutral, and based on a set of compelling considerations to protect student and university interests. The counterstories I share provide an alternative perspective on removing a program such as Upward Bound from campus, a set of interests potentially overlooked in the original decision-making process. In the tradition of Critical Race Theory (see Chapter 2) I honor the counterstories often rendered voiceless in dominant narratives. Specifically, I share the perspectives of two graduate students who exercised their personal agency and conviction to organize and lead faculty, community, and students in a movement they named "Bound for Social Justice." The concerns and perspectives they brought to light potentially contributed to a shift in the leadership's position and a renewed commitment to Upward Bound, as discussed in the concluding remarks of the chapter. The following stories honor student agency and self-empowerment and the potential role of students in shaping an institution's culture. These accounts were written by students to summarize experiences of and reactions to hearing the initial decision regarding Upward Bound and reflect their own opinions and perceptions at the time of submitting their respective class assignments. The narratives are presented in this chapter with their consent.

Student Narratives

Amy, Graduate Student and Bound for Social Justice Leader

"To Whom Much Is Given, Much Is Required"

Given my personal commitment and professional experience I felt it was incumbent upon me to challenge cultural and systemic oppression and re-educate well-meaning liberals who continually and most often *unintentionally* participate in keeping the cycle of oppression going. I am the beneficiary of those before me; therefore, it is of utmost importance to me that I shoulder the same responsibility, walk with conviction, and pave the road for those coming behind me. I knew as a parent whose children have had access to amazing academic institutions (including one currently enrolled at a Tier 1 university), I could not sit passively by and not fight for the same access to education for other black and brown children.

For those who know me, standing up and speaking truth to power is what I have spent the last few decades trying to model. However, in the particular moment hearing the news of Upward Bound's eviction in my Social Movements and Human Rights class, speaking up did not seem sufficient. On February 12, 2011, I found myself contemplating how I was going to be exiting off this *Social Movements Theory Freeway* and onto the *Student-Agency and Social Praxis Highway*. I wasn't sure a moral compass, a conviction map, and a justice-seeking flashlight were sufficient to shed the necessary strategic light to travel down *Equity Lane* successfully. But, I was sure that I could not sit submissively, looking out the window watching the signs of dehumanization and marginalization of young people passing me by.

The administration's uninformed, insensitive, and unilateral decision felt like a personal attack; and to not act on this, I would have knowingly been participating in keeping the cycle of exclusion and oppression going. As the saying goes, "you're either part of the solution or part of the problem"; I was determined to act out the first.

Accountability to Social Justice

Back in mid-January 2011, I had left my entire life behind in Boston bound for my first semester of graduate school on the other side of the country. After a decade or so of waiting to obtain a master's degree, I selected University West because of its program in International and Multicultural Education with a Human Rights emphasis. It was their stated beliefs and commitments to upholding Jesuit values that inspired me, the first one being an opportunity to do service-learning (an opportunity to apply what we learn in the class-room – the emphasis being on reciprocity and the equal benefits for both students and the community) or as the institution states: "work to create a more humane and just world." Second, it is "the belief that no individual or group may rightfully prosper at the expense of others." In other words, it was aligned with my own commitments to "walk the walk"; to stand up when staring eye-to-eye with injustice; to work on behalf of and in service to the marginalized and disenfranchised; to utilize my *full-self* to change the current educational landscape; and to strengthen the social fabric of my communities: people of color, teenage parents, economically unstable, and the learning disabled.

A few days into what we were calling a "rev-ah-lution," we read aloud a letter written by a faculty member in our student meeting. The content of the letter not only eloquently echoed and validated my convictions, it also had the hegemonic tone that I needed to hear and would later use. The willingness of faculty to put out such a critique was empowering and was followed by collective and individual letters to the President and dialogue with campus administrators. Nonetheless, I kept longing for more *action* from UW faculty and staff. Many encouraged us, provided ideas and information, and participated in the protests but most didn't get down and dirty with us to do the hard work of creating collective action and public demonstration.

So, like many other movements, the students were at the frontlines; *we* were *leading* the uprising against what we viewed as a racist, elitist, and flat out unjust decision, whether or not this was the intention. We set out to stop the university from denying equitable access to college readiness support for just over 150 currently enrolled, hard-working, and highly deserving under-served youth and lest we forget the potentially thousands of youth in the years to come. Over those two months and three days that we fought for keeping Upward Bound, I was determined to hold myself and the entire institution up to the standard of acting out our social responsibilities and not just spewing the social justice rhetoric we intellectuals are so good at.

Quite frankly, the defensive posturing of certain individuals who referenced their current diversity commitments (i.e., garden in Bayview Hunter's Point and the street legal counsel in the Tenderloin) is what I would categorize as false generosity. Paulo Freire describes false generosity as "relieving the guilty conscience of the oppressor rather than working to liberate the oppressed." When I heard comments around campus like "this is not in our mission," "we no longer have space," "youth need professional etiquette lessons," "youth need to wear polo style shirts," it made me feel disheartened but fueled my fire to keep fighting to promote a critical analysis of privilege and oppression and to expand people's limited understanding of the breadth of diversity on our campus.

Moving Upward and Onward

To be effective we had to create a message that would unite all the different students on campus, expose the inconsistent hegemonic messaging handed down from the administration, work collaboratively with the Upward Bound staff to build the counterhegemonic stories, and engage involvement from key stakeholders amidst several constituencies. Some of our initial steps were: immersing ourselves in our institution's written commitments; going on a fact-finding mission; and interviewing the Executive Director of the program, faculty members, and the Dean of our School of Education.

Through the deliberate acts of creating a unifying symbol (clinched fist with the globe and colors to represent the different peoples), naming our first resistance tactic (Circle for Justice) and building a Facebook page, a Gmail account and a phone line – the Bound for Social Justice student-movement was born! Capitalizing on the power of social networking to post testimonials from Upward Bound high school students, our current student body, and alumni of both our university and the program not only uplifted and catapulted our voices across the city and surrounding areas; it inspired others to join the efforts, which in turn brought resources and strategies we hadn't considered nor would have had access to otherwise. This helped with organizing protests and demonstrations to make noise and raise awareness about the issue beyond campus. Our first demonstration culminated in a march to the President's office to deliver a petition signed by approximately 800 students stating:

> We, the undersigned, UW Graduate & Undergraduate Students are joining in Solidarity to DEMAND that the UW Administration live up to its commitment to social justice and its Jesuit value: "the FULL, integral development of each person and all persons, with the belief that NO individual or group may rightfully prosper at the expense of others." We also want UW Leadership to understand that we agree to "SHARE SPACE" with deserving local High School Students.

It was frustrating to be told that Upward Bound was getting kicked out because of "space." The federal grant pays student and staff expenses, and pays rent for office space and some amount of indirect costs, so I couldn't understand why they wouldn't allow the UB students to use leftover classrooms. When we didn't get answers or the response we were looking for, we spent hours identifying, strategizing, and utilizing our allies, formal and informal. Ultimately starting with those closest to the decision-making, the Dean of School of Education and then working our way up the chain of command to the Provosts. The actualization of our idea to solicit political capital from influential people in the city came via a personal connection of Dr. Rev. Amos Brown, a major civil rights activist and leader for the surrounding community.

He coordinated a meeting for us with the former Mayor of the city. After spending over an hour in the meeting learning some new tactics, we left with a renewed spirit to move forward. The key advice was to put a "spotlight" on the issue, reach out to the Board of Trustees, make sure people in power were informed of the facts so they might question the decision when they are at "the table," and contact media outlets and community contacts.

Kim, Graduate Student and Bound for Social Justice Leader

The Perfect Moment for Movement

I would tell anyone that when you cannot deny what you think, when how you feel conjures up all your might, and when it leads you to yearning for something to happen or for change to occur, it is the perfect moment informing you that time and circumstance are calling you to take action. We have distinct moments in our lives when we are so moved by an experience that what we do with that moment will dictate our capacity to move others. In the matter of UW Upward Bound vs. UW Administration & Leadership, I was moved because my personal expectations and values were attacked and challenged by an intentional decision that seemed to carelessly impact the marginalized youth of the university. As a Black Woman and Youth Development Professional who knows well what it is to be marginalized in education and society, a sense of clarity was undeniable and I felt the impact, understood the conflict, and shared identity with the issue. Furthermore, as master's student in the School of Education, sitting in a Social Movements class no less, I was prompted to take responsibility and accountability to get informed, share my own knowledge, and project my personal perspective upon anyone that would listen.

In retrospect identity, access, and personal investment were key factors in stimulating movement building in solidarity with the staff and youth of Upward Bound. However, in the instant of inspiration and motivation, it was more about "the perfect moment" in which I was aligned with my emotions, will power, and intention. I was fully present and conscious of my role. My heartstrings were pulled and I found myself upset and feeling dismay when I was first informed of the decision to remove Upward Bound from the local community. In the moment I bellowed out "No" in disbelief. I repeated in question, "Upward Bound?" again and again as if eventually my professor would respond with some other answer. Immediately after class another classmate and soon to be partner in movement-building (Amy Cipolla-Stickles) looked at me with the same intensity that I felt going through me. It was no question that we both had already made a commitment to get involved as she said, "We have to do something, this isn't right!"

The "bottom line" truth of their decision to remove the program was the most authentic example of how power structures work when circumstances become challenging. The leadership of University West had to increase its revenue as well as survive in a time of financial downfall. Consequently, the uninformed, marginalized, and seemingly powerless were put on the line; a scenario supremely reflective of a legendary system in America.

As soon as I knew about what was happening I was clear more people needed to know and the administration had to be challenged and questioned. I immediately used a single tool and pursued two goals. I jumped on the Internet to develop my personal knowledge as best as possible while spreading the word. Only 12 hours after first being told of the circumstances I emailed and Facebooked every youth developer and teacher I knew in the city and jumped on the university website. By the time I walked out of my front door to meet up with Amy I had a list of the university's core values highlighting the ones in jeopardy by making the decision. I also had come to the conclusion that an "eviction" was taking place. I recalled my own childhood experiences of being told I was a burden. I recognized that regardless of intention these young people were being evicted. In regards to access to higher education and having a home base to prepare for entry into it, they were being evicted. Under the circumstances of being youth of color living in a gentrified city where many of their families were below the poverty line, this decision engaged in revictimization.

Accountability and Moving Forward

As a new student to the University West I made a commitment to the institution. I applied, enrolled, and paid tuition believing that through coursework in human rights education and as members of the school of education, I would collaborate with the university's stated commitment to social justice. I believed that this well-seasoned institution had a culture that would fine-tune me as a change maker. I never anticipated the need to defy the leaders that sat at the top of the mountain dictating decisions that reflected poor ethics. Unfortunately, before the end of my first semester I was experiencing neglect, classism, the oppressive gender politics of academe, the suppressive nature of maneuvering within institutional hierarchy while subdued in a grave reality check of living in the American Paradigm. I realized I was engaged in a place where our choice was intended to be taken from us.

The first opportunity to actualize a purposeful plan of action was in a meeting with the Black Student Union Executive Board. We made decisions to spread the word across campus, shake up the leadership with the perspective of the disenchanted, and make a demand for a reverse in the decision to evict Upward Bound from the campus. We made lists of suggestions that came from the greater community at the Town Hall meeting and in passing conversations. What was envisioned through the collective thought process was a demonstration around the university's prize: a historic church that serves as the centerpiece of the campus. What was most important was that we assertively communicated peace and provided a display of solidarity. Thus, we planned the demonstration as a peaceful circle of linked arms that wrapped a human chain around the church.

We had a short matter of time to make movement and a lot had to be done. Our adrenaline started to pump and we knew organization and detail would make a great difference. Personally my goal was to listen to what "the people" wanted and make sure there was an expectation of organization and structure to achieve our goals. We began making fliers for distribution, creating petitions and fact sheets for people on campus as well as delegating outreach goals in the number of people we needed to sign the petition. We spoke to people about their own connection to childhood and what programs may have supported them in gaining access to college. We asked people for their perspective of the administration, and if they ever experienced being dismissed from a democratic process. We asked people about their value for student voice and student choice.

Getting to a Win–Win: The Benefits to All Involved

The city surrounding UW has alarming drop-out rates, little to no summer school, night school, and course grade retention opportunities. In a state that bases college entry on a set of strict eligibility standards, Upward Bound was one of very few programs that provided a gateway for students to retain replacement grades through course retaking. Furthermore the program performed this great service for students as they pushed up against the odds of socioeconomic struggles that create an unbalanced playing field for candidates applying for college. Up until this disastrous dilemma [referring to the initial decision to discontinue Upward Bound] University West provided a platform for over 45 years for students of color below the standard poverty rate to compete, apply, and have a sense of self-worth beyond their uncontrollable circumstances.

Keeping Upward Bound was also in the best interest of UW. The benefits of Upward Bound are numerous. Upward Bound is a direct placement for Service Learning Students: for the past three years it has worked with students from professors in the School of Business and Professional Studies and in Computer Science. Likewise, the School of Education faculty has placed counseling student interns in the Upward Bound summer session and School of Education TEAMS participants have worked as UB instructors. UB currently has alumni enrolled as undergrads and three alumni in the School of Education grad programs and it hires an average of 10–15 students each year as tutors, advisors, and clerical assistants. There have also undoubtedly been additional applicants from UW and other local UB projects as a result of tours and presentations arranged and conducted by the UB staff for visiting UB projects.

We had to convince the leadership of these benefits but, no matter whom we spoke to on the leadership team, accountability was spread thin or redirected. I believed there was a need for humility from all parties involved so that we could open up conversation to better address the issues and circumstances of Upward Bound. The experience of being the group marginalized, removed, disregarded, of a lower class, and having the disenfranchised experience meant the experience of humility was already happening to us, whether it was being voiced or not. An initiation of humility needed to come from the leadership team, but it was like pulling teeth. I began to feel more hopeful when private meetings with administrators and leadership led to acknowledgment of making a mistake by being unaware of the level of value the Upward Bound program had in the community. But still, there was a need for humility and public accountability if we were going to move forward in a way that everyone could benefit from.

Discussion

Setting it apart from many universities across the country, University West has a strong institutional identity around social justice values, as exemplified in this statement by the President, highlighted in a press release by Upward Bound advocates:

> The underlying questions of higher education today should be: How does what our institutions are doing with the 1 percent of the world who are our students affect the other 99 percent? What is our role in helping our students be humanly in this world? We cannot educate in a vacuum. We cannot educate as though our focus is simply the 1 percent that we happen to have here at this moment. It has to be how is what we're doing with this 1 percent going to affect the lives of the 99 percent. The challenge, particularly now with the weak economy, is that people tend to resort back to a kind of rugged individualism. This puts a real strain on the social fabric. I think the fundamental reality is that we're all interrelated, and that we move forward together.[4]

These values are enacted in programming at UW such as a campus service-learning requirement, a multicultural requirement, efforts to recruit a diverse student body and faculty, and numerous service projects domestic and abroad. The university's actions have earned it distinction as being in the Top 20 Universities in student body diversity and consistently being placed on the Corporation for National and Community Service's President's Honor Roll, amongst other recognitions and awards.

Nonetheless, the counterstories shared in this chapter reveal that these university ideals and values felt like empty promises to student advocates of

Upward Bound (many of whom were students of color) at the moment of hearing the initial decision to discontinue the program. Based on the student narratives displayed in this chapter and 3 hours of follow-up conversations with each, it was clear that both perceived the decision to be inconsistent with the mission of the institution and a culture of inclusion for communities of color. Kim asserted that the values, priorities, and interests that guided this particular decision were "misinformed and inconsistent with the University's mission to be an agent for social change." Perhaps, it would be more accurate to say it was inconsistent with both students' interpretation of the mission and their desire for a particular type of social change. Indeed, their vision of the institution's mission and to whom the mission extends was different from what was expressed by the leadership in justifying the initial decision. Given that values and mission are important manifestations of an institution's culture, their challenges to the enactment of values in the mission reflect a desire to impact cultural change. Although the narratives were rich with descriptive content about the movement and specific strategies, I focus here on three themes – critical race theory lens, community-cultural wealth, and transformative resistance – as these themes were most relevant to the student leaders' sense of agency, empowerment, and motivation for social praxis.[5]

Critical Race Theory Lens

Although unknowingly, the student leaders adhered to three tenets of CRT as defined by Solórzano (1997, 1998) in their framing and discussion of the Upward Bound issue.

1 *Recognition of the pervasiveness of racism and its intersectionality with other forms of subordination.* The students recognized the pervasiveness of systems of power, privilege and oppression that operate throughout society and social institutions including higher education. This tenet of CRT reflects an understanding of the structural nature of racism, classism, and other intersecting forms of oppression. Specifically, they are perpetuated through organizational and individual actions not necessarily intended to be racist or exclusionary (Bonilla-Silva, 2006). Amy and Kim viewed the UB decision through a CRT lens and had a critique about its role in perpetuating the subordination of traditionally excluded racially and economically underserved people.

2 *Challenge to dominant ideology.* Amy and Kim questioned the neutrality, objectivity, and colorblindness of the decision, pointing to the overlooked impact of local communities of color and poor communities. Amy in particular felt some responsibility based on economic and educational privilege. Both recognized their access to higher education as a privilege over those who are denied access. Their perspective reflects this CRT tenet's

critique of meritocracy and the notion that social mobility is colorblind and earned through individual efforts and abilities, as opposed to being influenced by systematic advantages afforded to groups of individuals.

3 *Commitment to social justice.* From a CRT perspective, commitment to social justice entails a commitment toward (a) eliminating racism, sexism, and poverty and (b) empowering communities of color (Solórzano & Delgado Bernal, 2001). The student leaders interpreted the social justice agenda and mission of UW through this lens. For example, Amy described the mission and Jesuit values as aligned with her own commitments "to work on behalf of and in service to the marginalized and disenfranchised . . . and to strengthen the social fabric of my communities: people of color, teenage parents, economically unstable, and the learning disabled" (Amy's narrative).

Community-Cultural Wealth

Both student leaders exhibited what Yosso (2005) refers to as community cultural wealth: "Accumulated assets and resources in the histories and lives of communities of color" (p. 77). More specifically, "community cultural wealth is an array of knowledge, skills, abilities and contacts possessed and utilized by communities of color to survive and resist macro and micro-forms of oppression" (p. 77). It challenges the traditional interpretation of social capital theory, which frames students of color and their communities as deprived of the social capital deemed valuable for and to higher education institutions (Yosso, 2005). Amy's and Kim's understandings grew out of their personal backgrounds and experiences of racism, classism, sexism, heterosexism, and gender politics, and the tools of resistance they had developed through their communities and life experiences. Kim identifies as part of the Jamaican American and Black communities. She is first-generation Jamaican American, and grew up living on army bases or otherwise mostly low-income working-class neighborhoods, and was homeless for 1 year. She moved around frequently but credits learning "what it means to be a Black girl in America and how to fight systematic oppression" to the years she spent living in a low-income working-class community of Marin City, California. Amy identifies as a biracial-Black, lesbian teenage parent, transracially adopted into an upper middle-class background. In the follow-up interviews, Amy and Kim talked about relying mostly on their respective and collective intuitions in how they reacted to the decision and throughout the movement-building process. These intuitions and understandings were drawn from their life experiences and guided them in navigating the circumstances they faced. Both indicated in follow-up that their life experiences led them to a sense of group consciousness with marginalized communities and a desire to work toward advancing the entire community. Their general notion of family as including marginalized communities of color paralleled their perception of Upward Bound students as part of the UW community, and fueled their desire to advance the university community toward a greater commitment to racial justice. Their respective community-cultural wealth, including understandings, empathies, hopes, and resistance, helped them successfully navigate the movement-building process, create a collective voice, and contribute to change on campus.

Transformative Resistance

Amy and Kim exhibited a Freirean critical consciousness (Freire, 1970) through their knowledge of how oppression operates and recognition of their personal power and agency in creating change. Their actions can also be understood using transformational resistance (Solórzano and Delgado Bernal, 2001). Transformational resistance promotes change and is characterized by a critique of structures of domination, an understanding of one's own oppressive condition, and a need to struggle for social justice.

In line with transformative resistance, Amy and Kim had a CRT critique of structural inequalities in society and were conscious of their oppressive position in intersecting social structures of domination (as members of the Black community, as women, as Lesbians) and in the hierarchical structure of the university (as students). Although both students mostly focused on the oppressed position of Upward Bound youth, each expressed alignment with the Upward Bound students and their experience of oppression. In Amy's words, " the administration's uninformed, insensitive, and unilateral decision felt like a personal attack." Kim similarly wrote, "my personal expectations and values were attacked and challenged by an intentional decision that seemed to carelessly impact the marginalized youth of the university." Both perceived the university's decision as positioning their community as the "other" and not within the purview of university interests. Ultimately, they experienced the decision as an attack on local poor, marginalized, and racially disenfranchised communities, and on themselves.

A sense of injustice also came from feeling the decision was being made on their behalf as students of the university but without their consent. This perceived absence of what Kim referred to as "student voice and student choice" and a democratic process is conveyed in Amy's reference to the "administration's uninformed, insensitive, and unilateral decision" and Kim's reference to leaders sitting "at the top of the mountain dictating decisions." As noted previously, the experience of marginality within the university power structure and often authoritarian decision-making processes is common amongst students across higher education institutions (Chesler & Crowfoot, 2000) and reflects what Freire (1970) refers to as the banking method of education, in which students are expected to be passive receptacles of information.

Amy's and Kim's critical consciousness led each to feel personal responsibility and ownership over the environment and the values that had brought them to the institution. They believed the university was accountable to them; and they felt accountable to the students in Upward Bound. Demonstrating their transformative resistance, both felt compelled to struggle for social justice. Their narratives relay a strong sense of responsibility and desire for taking actions to pursue a reversal of the initial decision. For example, Amy explained, "I felt it was incumbent upon me to challenge cultural and systematic oppression . . . I could not sit passively by and not fight." Likewise, Kim described her "yearning for something to happen or for change to occur" and immediately feeling "prompted to take responsibility and accountability to get informed, share my own knowledge, and project my personal perspective upon anyone that would listen." Overall, in addition to their theoretical understandings, a sense of responsibility and ownership over interpretation and enactment of the university mission led Amy and Kim to engage in social praxis through the Bound for Social Justice student movement.

Resolutions and Implications for Campus Culture

Throughout history, as evidenced by literature on social movements, and in current times, it has been students who have identified individual instances or decisions as linked to a greater history of exclusion and demanded progress toward more racially inclusive campus cultures (Chesler & Crowfoot, 2000; Rhoads, 2000; Yamane, 2001). Indeed, during the 3-month time period that student unrest and protest ensued at UW, students at UC Berkeley engaged in an 8 day hunger strike to protest the university's unilateral decision to downsize and consolidate Ethnic, Gender, and Women's Studies programs. Around the same time, graduate students at Harvard's School of Education expressed their outrage over the school's failure to retain and tenure faculty who study issues of justice and equity and a perceived lack of social justice-based curriculum. In all cases, students presented institutions with an opportunity to reconsider their actions in light of their implications for racial equity and for creating an inclusive culture for students of color on the campus. Only by valuing the community cultural wealth of students of color and their perspectives can institutions move in this positive direction.

In the case of Upward Bound at University West, the President and other members of the university's leadership were eventually convinced of the need to maintain Upward Bound at UW, not only agreeing to continue sponsorship of the program but *initiating* the creation of additional structures to ensure the program's continued success and full integration into the university community. The additional support structures include an advisory board with representation from the university and the community, and a university-wide integration committee composed of faculty and staff. The agreement was made at a meeting, which included Amy, Kim, UW administration, members of the Board of Trustees, and community leaders. Inviting Amy and Kim to be a part of the decision-making process was a clear sign of the university leadership's willingness to embrace these student of color leaders and protest organizers as valued allies. Both Bound for Social Justice leaders were also invited to be on the Advisory Board. The announcement of the new decision to the campus community proclaimed:

> Everyone benefits from this arrangement: the program, the community, and the university . . . I also applaud our students, staff and faculty who championed social justice and the rights of the less privileged. This goes to the heart of UW's mission and rich history. (university-wide communication, April, 15, 2011)

I can only speculate that the Bound for Social Justice student-initiated movement at UW played a critical role in reversing the university's initial decision to discontinue sponsorship of Upward Bound, encouraging a more democratic decision-making process, and bringing forth a renewed commitment to the program. The impact on more pervasive campus norms and cultural values is yet to be determined; nonetheless, it is safe to say that, from the perspective of promoting an organizational culture of racial inclusion, this action signals a recommitment to (1) fighting the systematic racism and organizational structures that generally reify the accumulated wealth and privilege of advantaged groups, and (2) disrupting a cycle of exclusion from higher education and social mobility for low-income students and students of color. It is also safe to say that the student leaders of Bound for Social Justice viewed their empowerment and social praxis as a way to redefine the campus culture and educational environment, as demonstrated in this statement made by Amy in the follow-up interview and echoed by Kim:

> I believe the institution moved closer to living up to its Jesuit and social justice mission and values. Because the institution reconsidered its initial decision, collaborated with us, and ultimately plans to facilitate Upward Bound's full integration, I feel like it's my university and it's up to me to continue to create the kind of space I and other students of color need to have to be successful here. I sharpened my own analysis of structural oppression within a university setting and raised my own expectations. I believe we not only impacted the School of Education community, but we shifted the culture within it and I would dare to say throughout the entire campus. I feel powerful and hopeful that I can continue to navigate other institutional structures given the struggles and successes we experienced fighting for Upward Bound.

Recommendations

This success story of institutional change and demonstration of student agency and empowerment holds many lessons for higher education institutions interested in promoting inclusive campus cultures that foster success among diverse students. As argued at the outset of this chapter, true transformation and organizational change must transpire from those who are in oppressed positions (Freire, 1970). They are the ones with the greatest understanding of the circumstances of their oppression and have the greatest capacity for viewing institutional practices and everyday decisions through this alternative lens. When institutions value community cultural wealth and the transformative potential of students of color as change agents, they create the potential to engage in problem-solving pedagogy as a rejection of the banking method of education. Unlike the latter, which positions students as passive receivers of education, the former envisions students as active participants of their educational environments in which they are not only taught and led by the university but also contribute as teachers and leaders. Furthermore, universities are not simply leaders but leader-learners, or leaders willing to learn as well. Institutions can best adapt their cultures to ones of racial inclusion for the potentially growing number of students of color on their respective campuses, by embracing dissenting student views and calls for reconsideration or reflection on institutional practices perceived as contributing to racial inequalities.

What does this mean about the importance of universities' having a social justice mission? The overall story told in this chapter suggests that having an explicit focus on social justice and equity in the mission can serve as a starting point for conversations about inclusion. Instituting a focus on social justice that explicitly includes racial equity, reflecting a CRT definition of social justice, would be even more conducive to these conversations. The story also reveals the level of dedication and hard work it takes to be accountable to social justice ideals that institutions striving for such an agenda should be ready to undertake. Amy and Kim were remarkable in that they not only had strong values and beliefs about equity but were accountable to those beliefs and committed to putting in the work to enact their values. We can all learn from their inspiring example. Likewise, institutions that are truly accountable to social justice are willing to re-examine practices and policies and bring them into alignment with this agenda when necessary. Having a social justice mission and agenda to be inclusive of diverse students means being accountable to those students and their perspectives of social justice. This level of accountability and willingness to embrace the perspectives of students of color and their social praxis is what University West demonstrated through its final decision to create a sustainable plan to maintain its sponsorship of Upward Bound.

Notes

1 University West is a pseudonym for a private Jesuit university. It is one of 953 institutions with an Upward Bound program. To maintain anonymity this pseudonym is used throughout this paper and all identifying information has been modified throughout the document, including in the student narratives and the public documents shared.
2 *TRIO* refers to a family of federally funded outreach and support programs that seek to increase access to college amongst individuals from underserved and marginalized groups such as low-income students, first-generation college students, underrepresented minorities, and individuals with disabilities. The Federal TRIO Program emerged in the 1960s with the Economic Opportunity Act of 1964 and the Johnson Administration's War on Poverty. Although it began with three initiatives – Upward Bound, Talent Search, and Student Support Service – at which point the name TRIO was coined, TRIO now includes eight programs targeting low-income and underserved student populations.
3 The citation for a YouTube video featuring this statement made publicly to UW students has been removed for anonymity purposes.
4 This quote appeared in a 2010 publication of a reputable national organization dedicated to promoting community service. The citation has been removed to preserve anonymity.
5 Social praxis is the application of theoretical understanding toward action and change.

References

Bonilla-Silva, E. (2006). *Racism without racists: Color-blind racism and the persistence of racial inequality in the United States* (2nd ed.). Lanham, MD: Rowman & Littlefield.

Burd, S. (2011). *Lack of coordination harms federal college outreach efforts* [Web log comment]. Retrieved May 31, 2011, from http://edmoney.newamerica.net/blogposts/2011/lack_of_coordination_harms_federal_college_outreach_efforts-52139.

Chesler, M. A., & Crowfoot, J. (2000). An organizational analysis of racism in higher education. In Brown, M. C. (Ed.), *Organization and Governance in Higher Education (5th Edition)*. Boston: Pearson Custom Publishing.

Douglass, F. (1988). The significance of emancipation in the West Indies. In G. Carruth and E. Ehrlich (Eds.), *The Harper Book of American Quotations*. New York: Harper and Row. (Original speech August 3, 1857.)

Foucault, M. (1980). *Power/knowledge: Selected interviews and other writings*. New York: Pantheon.

Freire, P. (1970). *Education for critical consciousness*. New York: Continuum Publishing Company.

Geertz, C. (1973). *The interpretation of cultures*. New York: Basic Books.

Giroux, H. A. (1983). *Theory & resistance in education: A pedagogy for the opposition*. South Hadley, MA: Bergin & Garvey Publishers.

Kuh, G. & Whitt, E. (1988). *The invisible tapestry: Culture in American colleges and universities*. ASHE-ERIC Higher Education Report Series. Washington, DC: Association for the Study of Higher Education.

Maldonado, D., Rhoads, R. & Buenavista, T. (2005). The student-initiated retention project: Theoretical contributions and the role of self-empowerment. *American Educational Research Journal, 42*(4), 605–638.

Manning, K. (1993). Properties of institutional culture. In G. D. Kuh (Ed.), *Cultural perspectives in student affairs work*. Lanham, MD: American College Personnel Association.

Masland, A. (1985). Organizational culture in the study of higher education. *Review of Higher Education, 8*(2), 157–168).

McElroy, E. J., & Armesto, M. (1998). TRIO and Upward Bound: History, programs, and issues – past, present, and future. *Journal of Negro Education, 67*(4), 373.

Museus, S. D. (2007). Using qualitative methods to assess diverse campus cultures. In S. R. Harper & S. D. Museus (Eds.), *Using qualitative methods in institutional assessment* (New directions for institutional research, no. 136, pp. 29–40). San Francisco: Jossey-Bass.

Rhoads, R. (2000). *Freedom's web: Student activism in an age of cultural diversity*. Baltimore, MD: Johns Hopkins University Press.

Schein, E. (1992). *Organizational culture and leadership* (2nd edn.). San Francisco: Jossey-Bass.

Solórzano, D. (1997). Images and words that wound: critical race theory, racial stereotyping and teacher education. *Teacher Education Quarterly, 24*, 5–19.

Solórzano, D. (1998). Critical race theory, racial and gender microaggressions, and the experiences of Chicana and Chicano scholars. *International Journal of Qualitative Studies in Education, 11*, 121–136.

Solórzano, D., & Delgado Bernal, D. (2001). Critical race theory, transformational resistance and social justice: Chicana and Chicano students in an urban context. *Urban Education, 36*, 308–342.

U.S. Department of Education. (2011). Federal TRIO programs. Retrieved April 28, 2011, from http://www2.ed.gov/about/offices/list/ope/trio/index.html.

Yamane, D. (2001). *Student movements for multiculturalism: Challenging the curricular color line in higher education*. Baltimore, MD: Johns Hopkins University Press.

Yosso, T. J. (2005). Whose culture has capital? A critical race theory discussion of community cultural wealth. *Race Ethnicity and Education, 8*(1), 69–81.

8

SHARED LEADERSHIP FOR CREATING CAMPUS CULTURES THAT SUPPORT STUDENTS OF COLOR

Adrianna J. Kezar

Melissa is the Director of a Multicultural Center at a research university and has been working for years to help support students of color. When she first came to campus, she was a strong advocate for undergraduates of color and knew she wanted to be an agent of change. However, quite early on she recognized that her strong advocacy was leading to a loss of her credibility and the perception that she was always complaining. Melissa was frustrated at how people misinterpreted her actions and were taken aback. She was unsure how she could move forward in trying to do the work that she knew was important: creating the condition for college students of color to be successful on campus.

Juanita is a college president at a community college. She has long been committed to equity and access for students of color. After a successful career as a lawyer, she decided to assume a leadership position at a community college. She wanted to work with an institution that serves large numbers of students of color, but that had not always been supportive of them. She started her presidency with the strategic planning process in which she emphasized the importance of diversity as one of her main priorities. After a year-long strategic planning process in which the campus created a new vision and mission statement emphasizing diversity, she obtained feedback from the board of trustees that several stakeholders throughout campus were concerned about her emphasis on diversity at the expense of other priorities. There were some fairly serious fiscal conditions, which needed her attention, and a failing community outreach program that had gained community outrage.

Paul is a faculty member of color in Political Science at a small liberal arts college. All through his education, he had been one of the few students of color within his academic programs and he suffered a lot of emotional damage from the racism that he experienced. He vowed that if he became a faculty member – his long-held dream – he would make sure students received the support he had not and that the departmental climate for students of color was much more positive. Paul also took steps toward increasing the representation of students of color in programs with which he was associated. As an early career faculty member, he offered to be on the recruitment and admissions committee for his department and was an outspoken advocate for recruiting students of color. Although he knew he had to be careful about strongly voicing his opinions before tenure, he positioned himself to make the most difference possible on local decisions being made within the department related to curriculum, hiring, and other areas which could be altered to support students of color. However, when he went up for his third-year review, he was informed that he should perhaps not be so vocal on issues within the department.

Melissa, Juanita, and Paul are like many champions and change agents who have entered the academy and are helping to make positive changes. Their leadership is crucial to creating an environment that supports students of color. Yet, as their stories demonstrate, lone champions and change agents often find themselves in difficult situations that limit the potential impact their advocacy can have on creating a supportive culture for students of color. The non-collaborative nature of the Academy, in which faculty are left to work on their own, staff are often siloed into a unit, and presidents are forced to work unilaterally, can lead to the type of individualized and isolated leadership described in these stories. Although lone change agents can make important contributions, they often experience many difficulties, ranging from losing their credibility, through jeopardizing promotion and tenure, to sacrificing their commitment to an issue, or becoming so frustrated that they leave the Academy. As a result, they do not make the kind of impact that they might have had if they collaborated with a larger group of people to create change.

Melissa, Juanita, and Paul work in environments that do not encourage collaboration. They are not the only ones. Today, change agents function in a world where leadership tends to be conceptualized as the "Lone Ranger." This view of leadership is prevalent within our society and prevents people from seeing the value and perhaps the necessity of a shared or collective leadership process (for discussion of the lone ranger view of leadership, see Kezar, Carducci, & Contreras-McGavin, 2006). In this chapter, I offer data and evidence to support the notion that shared or collaborative leadership is essential to alter campus culture and support students of color. First, I describe the important role that leadership plays in altering campus culture as a foundation for why leadership is important. Next, I encourage change agents to search for allies on campus and work in tandem to create change. In addition to broadly advocating for a more shared leadership process, I provide specific advice about shared leadership that has proven successful in creating more supportive campus cultures for students of color.

Building Campus Cultures Supportive of Students of Color through Leadership

Whereas some studies suggest the importance of leadership for creating change (Hurtado, Milem, Clay-Pederson, & Allen, 1999; Kanter, 1983; Kezar, 2001; Kezar et al., 2006; Komives & Wagner, 2009), others point more specifically to the importance of leadership for altering organizational cultures (Schein, 1985). Schein provides one of the most comprehensive examinations of the relationship between leadership and organizational culture. He demonstrates how leaders are looked at within organizations in order to understand the values and norms to ultimately guide behavior. People within the organization understand that values and norms often determine the allocation of rewards and the understanding of performance. Schein highlights three levels of culture that leaders can shape to alter the culture fundamentally.

The most important level is the underlying assumptions, which are the most intangible and hidden aspects of culture. People often do not directly acknowledge or talk about underlying assumptions, which makes them hard to recognize, especially for those entrenched in the organization for a long time. One example of such an underlying assumption on a college campus might be that, because students of color are less likely to be in honors courses, they are therefore less talented. Faculty and staff develop these basic assumptions over time and often do not recognize it. Indeed, they are unlikely to ever espouse this particular belief, but they hold and act on this belief. In order for students of color to be successful, leaders need to make visible and also question these underlying assumptions so that people can become more conscious of and hopefully alter these problematic assumptions that structure the overall culture. These deep-rooted assumptions are of course the most difficult to address, but are the most important for creating needed changes in mindset to ultimately alter behavior.

The next level is the espoused values or norms articulated by the campus. Examples of explicit values or norms might be "we value diverse perspectives" or "we value excellence." Mission and vision statements often communicate these types of espoused values, but they also can be found in less explicit places such as in conversations when people describe how community is valued within the institution. Leaders can identify or alter these explicit values and norms by examining key documents, reformulating speeches, and paying attention to the language of others throughout the organization. Change agents and leaders can use these strategies to alter language patterns or understood priorities to reshape behavior on campus.

The most visible level of culture is artifacts, such as diversity policies, recruitment practices, and rituals and events (e.g., separate graduation ceremonies for students of color). These more explicit and visible manifestations of culture are more apparent to people throughout campus. When the campus establishes a separate graduation ceremony for students of color it becomes symbolic of the importance of these students and their success to the institution. Leaders can take actions to establish these types of visible artifacts that help guide and change values and underlying assumptions. However, Schein (1985) is clear to note that people tend to operate unconsciously off, and rely most on, their underlying basic assumptions; thus, altering artifacts alone may have limited influence in the context of change efforts. Basic assumptions can override other cues people receive from their environment. Thus, although difficult to do, it is particularly crucial for leaders to alter both basic underlying assumptions and artifacts that can sometimes be easier and more straightforward.

Schein's (1985) framework provides a clear articulation of how leaders can shape organizational culture, but that does not mean that leaders always necessarily desire to play this role or recognize the important role they can have in altering the culture. It is important to note that there are a myriad of leadership strategies that people can use to create or shape culture: allocation of resources; creation of new offices or structure such as a multicultural center; revision of policies such as recruitment, the type of people hired, the socialization of new members; symbolic decisions such as honoring Black history month; formulation of a vision and an agenda for change; and commission of conversations that focus on diversity. However, it is important that leaders think through how the use of a particular strategy has implications for shaping artifacts, values and norms, and underlying assumptions. For example, creating new offices and revising policies are unlikely to shape underlying values and assumptions. Many of the strategies leaders adopt are what Bolman and Deal (2007) identify as structural strategies. In general, leaders tend to favor alteration of policies and structures over cultural approaches such as deciding to honor Black history month or leading conversations on race that can dig more deeply into underlying values and assumptions.

Although this last section has examined the potential for leaders to alter campus cultures, studies have also demonstrated the importance of leadership for improving the campus culture for students of color. For example, Kezar (2007) demonstrated how presidents carefully aligned their leadership strategies to different stages of institutionalization (mobilization, implementation, and institutionalization) to alter the culture of college campuses. At the start, when the campus is beginning to mobilize support for a new culture, presidents are most successful when they work on developing a vision for a multicultural campus, increasing motivation and energy toward the vision, and creating an infrastructure such as a diversity office or budget to support the vision. Through all this work, people begin to consider a new set of values: the importance of diversity. As the change becomes implemented, the president needs to broaden ownership by supporting people who help students of color and move from rhetoric to action by measuring success (better retention and graduation rates) and demonstrating progress (students report a better climate). Also, leaders focus on artifacts such as targeted hiring policies or new student recruitment processes that will help solidify the new understandings that were developed in the mobilization phase; all this activity moves people from considering to adopting the new values system. In the institutionalization phase, presidents help to ensure the new values are deeply embedded by facilitating difficult dialogues that can help foster necessary learning among people who were initially reluctant to embracing the new set of espoused values.

Understanding Shared Leadership

We can conceptualize shared leadership in several different ways. Traditionally, most scholars and practitioners have understood and studied shared leadership in a more hierarchical way, whereby those in positions of power such as presidents or provosts work more broadly with leaders across campus such as deans and department chairs. Bensimon and Neumann (1993) conducted one of the best-known studies of shared leadership. They examined presidential leadership teams that bring together collective expertise from various units to inform presidential decisions. The advantage of this approach to shared leadership is that those in positions of power often have the ability to mandate change, alter reward structures, use leverage devices such as strategic plans, refine mission and vision statements, and have other mechanisms to support changes that may be counter to the current culture. The downside to this approach is that it does not capitalize on the full set of human resources available on campus, may lack buy-in from constituents, and may not foster the commitment, energy, and enthusiasm of faculty and staff needed to execute changes.

Another way to conceptualize shared leadership is to look at collectives of individuals working in a coordinated way but not necessarily sanctioned or orchestrated by the formal administration or others in positions of power. For example, Astin and Leland (1991) studied women faculty and staff on campuses who participated in the women's movement and who created a variety of different changes on college campuses to support women and people of color, including curricular change, development and support services, and recruiting and admitting more women and students of color. This inquiry demonstrated that collectives of faculty and staff working together could make significant and important changes in the face of significant barriers and in a culture that is not open to the types of changes they were trying to make. The advantage of bottom-up[1] grassroots leadership is that it engages and draws on the expertise of people close to the students of color, leaders who often have the needed expertise to resolve and create solutions. Bottom-up leaders can also capitalize on the commitment and interest of faculty and staff, as well as create needed energy and buy-in to sustain the change. One potential disadvantage to grassroots groups is that these groups can be fragile because they do not have any institutional support. If a few of the champions lose energy or momentum, the entire effort can fall apart. In addition, as resistance emerges within the institution, people can burn out and the initiative can falter.

More recently, Kezar and Lester (in press) examined a third version of shared leadership in which bottom-up faculty and staff grassroots leaders worked to advance changes on campus that support students of color, but they also converged with top-down leadership efforts among those in formal positions of power. The difference from the first approach is that the bottom-up leaders have equal power and are driving the change, as opposed to being delegated power from the top. This type of shared leadership involves both the bottom and top collectively working together to recreate campus culture. The advantage of this merged approach to shared leadership is that it can capitalize on the support system and structures that formal leaders can put in place to support students of color. In addition, this approach has the support and buy-in from bottom-up leaders. Although this approach can be very difficult to achieve, if a balance can be struck between bottom-up and top-down leaders (in which the bottom-up have true power) it can create the type of collective leadership that can lead to swift and deep changes throughout the institution. I believe this form of leadership has the most potential to alter campus cultures because it capitalizes on the various levers of top-down leaders that can promote broad-scale transformation through changing rewards or strategic planning. In conjunction, bottom-up leaders tend to add more depth by working closely with others to change their underlying values and assumptions through relationship building, networks, and intense dialogue.

It is important to understand that these three approaches (hierarchical, bottom-up, and convergent) to shared leadership exist and each has the potential to support and progress changes for students of color. Because achieving the last type of shared leadership (bottom and top working together as "relative" equals) is complex and uncommon on campuses, I think it is important to advocate for any form of shared leadership that can be produced within a particular campus culture. Convergence is so difficult because it entails those in positions of power negotiating with bottom-up leaders and that shared purposes override status and authority in decision-making. Convergence does not mean getting rid of distinctions in authority, but rather creating a space for dialogue and negotiation.

The research on grassroots networks and groups also identifies the benefits of working in a collective fashion (Pearce & Conger, 2003). One of the major advantages of working in a shared leadership fashion is that you have an automatic support network that can help you maintain resiliency in the face of difficulties. Another major advantage of a shared leadership approach is that it can draw on ideas and information from across various networks on campus and develop more complex and complete solutions in terms of intervention for students. Also, the network has many more nodes than isolated individuals working in pockets and can have a broader impact across the entire culture of the campus. Rather than only impacting a particular subculture or group on campus, a network can attempt to work broadly and create changes across various departments and units. In general, working with a shared leadership approach creates more buy-in for the change as more people are brought into the change process. Particularly, bottom-up leaders face a lot of backlash of resistance for their efforts; working in groups helps them to have people who can support them and comfort them in difficult times. Also, in working collectively, an individual is less a lightning rod for backlash and resistance as there is no single individual that can be seen as driving the effort. Another advantage of working in a shared leadership fashion is that, as resistance to changing the culture emerges, people who are experiencing more backlash can temporarily move into the background behind the scenes, while others take up the more visible leadership roles and responsibilities. In this way there is a sharing of the resistance/backlash. The myriad benefits of working in a shared leadership fashion emerged from examining the challenges that lone grassroots and top-down leaders face as they attempt to create culture change.

Evidence to Support a Shared Leadership Process

Various studies have suggested the importance of leadership for changing campus culture and putting in structures and supports for students of color (Hurtado et al., 1999). Yet the studies tended to examine or define leadership in terms of the support of the college president. Kezar, Eckel, Contreras-McGavin, and Quaye (2008) followed up on these findings about the importance of leadership – specifically presidential leadership – and explored 30 campuses that had made advances for students of color. Individuals at the American Council on Education nominated these campuses because they were known nationally for making significant progress in advancing a comprehensive diversity agenda and changing campus culture. The campuses varied by institutional type from small liberal arts colleges to community colleges to large research universities and were located in every region of the country. In conversations with college presidents about their leadership and ways they altered the campus culture, the presidents noted that they had many levers that were important for creating change, particularly allocating resources, strategic planning, creating a vision for diversity, shaping and framing conversations, asking hard questions, and facilitating dialogues about diversity.

Yet they noted that their leadership alone is not sufficient for altering campus culture to make students of color successful. Presidents spoke about a web of leadership that they created across campus (or capitalized on, as it already existed on most campuses) with change agents who could identify and understand the needs and resultant support systems that would create more opportunities for students of color to be successful. Rather than look to the usual groups who might work on other leadership initiatives (a prominent faculty member to lead a curricular change), successful presidents knew that they had to identify change agents on campus that were closely connected with students of color and understood the types of changes that were truly needed. They stated that their colleagues that were less successful often depended on a small group of more formally appointed officers, such as a vice president for multiculturalism or associate deans who were in charge of diversity and multiculturalism. Although these individuals were important to include, they often lacked important information about critical success: (1) close connection to the students and the problems faced by students of color, (2) information about possible solutions on the ground, and (3) knowledge of the informal work going on to help students of color. In order to create effective solutions for making students of color successful, the leadership on campus needs to be aware of current issues and problems. Presidents noted that their vice president for multicultural affairs might be operating from assumptions based on once being a student of color or just be too removed from the students after years of administrative work. Connecting to entry-level staff who are working more closely with multicultural student groups, for example, is important because they can talk about newer issues such as students wrestling with multiethnic identity or virtual/on-line racism.

The study demonstrates that presidents also engaged in several activities to build this web of support or shared leadership for students of color that worked to change the culture. Presidents became actively involved in hiring processes so that new faculty and staff were aligned with commitment to the success of all students. Presidents also mentored faculty of color and set up intergenerational mentoring networks so that individual faculty did not feel isolated. Further, successful senior leaders created partnerships with faculty to transform the teaching and learning environment so that it better supported students of color, and leaders supported student affairs staff to create safe havens for students outside class. An important area that many leaders would not think about is the direct contact presidents have with students of color. Presidents can ensure they were themselves in touch with the needs of students of color. Many set up an advisory board of students of color. So, not only did they rely on a shared leadership approach but also on successful presidents that actually fostered and nurtured the web of leadership.

In a follow-up study focused on bottom-up leaders who support students of color on campus, Kezar and Lester (in press) demonstrated that there is an invisible web of leadership that exists on many college campuses and that is working to change campus culture. These different groups of leaders are an extremely powerful mechanism for challenging underlying assumptions and values among various pockets of staff, faculty, administrators, and students. Even the informal conversations that members of the campus networks have with different stakeholders can alter values and eventually behavior among their colleagues who may not have initially supported racially diverse students.

A case study of five institutions that had created supportive environments for students of color demonstrated that they had a rich web of bottom-up leaders that were networked across the institution. Together they had worked over an extended period of time to change the underlying values and assumption of the campus. One example is Activist Community College, which is located in a suburban area outside a major metropolitan area. The campus has long served (1960 to the early 1990s) a largely White middle-class population but found itself increasingly with more students of color (last 15 years). A set of faculty in the ethnic studies area noticed that, despite the shift in demographics, support services for diverse students were not available, curriculum did not represent diverse perspectives, and the faculty remained largely White. They began talking about ways to recruit more faculty of color so that students saw more faculty that looked like themselves. Furthermore, they began discussions in the faculty senate curriculum subcommittee about the nature of the curriculum and changes that might be made.

Simultaneously, across the campus a group of women – both White women and women of color – from a variety of disciplines began to meet over lunch to address a challenge they observed – a variety of populations including returning female students, women in science, and underrepresented/minority students were not well served by the campus. They met over a three-year period to read and discuss issues around diversity and equity and come to some consensus about solutions they thought could address the problem. They also began to work through various committees on campus including the curriculum committee to create changes in terms of the curriculum and support services. Because their discussions had been so rich and important, they also began a dialogue series about diversity and equity for the broader campus.

A group of staff members of color also began meeting to propose changes they saw necessary, such as multicultural student groups, tutorial services, and leadership opportunities for students of color. In addition to setting up these visible artifacts for supporting students of color, they also led an informational campaign among staff trying to help them with understanding the characteristics of racially diverse students and strategies for altering any stereotypes that might exist. All of these efforts began separately, but over time coalition-building took form among common efforts and the need to support one another's efforts. The faculty groups, in particular, were very successful in recruiting many faculty of color on campus and creating a powerful network of faculty across a variety of departments. The changes to the curriculum, support services, recruitment and retention processes, and discussion of the underlying values all happened without support from the administration. Rather, the efforts were all largely from the bottom up. This case shows the potential of strong collective bottom-up leadership.

Strategies of Success for Shared Leadership

Shared leadership must be carefully created, however. Because we are used to working individually, we often need to think through ways to work in a shared fashion that is respectful of individual and collective talents to overcome interpersonal and intergroup challenges that emerge. I divide the suggestions for enhancing shared leadership into advice for top-down leaders and for bottom-up leaders. First, I note one dynamic that cuts across the advice for both groups: the importance of trust. Although trust is quite an amorphous topic, many of the suggestions address bottom-up leaders not trusting those in positions of power and different grassroots leaders not trusting each other. Because White students have historically been and continue to be privileged, and racially diverse students discriminated against, lack of trust is likely inherent in this process of moving to a changed culture. Because trust is still likely to be missing between groups and individuals, one-on-one relationship building and substantial dialogue among people is required to make shared leadership work. Campuses that have had success altering culture recognize that change will be slow, given that relationship-building and trust development are delicate and long-term processes. The many successful presidents I have studied were able to foster and nurture shared leadership precisely because they had earned trust first, and subsequently were seen as credible agents of change by stakeholders from both the bottom and the top. For those in positions of power, for example presidents, deans, provosts, and department chairs, I offer the following advice.

Support and Acknowledge Those Who Have Been Working to Change the Culture for Years

Bottom-up leaders have most likely been working on change for many years on your campus with little reward or appreciation. Although these bottom-up leaders are committed to supporting students of color and do it because of their dedication and passion, they can still benefit from acknowledgment of their long-standing commitment to try to transform the culture. Often a new leader will come to campus and be committed to diversity, but will overlook the good work that has been done tirelessly over the years. When these leaders do not acknowledge the work that has been going on for years, they often take the wind out of the sails of bottom-up leaders and make trust and shared leadership more difficult.

Do Not Co-opt the Progress Made by Other Leaders

Those in positions of power who support racially diverse students often do so by making bold pronouncements about the way diversity will become a priority on campus and included in strategic plans and vision. As they begin promoting the importance of diversity, they might build on the important work that has already been done in pockets of the campus and innovative programs. The work of administrators is often to take small and good ideas that have been developed within particular units among grassroots leaders and to make them more widespread across campus. However, in many instances, top-down leaders have not acknowledged the people who created these programs. Instead, they have ended up co-opting the work and ideas of others and taking them on as their own. Because bottom-up leaders have been working for 10 to 15 years to create these interventions, as programs, and tools that are supportive of students of color, they become very invested with these ideas. Although they are happy to see their interventions used more broadly, those in positions of power can dishearten bottom-up leaders by not acknowledging their involvement in creating these programs. This co-optation invites suspicion and undermines trust that can hinder efforts to work in a shared way.

Look Broadly for Support and Change Agents

In order to acknowledge these bottom-up leaders, administrators need to look broadly to understand who have been supportive of students of color and been working to change the campus culture. Grassroots leaders can be found across all sorts of units and among different stakeholders from student groups, custodial and secretarial staff, faculty in various disciplines, and maybe staff in diverse units across academic and student affairs. Also, it is important to look for allies who have been working on gender issues, gay and lesbian issues, disabilities, first-generation or low-income students, and other equity issues, as these individuals often want to lend support to students of color and understand interventions and strategies for promoting racially diverse students. In the previous example of grassroots leadership at the community college, women came together initially to think about gender issues and they quickly expanded into other areas of diversity. Diversity issues are all interlinked; racially diverse students will also be women, gay and lesbians, disabled, and of low income.

Create Networks

Those in positions of power can provide support to formalize what are often informal networks by providing more resources for them to meet, nicer venues, and amenities such as food for lunches that can enhance the network. My research on grassroots leaders demonstrates that they are very adept at creating informal networks to formulate interventions and ideas that support students of color. However, these informal networks typically do less to alter the campus culture, as the networks tend to be more insular and working with those who already have adopted values favorable to supporting students of color. A more formal network supported by those in positions of power can broaden the network and bring in people who might be interested in learning more about diversity. A formal network can also bring in people who have not historically been supportive of such issues, thus creating more allies for the change in campus culture.

Balancing Power Dynamics and Keeping the Lines of Communication Open

As the power of grassroots leaders begin to grow it can evoke fear and suspicion in top-down leaders who become threatened, and backlash can ensue. This can destroy the relationship between members of the top-down and grassroots groups and the potential chances for shared leadership. For example, in the previous case of the women at the community college, top-down leaders felt threatened by the women faculty as their power began to grow. Top-down leaders felt the women faculty were influencing too many decisions on campus. Rather than communicate their concerns, administrators took unilateral actions to stifle the growing power base. In order to equalize power, top-down leaders stopped reassigning members of the women's group to committees and took away the leadership roles they had acquired. The administration's efforts destroyed the relationship between members of the top-down and grassroots groups that had been working in concert. As these dynamics unfolded, they damaged the alliance between the top and bottom. Top-down leaders can address misperceived power imbalances by communicating with groups, being less suspicious, and embracing opportunities for collaboration and developing trust, rather than operating in a defensive way. In addition to advice for those in positions of power who are part of a shared leadership process, I also offer suggestions for bottom-up leaders as they work together to alter the campus culture.

Embrace and Work with White Allies

On campuses that altered their culture related to racially diverse students, they reached broadly for allies and included White administrators, faculty, staff, and students. Changing culture requires that basic assumptions and values be altered among a large number of people on campus. If White administrators, faculty, staff, and students are ignored as potential allies (who may already understand issues of diversity) or are dismissed because they are considered too difficult to change their mindsets, it will be extremely difficult to alter the campus culture. To identify possible White allies, grassroots leaders looked for evidence that certain White staff, faculty, or students had made explicit remarks or engaged in actions that suggested that they had a commitment to supporting students of color. Too often, bottom-up leaders of color connect only with other faculty, staff, administrators, or students of color in their efforts to create change because they are suspicious of the intentions or true commitment of White members of the organization. Although this suspicion can be understood, given the historical and current privilege and power that Whites maintain, this skepticism can prevent meaningful connections to potential White allies and opportunities for altering the basic values and assumptions of faculty or staff. I found that many bottom-up leaders maintain a level of suspicion and concern that is detrimental to creating shared leadership. Campuses have different ways of overcoming the suspicion of White colleagues. When White faculty, staff, and administrators acknowledge their privilege and awareness of racial inequalities, it can help build trust. For example, on one campus, White allies felt it was their responsibility to create trust by wearing, throughout the semester, t-shirts that dealt with White privilege and power as an effort to demonstrate to their colleagues that they understood these issues and wanted to create dialogue on campus about them.

Look for Opportunities to Create Coalitions

Successful grassroots leaders working collectively recognized that there were many other groups on campus that had related interest that they could capitalize on to drive culture change. For example, those interested in environmentalism and sustainability issues recognized that people in the most polluted places tend to be low-income and racially diverse populations. Through their work to create less pollution and protect the environment, they became intimately familiar with the struggles of low-income and racially diverse groups and were strong allies who could be tapped into to assist with creating a greater power base on campus for culture change. On several campuses I visited, coalitions were built with interdisciplinary groups, environmental advocates, immigration and human rights lobbyists, staff equity champions, unions, and other groups that look at issues of equity. Not only do these groups understand the issues of power and privilege, but also they are often intimately familiar with the needs and concerns of racially diverse populations. However, too often these groups are overlooked.

Constructively Deal with Intergroup Conflict Related to Disparate Notions of Diversity

There are very different views about diversity and priorities related to diversity. This can lead to conflict and hinder progress toward supporting racially diverse students. Some people believe that race should be the most important issue whereas others think that it is socioeconomic status. Some believe that, when thinking about race, only African-Americans and Hispanics deserve focus and that Asians and other groups should not be part of efforts to create better support on campus. Still others like to think of diversity in a broad perspective, with an emphasis on issues of power and privilege, giving groups that have experienced particularly harsh power conditions, such as African-Americans, some priority in terms of support. These are only a few of the many views related to diversity and creating campus environments that support racially diverse students. These views often cause conflict within bottom-up groups that are trying to create supportive cultures for racially diverse students. My research demonstrated that many grassroots groups are ill equipped to talk through and address these differences in perspectives related to diversity; the collectives created often disband because of disagreements about these issues. These types of interpersonal and intergroup issues can be effectively dealt with through strategies of intergroup dialogue offered in the work of scholars such as Ximena Zuniga et al. (2007). However, I found most bottom-up grassroots groups neither anticipated these types of challenges nor dealt constructively with them through any form of dialogue.

Look for Opportunities to Converge with Top-Down Efforts

Another challenge I found in examining grassroots leadership teams working to support students of color is that they often overlook opportunities to merge with top-down efforts to support students of color on campus. Because of their suspicion and lack of trust about administrative motives, bottom-up leaders looked warily on strategic plans and visioning processes around diversity. Some grassroots leaders had already been through strategic planning processes related to diversity that had resulted in a great investment of work and little to no progress and they had lost faith in this process. Other grassroots leaders did not pursue top-level support because they were not sure if administrative motivations around diversity were authentic and matched their own intentions. Often administrators might seek to diversify the campus to increase revenue or they might take a more celebratory view of diversity and not look at the power and privilege disparities of different racial groups that are inherent in their history. Yet bottom-up groups that never receive any support from the top are often extremely fragile and have difficulty achieving their goals because of lack of resources, clerical support, rewards and incentives, and other institutional supports that can help implement changes that they would like to see. When the grassroots leaders were able to converge with the leadership from administrators successfully, the synergy created a much more powerful and deep change process for campuses.

Look for Translators (or Boundary-Spanners) between the Levels of Leadership

In order to successfully converge with administrators, grassroots leaders should look for individuals within the administration or their own network that can serve as translators between the two levels of leadership. Grassroots efforts typically speak a different language than the administration and vice versa. The administration is often thinking in terms of budgets, planning, state-level legislation and initiatives, stakeholders, customer concerns, assessment, and a set of management and political dynamics and language, whereas the grassroots leaders often conceptualize issues in terms of practical, micro interventions (staff) or theoretical concerns such as Critical Race Theory (faculty). Faculty and staff also tend to think about diversity in terms of individual students and their experiences; meanwhile the administration tends to think about diversity in broader terms of overall recruitment plans or educational outcomes. Because of the difference in language and mindset, individuals who understand both languages and mindsets become critical to creating a culture of shared leadership. For example, the director of multiculturalism on one campus was part of the administration, but also worked closely with faculty and staff grassroots leaders as part of her advisory group. Because she spoke with both groups regularly, she could translate plans and ideas between the two groups. These types of individuals are critical to creating a broad network that can alter the culture of the campus.

Sensitize Those in Power to a Culture Supportive of Racially Diverse Students

Successful grassroots leaders who created a more shared leadership environment were careful to sensitize those in power to the way they conceptualized a racially diverse campus. An example of sensitizing administrators to the grassroots vision of a campus supportive of students of color is demonstrated in the story of a liberal arts college. A set of faculty regularly sent articles and books to administrators that articulated their ideas about how to support students of color. The faculty met to develop a concept paper that drew from articles and books, and they created a summary of the key ideas necessary to foster new values for the campus. They later forwarded the concept paper to various influential individuals on campus asking for feedback, so that they were reading and engaging with the ideas. They set up a speaker series and invited administrators to attend. Although administrators did not always attend, over time the variety of administrators who did attend these events began a dialogue with the faculty about their ideas. Through these various avenues (speaker series, concept papers, articles, and books) the faculty communicated their ideas about culture change. Unsuccessful grassroots leadership teams continued dialogue only amongst themselves and allowed the administration to create quite separate discussions about the best strategies and interventions to help students of color, which reflected few or none of their grassroots ideas. Because those in the administration had more power and resources at their disposal, it was their ideas rather than the grassroots leaders' concepts that became instantiated within the culture.

Balancing and Respecting Differing Leadership Styles

In my studies of grassroots leaders, I found a variety of different leadership styles based on varying motivations, backgrounds, and life experiences. Different leadership styles often lead to conflict within grassroots leadership groups about how to approach creating culture change on campus. The most significant difference in leadership approaches is that between those who take a confrontational and a more tempered approach. A confrontational approach views the administration and status quo of the campus culture as intractable, and the only way to achieve change as to force, push, and cajole. This approach assumes that those who have power and privilege are unlikely to relinquish it. A more tempered approach to leadership suggests that, although there is a dominant system of power in place, there are opportunities for learning and altering values through relationship-building and dialogue. Often those who take a confrontational approach have experienced discrimination in the past and continue to have a strong awareness of being oppressed. Grassroots leaders talked about the importance of reflecting on and healing from experiences of oppression that can prevent functional interactions with members of the status quo society whom they are attempting to work with in order to alter the overall culture. Leaders that have not dealt with lingering rage from previous oppression can experience intra-group dysfunction and strife, a finding quite prevalent within my research. It is important to note that, in my studies, a tempered approach to grassroots leadership was more successful for achieving change and meeting goals. Although I found that other approaches – such as confrontation – have their utilities, they should be used strategically and sparingly. Thus, leadership styles need to be carefully examined and reflected on as groups work together.

Suspicion as a Tool for Converging

Although too much suspicion tended to paralyze work across important allies/coalitions, with White faculty and staff, or with the administration toward converging into shared leadership, some suspicion was helpful particularly when working with the administration. Various grassroots leadership groups felt that they had alignment with the administration on how to create a campus culture supportive of racially diverse students only to find out later that the administration was only parroting alignment with their values, but in other circles or through its actions promoting a very different perspective on diversity. It is important for grassroots groups to be clear about their underlying values and commitments, for example dedication to undermining power and privilege, and to ensure that these commitments are part of the new value structure that is being put in place. It is often difficult for the administration to embrace a less than celebratory approach to diversity, and this approach may not match the commitment of the grassroots leadership group. However, some grassroots leadership groups are willing to compromise on certain values in order to make students of color a priority and part of the value system. Nevertheless, holding some suspicion about the intentions of the administration is probably healthy in order to ensure that shared leadership results in the kind of outcomes that are desired.

Perceived Little Support for Shared Leadership

What if you find yourself on a campus where there appears to be only a handful of people that want to support students of color and the culture seems overwhelmingly against your efforts? Some leaders that I have spoken with described a time on their campus when they felt that they were mostly alone in caring about these issues. On some campuses, allies are not identifiable, coalitions and networks are not likely, and people are isolated within a few departments and perhaps are not even accessible to one another. Grassroots leaders at these institutions focused on the need to work with the few individuals they could access to impact hiring processes so that over time more like-minded people could be hired. Certainly there are times that you need to act alone (for example, creating a campus dialogue about diversity or sending a letter about concerns for students) because broader support cannot be created. These individual acts can change the consciousness of others who may in the future become fellow change agents. I recognize that, at times, individual leadership may be necessary, but I advocate for and highlight the value of operating in a shared fashion when feasible. However, passionate change agents cautioned that they are often likely to act without looking for allies and for ways to share the burden.

Conclusion

Leadership is critical to any change process and recent research on leadership suggests that a shared leadership approach has many advantages or benefits when compared with the impact of individual leaders (Kezar et al., 2006; Pearce & Conger, 2003). Research on shared leadership that can transform campus cultures to support racially diverse students underscores the potential and promise of people working in a collective fashion across campus. Yet this journey is fraught with challenges because of our lack of experience working in a shared leadership fashion. Furthermore, issues of racial diversity bring up complexities around power and privilege, trust, suspicion, and skepticism that make the relationship-building and dialogue necessary to change cultures much more complex. Nonetheless, if shared leadership groups can anticipate particular barriers and follow proven strategies – both highlighted in this chapter – they can move forward to create positive cultures for students of color.

Note

1 For the purposes of this chapter *bottom-up* refers to individuals at the "bottom" of the university employee (administration, staff, and faculty) hierarchy.

References

Astin, H. S., & Leland, C. (1991). *Women of influence, women of vision: A cross-generational study of leaders and social change.* San Francisco: Jossey-Bass

Bensimon, E., & Neumann, A. (1993). *Redesigning collegiate leadership: Teams and teamwork in higher education.* Baltimore, MD: Johns Hopkins University Press.

Bolman, L. G., & Deal, T. E. (2007). *Reframing organization.* San Francisco: Jossey Bass.

Hurtado, S., Milem, J., Clayton-Pederson, A., & Allen, W. (1999). *Enacting diverse learning environments.* ASHE-ERIC Report Series. Washington, DC: George Washington University.

Kanter, R. M. (1983). *The change masters: Innovation for productivity in the American corporation.* New York: Simon & Schuster.

Kezar, A. (2001). *Understanding and facilitating organizational change in the 21st Century: Recent research and conceptualizations.* ASHE-ERIC Higher Education Reports, 28(4). San Francisco: Jossey-Bass.

Kezar, A. (2007). Tools for a time and place: Phased leadership strategies for advancing campus diversity. *Review of Higher Education, 30*(4), 413–439.

Kezar, A., Contreras-McGavin, M., & Carducci, R. (2006). *Rethinking the "L" word in higher education: The revolution of research on leadership.* San Francisco: Jossey-Bass.

Kezar, A., Eckel, P., Contreras-McGavin, M. & Quaye, S. (2008). Creating a web of support: An important leadership strategy for advancing campus diversity. *Higher Education, 55*(1), 69–92.

Kezar, A., & Lester, J. (in press). *Enhancing capacity for leadership: Stories and lessons from grassroots leaders in Higher Education.* Palo Alto: Stanford Press.

Komives, S. R., & Wagner, W. (2009). *Leadership for a better world: Understanding the Social Change Model of Leadership Development.* San Francisco: Jossey-Bass.

Pearce, C. L. & Conger, J. A. (2003). *Shared leadership: Reframing the hows and whys of leadership.* Thousand Oaks, CA: Sage.

Schein, E. (1985). *Organizational culture and leadership.* San Francisco: Jossey-Bass

Zuniga, X., Nagda, B. A., Chesler, M., & Cytron-Walker, A. (2007). *Intergroup dialogue in higher education: Meaningful learning about social justice.* ASHE Report Series, 32(4). San Francisco: Jossey-Bass

9

ENGAGING FACULTY IN THE PROCESS OF CULTURAL CHANGE IN SUPPORT OF DIVERSE STUDENT POPULATIONS

Jay R. Dee and Cheryl J. Daly

One of the most consistent findings in the research on college student development is the important role that faculty members play in both fostering students' adjustment to college and shaping their degree aspirations and educational outcomes (Astin, 1993; Kuh, 2003; Lamport, 1993; Pascarella & Terenzini, 2005). As teachers, mentors, and advisors, faculty have the capacity to create interactive learning environments that foster student success. When these learning environments foster high levels of good-quality faculty–student interaction and contribute to a welcoming and supportive campus culture, positive outcomes for learning, personal growth, and degree attainment are likely to be achieved.

These positive effects can be attributed in part to the role that faculty members play as cultural agents. A cultural agent is an individual who has the capacity and commitment to transmit cultural knowledge of an institution or system to others (Stanton-Salazar, 1997). Various forms of cultural knowledge can help students navigate complex social systems, and gain access to institutional resources and opportunities (Bourdieu, 1986; Giroux, 1992). Within the context of higher education, important forms of cultural knowledge for students may include norms and expectations regarding studying, involvement in academic work, and participation in campus life (Kinzie, Gonyea, Shoup, & Kuh, 2008; Kuh & Love, 2000). As students become more experienced in the use of cultural knowledge, they are better able to identify and access resources and opportunities that advance their educational goals.

Cultural knowledge is conveyed to students through their communications and interactions with knowledgeable cultural agents, such as faculty. Frequent, high-quality communication with cultural agents may be particularly important for students whose cultures of origin are quite different from the cultural norms privileged within the college in which they are enrolled (Rendón, 1994; Tierney, 1999). Specifically, students of color who attend predominantly White institutions may perceive a high level of incongruence between their precollege cultures and the dominant culture of the campus (Museus & Quaye, 2009). This level of incongruence generates stresses and tensions that students of color are compelled to address. These tensions manifest themselves when the values of one culture are in conflict with the other culture, or when knowledge and skills developed within the home culture are not valued by the campus culture. Whereas all students must learn the cultures of their institutions to succeed, students of color must also develop strategies to mitigate the stress of cultural incongruence.

In order to reduce the stress of cultural incongruence, students can assimilate to the dominant culture, but this comes at the price of dissociating from their cultures of origin. This can generate yet another set of stressors that negatively impact student learning and persistence (Tierney, 1992). Another alternative is for students to develop skills for participating as members of multiple cultures (Giroux, 1992; Rhoads, 1994), including their culture of origin and the new campus culture. Developing these types of code-switching[1] skills, however, is incredibly complex, because students first need to decode a culture that is unfamiliar to them, and then they must work diligently to gain access to resources and opportunities that are routinely made available to members of the dominant culture (Stanton-Salazar, 1997). When the onus for this type of cultural work is put entirely on students, they become taxed with a significant burden on their time and energies. Thus, many scholars have argued for institutions to assume a greater responsibility to facilitate cultural learning among students from underrepresented minority groups (Rendón, Jalomo, & Nora, 2000; Tierney, 1992, 1999). And faculty members can serve as one of the primary conduits through which higher education institutions foster cultural learning among students.

Through various practices and strategies, faculty members can address the unique cultural learning needs of diverse students. They can take actions that validate students' ongoing connections to their cultures of origin, while also conveying the norms and practices of academic work within the campus culture. Collectively, faculty members also have the ability to serve as cultural change agents who seek to reduce the gap between students' cultures of origin and the campus culture. Given their roles in curriculum development and in structuring learning environments for academic programs, faculty members have the capacity to reshape campus cultures so that students of color experience less cultural incongruence. In other words, faculty can work to reinforce and enhance campus cultural values that promote success for all learners.

In this chapter, we focus on the role of faculty members as cultural agents. First, we use the literature on cultural capital, as well as research on student engagement, to delineate four dimensions of the faculty member's role as cultural agent: (1) decoding the text, (2) building the network, (3) validating students' cultures, and (4) structuring supportive learning environments. Then, we examine how faculty can work collectively to serve as cultural change agents on their campuses. In this last section of the chapter, we posit a central role for faculty development centers as venues for faculty to engage the components of campus culture that promote student success. We draw from some of our research on innovative faculty development programs (Dee & Daly, 2009) to develop recommendations for faculty, faculty development staff, and other academic leaders who seek to reshape campus cultures and increase levels of academic success among diverse student populations.[2]

Faculty as Cultural Agents

The quality and quantity of faculty–student interactions are key variables in predicting the success of underrepresented minority students in college (Bensimon, 2007; Kinzie et al., 2008). Through their interactions with students, faculty members are able to set high expectations and expose students to new opportunities for learning and personal growth. Yet, as Museus and Quaye (2009) point out, few researchers have examined how faculty members, as cultural agents, positively shape the experiences of students of color. Therefore, we need to identify more precisely the ways in which faculty members can and should convey cultural knowledge to students from underrepresented groups.

In this section, we use cultural capital theory and research on student engagement to explain how faculty, as cultural agents, can build meaningful connections with students of color. The concept of cultural capital helps explain the high levels of cultural incongruence that many students of color encounter on campus. This theory also provides insight into how faculty can connect students with resources and opportunities that make new sources of capital available to them (Bourdieu, 1986; Giroux, 1992). Similarly, the research on student engagement points toward the importance of academic norms and behaviors that are central to student achievement, yet remain largely tacit and seldom communicated directly to students (Kuh & Love, 2000).

In contrast to academic knowledge, which is conveyed explicitly through codified mechanisms such as textbooks, cultural knowledge is tacit; it is difficult to formalize or communicate (Lam, 2000). Therefore, tacit knowledge is acquired primarily through practical experience in relevant settings (that is, learning by doing). Learning how to participate in a class discussion, for example, involves gaining tacit knowledge. As students gain more experience in the classroom, they learn how to frame constructive responses to questions, pose new questions that pertain to the course's learning objectives, and offer relevant information that builds on previous discussion. They also learn how to regulate their participation based on the current context of the discussion;

that is, they understand when it is appropriate to ask questions, disagree with another viewpoint, or remain silent to allow others to join the dialogue.

Various forms of tacit knowledge provide a critical foundation for student success. These forms of tacit knowledge are often conveyed experientially through high-impact learning activities, such as first-year seminars, learning communities, undergraduate research projects, and service-learning programs. Unfortunately, research indicates that students of color are less likely to participate in the types of learning activities that promote high levels of academic engagement (Kinzie et al., 2008). Thus, students of color are less likely to participate in the venues through which tacit knowledge can be learned. Cultural agents, such as faculty, therefore, need to be intentional in their efforts to develop learning activities that convey not only academic knowledge, but also forms of tacit knowledge that are critical to student success.

Our analysis of these bodies of literature has led us to identify four dimensions of the faculty role as cultural agents who can assist students of color in learning how to successfully navigate the cultures of their campuses. Here, we conceptualize faculty roles as sets of expected behaviors (Katz & Kahn, 1978). If one of the roles of a faculty member is to serve as a cultural agent, then we need to be explicit regarding which faculty behaviors constitute that role. Specifically, we suggest that faculty, as cultural agents:

1 help students decode the text of higher education so that they understand the norms and expectations of academic work within their college cultures;
2 help students build peer and professional networks that improve students' access to resources and opportunities;
3 validate students' cultures of origin (e.g., through content reflected in curriculum, class discussions relevant to students' home communities), so that they are not compelled to dissociate themselves from their home cultures;
4 structure the learning environment so that it promotes academic engagement, especially during students' first year on campus.

Decoding the Text of Higher Education

We focus on the concept of "text" in order to recognize the powerful role that written and unwritten language plays in the ability of students to navigate the cultures of higher education institutions (Giroux, 1992). Text can be defined as a "means of organizing language in order to construct what people come to think of as 'knowledge'" (Allison, Wee, Zhiming, & Abraham, 1998, p. ix). Knowledge about the social world is constructed through language (Derrida, 1976). Once members of a social system arrive at a consensus regarding what constitutes knowledge, they convey their knowledge claims as text. Text, therefore, can be viewed as an outcome of knowledge production (e.g., facts and theories), but text also supplies the rules for engaging in knowledge production (e.g., norms and values regarding what constitutes valid knowledge). Those in positions of authority within a particular knowledge domain, such as faculty members within academic disciplines, have the power not only to create text, but also to establish the rules and processes through which text will be created (Foucault, 1986).

To gain knowledge within a particular academic domain, students must become conversant in the text associated with that domain. Becoming conversant in the text of an academic domain, however, is extraordinarily complicated and entails much greater effort than simply memorizing a set of terms or definitions. Students must learn to decode language systems that contain implicit meanings that are not easily decipherable (Derrida, 1976). The idea of developing an academic argument, for example, is very different from having an argument with family members or friends. These types of words and phrases in academic discourse must be unpacked and explained, before students can participate effectively in an academic community.

Given the complexity of academic language systems, students can benefit greatly from having faculty members who assist them in developing the skills associated with decoding the text of higher education. In particular, first-year seminars can be designed with the explicit intent of socializing students into the language system of higher education. Faculty in first-year seminars can unpack academic terminology that is likely to be unfamiliar to new students. They can also coach students in the development of study habits (e.g., note-taking skills) that enable them to extract meaning from written and spoken texts.

When understanding the experiences of students of color in particular, we must recognize that members of the dominant culture construct academic texts. Those in positions of power are able to shape texts in ways that advance their ideologies and interests (Bloland, 1995; Foucault, 1986). A group of powerful researchers within a particular field, for example, can shape the criteria used to make grant awards and publication decisions, thus advantaging their particular conceptualization of what constitutes knowledge. The perspectives of less powerful groups, therefore, may not be reflected in the texts of particular academic fields.

Faculty members can take several steps to unpack the power-laden dynamics of academic texts. First, they can encourage students to view a text as one interpretation of reality among many that are possible and potentially equally valid. Put another way, rather than seeing text as the "truth," students can be socialized to the value of seeing multiple truths. Second, faculty can incorporate texts into their courses that convey perspectives that have been marginalized within their respective fields. In this way, multiple truths and contrasting voices can be brought into the classroom (Kingston-Mann & Sieber, 2001). Finally, faculty members can help students realize that those undergraduates, too, can contribute their own voices to the text of higher education. Through writing and research projects, students can learn the conventions of academic discourse (e.g., how to structure an argument, how to marshal evidence to support the argument), while also creating texts that expand and challenge the range of perspectives within a given academic field (Giroux, 1992; Gonzalez, 2000/2001).

In summary, faculty members, as cultural agents, can help students decode the text of higher education by unpacking academic terminology, coaching students in effective study habits, and teaching students the rules of knowledge production so that they can also contribute to the text of higher education. These efforts to help students decode text may need to be offered as part of a developmental sequence within the curriculum. For instance, first-year seminars could focus on academic terminology and study habits, whereas upper-level courses within the major could focus on developing knowledge production skills.

Building Peer and Professional Networks

In addition to understanding the text of higher education, students must also be able to leverage their knowledge so that it opens new opportunities for further learning and development. According to cultural capital theory, social networks are the primary vehicles through which students can leverage what they know in exchange for access to new educational opportunities (Bourdieu, 1986; Wellman, 1983). Social networks include individuals who possess some degree of control over the distribution of cultural resources, such as opportunities for mentorship, financial assistance, or specialized training (Stanton-Salazar, 1997).

Not all students have access to social networks that foster success in college. Some students may have a multitude of college choices, not necessarily because of their academic accomplishments, but because they were born into families with social ties that help these students gain access to important personal and financial resources, such as mentors and scholarships. Other students may also grow up in rich cultural traditions, but those cultural frameworks may not translate into forms of capital that have been privileged and viewed as requisite for entrance into the academy. The social networks of these students and their families, moreover, may not include those who serve as the gatekeepers of educational resources.

Stanton-Salazar (1997) suggests that networks:

> are analogous to social freeways that allow people to move about the complex mainstream landscape quickly and efficiently. In many ways, they

function as pathways of privilege and power. Following this metaphor, a fundamental dimension of social inequality in society is that some are able to use these freeways, while others are not. (p. 4)

To extend the metaphor further, faculty members, as cultural agents, can create more "on-ramps" to these social freeways by intentionally developing opportunities for students to enlarge and diversify their networks.

We suggest that there are at least three ways in which faculty can help students build larger social networks. First, faculty should view themselves as important members of students' current social networks. Faculty members have access to information and contacts that may not be readily available to all students, and they can work to convey these cultural resources to a wider range of students (Chang, 2005). Some students, however, may not yet have sufficient confidence in their ability to leverage their knowledge in exchange for these resources. They may not apply for scholarships or seek to participate in honors programs, for lack of confidence. Thus, in some instances, faculty will also need to work at instilling among students a confidence that they can succeed (Treisman, 1992).

Second, faculty can establish peer networks within their courses. Peer networks can serve as important communication venues in which students share information and resources. The benefits of peer networks have been established by studies that show that students who report more participation in group projects and who more frequently discuss courses with other students tend to have a higher probability of academic success and retention (Kinzie et al., 2008).

Faculty can build peer networks by facilitating the formation of study groups, or by assigning team projects in their courses. Peer networks can also be extended to include connections between first-year students and upper-level students. Many first-year seminar models, for example, include the use of upper-level students (juniors and seniors) as peer mentors, who work closely with new students on developing their study skills (Barefoot & Fidler, 1996). The use of upper-level peer mentors can enable new students to learn what successful students do. This type of role modeling may also help students gain confidence in their own abilities, especially if the peer mentors reflect the cultural diversity of the student population (de Anda, 1984).

Third, faculty can help students gain access to important professional networks that provide career-related information and resources. Undergraduate research programs, for example, can connect students to faculty and researchers who are themselves linked to funding sources and contacts that could enable students to advance to graduate programs and greater professional opportunities. Several federal programs in the sciences are designed specifically to increase the number of underrepresented minority students who pursue scientific and technological careers (National Science Foundation,

2009). Faculty in these fields can seek funding from federal agencies to support and mentor students of color. Faculty in other fields can design internships or service-learning opportunities that link students to influential individuals in the community or in business and industry.

Validating Students' Cultures of Origin

Even if underrepresented minority students are able to decode the text of higher education and gain access to social networks, they may still feel isolated or alienated from their institutions. While students are learning the culture of higher education and networking with influential agents, they may feel as if they are losing their connections to their home cultures. The emphasis on adopting new norms and values may be interpreted by some students as a criticism of the norms and values of their cultures of origin. As a result, students may feel pressured to abandon their home cultures in order to succeed in the academic culture (Tierney, 1992).

Tierney (1999), however, argues that colleges and universities can both socialize students to the norms and practices of academe, and validate and affirm students' own cultural identities. *Cultural integrity* is a term adopted by Deyhle (1995) and used by Tierney (1999) to describe academic programs and pedagogical practices that validate students' cultures of origin. When faculty members validate students' cultural identities, they enhance the likelihood that their students will persist and succeed. As Museus and Quaye (2009) argue, "empirical evidence supports the importance of cultural integrity by illuminating how racial/ethnic minority college students benefit from being secure in their own cultural heritages" (p. 71).

Faculty members can validate students' cultural identities through several practices. They can call students by name and pronounce those names correctly, offer praise and encouragement, and work one-on-one with students (Rendón, 1994). Incorporating diverse cultural perspectives into course content can also affirm the value and significance of students' home cultures. Faculty can engage students' racial and ethnic backgrounds as resources that contribute to the development of relevant and meaningful learning activities (Kingston-Mann & Sieber, 2001).

In order to validate students' cultural heritages, faculty members need to develop knowledge regarding students' precollege cultures (Kuh & Love, 2000). This knowledge can be developed at both organizational and individual levels. At the level of the college organization, institutional research offices can supply faculty with data regarding the racial and ethnic composition of the student body, and faculty development centers can convene discussion groups in which faculty members read and respond to texts and articles that address the college-going experiences of students from diverse cultural backgrounds. At the individual level, faculty members could have students write an autobiographical personal narrative, in which they describe their previous educational experiences at school and home. In this way, faculty members can develop an understanding of the educational cultures that their students have previously navigated. Faculty members can also disclose information about their own cultures of origin and their own experiences and challenges as a college student. These types of self-disclosures can help build trust in the classroom and foster faculty–student relationships based on mutual understanding (Altman & Taylor, 1973; Chang, 2005).

Tierney (1999) argues that efforts to validate students' cultural backgrounds must transcend superficial gestures, and instead be grounded in educationally sound teaching:

> By [cultural integrity], I do not mean to suggest that the mere celebration of minority cultures on college campuses is sufficient to enable individual students of color to overcome any socioeconomic obstacles they may face. However, if postsecondary institutions make concerted and meaningful efforts to affirm these students' cultural identities, they stand to gain increased possibilities for ensuring the latter's success in college – if the structure of the education these students receive also involves a commitment to high academic and social goals and active learning. (pp. 84–85)

Thus, pedagogical practices associated with promoting cultural integrity need to be linked to learning environments that promote academic engagement.

Structuring Learning Environments that Promote Academic Engagement

We suggest that a fourth component of the faculty member's role as cultural agent pertains to efforts to structure academically engaging learning environments. Student engagement refers to "the extent to which students take part in educationally effective practices and the degree to which the institution organizes productive activities for student learning" (Kinzie et al., 2008, p. 23). Researchers associated with the National Survey of Student Engagement have identified five clusters of educationally effective practices: academic challenge, active and collaborative learning, faculty–student interaction, enriching educational experiences, and supportive campus environments (Kuh, 2003). Academic programs that promote high levels of student engagement include first-year seminars, learning communities, service-learning, undergraduate research projects, study abroad, internships, and capstone courses. However, research indicates that "underrepresented students participate in these experiences at lower levels than their peers" (Kinzie et al., 2008, p. 32). Underrepresented minority students may, therefore, be less engaged in the pedagogical practices that research has shown to be most closely linked to learning gains, persistence, and degree attainment.

Faculty members can take steps to increase minority students' engagement in educationally purposeful activities. They can incorporate into their courses pedagogical practices that promote student engagement. These practices include group research projects, service-learning activities, classroom-based problem-solving, writing assignments that require multiple drafts, and participation in online forums and blogs. These pedagogical practices not only increase the amount of time and participation that students devote to academic work, but, when coupled with efforts to promote cultural integrity, can also empower students to express their voice in the context of academic discourse. Promoting student voice in the classroom may combat the silencing that some students experience when the dominant campus culture is inconsistent with their perspectives and beliefs (Gonzalez, 2000/2001).

Two important caveats, however, must be issued in relation to faculty efforts to promote student voice in the classroom. First, faculty should avoid typifying students of color as the "class expert" on their racial/ethnic group. Such efforts minimize the role of students to mere cultural symbols to be displayed. Moreover, the student's identity is reduced to one dimension when other identity constructs such as gender, sexual orientation, and social class are inextricably linked to his or her racial or ethnic identity. Second, faculty must be prepared to address the cultural conflict that is almost certain to emerge when multiple voices are empowered to shape the text of higher education (Kingston-Mann & Sieber, 2001). Students from the dominant culture may react defensively when students from underrepresented groups raise issues of racism and cultural privilege. Students of color may experience retaliation within the class by White students who are threatened by their perspectives. Faculty members themselves may be the targets of hostility by students from the dominant campus culture who resent that their learning environment has been destabilized. Although it is beyond the scope of this chapter to delineate strategies for dealing with cultural conflict in the classroom, many other sources can provide faculty with guidance toward structuring learning environments that empower all learners to succeed (e.g., Brown-Glaude, 2008; Garcia & Hoelscher, 2010).

To summarize the first section of this chapter, we have described four dimensions that comprise the role of faculty member as cultural agent (see Table 9.1). Faculty cannot focus on only one dimension to the exclusion of the others. Helping students decode the text of higher education without validating students' cultural identities, for example, is a recipe for alienation and detachment. Similarly, if faculty validate cultural identities without making connections to academically engaging pedagogies, then their efforts are likely to yield superficial celebrations of diversity, rather than improvements in

TABLE 9.1 Faculty as Cultural Agents: Dimensions of the Role

Role	Related Actions
Decoding the text of higher education	• Unpack academic terminology that is likely to be unfamiliar to students • Coach students in the development of study habits that enable them to extract meaning from texts in your field or discipline • Help students contribute their own voices to the text of higher education, through writing and research projects
Building peer and professional networks	• Widely distribute information regarding educational opportunities (e.g., scholarships, internships) and link students to specific contact people for each • Establish student peer networks (e.g., study groups) and/or bring peer mentors (juniors and seniors) into classes to work with new students on study skills • Link students to professional networks in your field or discipline
Validating students' cultures of origin	• Use teaching practices that promote cultural integrity • Develop your own knowledge regarding students' precollege cultures • Share with students information about your own cultural background and educational experiences and challenges
Structuring learning environments that promote student engagement	• Use pedagogical practices that promote student engagement • Address issues of voice and silence in the classroom • Avoid positioning students as representatives or experts regarding their own racial and ethnic group

academic achievement and degree attainment. Academically engaging pedagogies certainly help students build knowledge and skills, but, if students lack the social networks with which to leverage these new knowledge resources, then their educational experiences may seem devoid of meaning – a mere exercise toward no tangible end. We view each of these dimensions as interconnected and necessary requirements for serving as a cultural agent and argue that faculty who seek to socialize and convey cultural knowledge to students from underrepresented groups must engage all four dimensions of the role.

In the second part of this chapter, we shift the focus from the faculty member as cultural agent in the classroom to the faculty member as change agent. We acknowledge that, even when faculty members are actively engaged as cultural agents who support students of color, the larger power disparities present within the dominant campus culture remain unchanged. Although faculty can help students deal with differences between their home and dominant campus cultures, the gap between those cultures often remains wide.

Fundamental changes in campus culture are needed to reduce the cultural dissonance experienced by students from underrepresented groups. The collective efforts of faculty will need to be mobilized to counteract cultural values that hinder the success of underrepresented minority students. We argue that faculty development centers can harness the collective capacity of faculty to serve as cultural change agents.

Faculty as Cultural Change Agents

Change agents are individuals who have the capacity to diagnose organizational problems, make sense of complex trends, and recognize opportunities for improving performance (Gilley, Quatro, Hoekstra, & Whittle, 2001). Collectively, faculty members have the capacity to initiate and implement significant change on college campuses. Previous literature has suggested that faculty development centers can promote organizational learning and change (Lieberman, 2005).

Faculty development programs can be organized to strengthen and enhance cultural values that promote inclusive teaching and learning and that view all students as capable of academic success (Dee & Daly, 2009). Most of the research on faculty development programs, however, has focused on the effects of these programs on the practices and effectiveness of the faculty participants (Akerlind, 2005). Few empirical studies have examined the effects of faculty development programs on the organization as a whole, including the potential effects of such programs on campus culture (Duponte & Dee, 2009).

In this section, we draw from our previous research on a grant-funded project that sought to redesign faculty development programs at seven postsecondary institutions (Dee & Daly, 2009). The goal of the project was to develop a campus-wide approach to encourage faculty members to use pedagogical practices that promote inclusive teaching and learning. The faculty development center at each campus served as the hub around which faculty organized activities to promote pedagogical change. These faculty development activities served as venues through which faculty examined and critiqued the cultures of their campuses, built and extended their knowledge of students' home cultures, promoted the use of inclusive pedagogical practices, and strengthened values that are consistent with the premise that all students are capable of success.

First, we provide a brief description of the grant-funded project that sought to redesign faculty development programs in order to promote inclusive teaching and learning. Then, we examine how the work of faculty members within these programs advanced a greater understanding of campus and student cultures.

The seven institutions that participated in the grant-funded project included three public universities, two private liberal arts colleges, and two community colleges. A faculty team of six to eight members was formed at each campus. Their first task was to conduct a faculty development needs assessment for their campus. They developed surveys and conducted focus groups to gain an understanding of current faculty perceptions, attitudes, and assumptions regarding faculty development, student achievement, and diversity. Then, each team gathered resources and readings to develop its own knowledge base regarding inclusive teaching and the experiences of diverse college student populations. Faculty team members met each week for a full semester to discuss these readings, analyze their needs assessment data, and engage in professional reflection on their own teaching practices. Finally, each faculty team designed a faculty development program (a series of workshops, online resources, and faculty reading groups) that addressed the unique needs of each institution.

Analyzing Campus Culture

The needs assessment surveys identified three assumptions within the faculty culture that were potentially detrimental to efforts to promote inclusive teaching and learning. The first problematic assumption was that a focus on diversity weakens academic quality. Faculty comments on open-ended survey items, especially at the three universities that participated in this project, revealed concerns regarding whether a focus on diversity would lead to lower admissions standards and the presence of more underprepared students in their classes. Faculty members who held this assumption equated underrepresented with underprepared.

The second problematic assumption in the faculty culture pertained to how faculty identified the sources of student failure. The needs assessment survey responses indicated that faculty members tended to attribute lack of success to characteristics of the students. Faculty at the three universities and two liberal arts colleges attributed student failure to lack of motivation or lack of seriousness about academic work, whereas the community college faculty were more likely to focus on limitations in the students' backgrounds, such as lack of financial resources and the need to work excessive hours at jobs while enrolled in college. Few faculty members suggested that teaching practices may interfere with academic success and persistence.

The third problematic assumption pertained to whether diversity, as a construct, was viewed as germane to all academic disciplines. This assumption became evident in needs assessment survey responses to items that pertained to how faculty members incorporate perspectives on diversity into their own courses. Some faculty indicated that diversity was not relevant to content within their disciplines. A faculty member in the physical sciences at one of the participating universities, for instance, stated that diversity-related course content "might be fine for a social science class, but I don't see how it is relevant for what I teach."

Following the needs assessment process, the members of the faculty teams from each campus met to discuss their findings and create some guiding principles for the faculty development programs that they would soon develop. Several of these principles were constructed as responses to the problematic faculty assumptions that were uncovered in the needs assessment surveys (see Box 9.1). Faculty team members used these guiding principles to design and implement faculty development activities that espoused a different set of assumptions.

Build and Extend Knowledge of Students' Home Cultures

While faculty members used the needs assessment process to develop a more thorough understanding of campus culture, they also sought to build and extend their understanding of students' backgrounds and educational experiences. The faculty at the three universities began their inquiry at the organizational level. They sought data from their respective institutional research offices regarding the racial and ethnic composition of the student body. In addition to this information regarding structural diversity, they sought to identify the academic majors at their institutions that tended to attract underrepresented minority students, as well as the majors that had few students of color. At one campus, this led to a further inquiry regarding students' grade point averages in various majors and whether grade outcomes differed by students' racial and ethnic backgrounds.

At the two liberal arts colleges and two community colleges, the faculty teams began their inquiry at the individual level. The faculty team members sought to learn more about the backgrounds of the students who were currently in their classes. Some faculty had their students write autobiographical

BOX 9.1 Guiding Principles of Faculty Development Practice

- We seek to legitimize and highlight the intellectual rigor and quality associated with inclusive teaching and learning.
- We seek to promote the idea that all students have the capacity to learn.
- We emphasize the obligation of faculty and institutions to change their practices to enhance the likelihood of student success.
- We emphasize the relevance of inclusive teaching and learning for all disciplines and fields of study.

narratives about their backgrounds and experiences in education. Other faculty, especially those teaching first-year seminars, had students keep a journal throughout the semester to record their thoughts and questions about the educational process.

Promote the Use of Inclusive Pedagogical Practices

During the first semester of their work together, the faculty teams conducted needs assessments, identified relevant readings and resources on inclusive teaching, and examined student backgrounds at organizational and individual levels. Then, in the following semester, they designed and implemented a faculty development program that included workshops, reading groups, and online resources, which aimed to promote the use of pedagogical practices that foster inclusive teaching and learning.

In particular, faculty organized several workshop series that focused on the pedagogical practices that promote high levels of student engagement. One of the liberal arts colleges developed a workshop series that focused on collaborative learning strategies for first-year seminars. At one of the universities, faculty created a discussion group in order to share approaches for fostering student engagement in large lecture classes. A workshop series at one of the community colleges focused on service-learning as a way to connect students' learning to their home communities and cultures. As one faculty member explained, "our students are not just temporary visitors. They live here, in the community. And we can have their learning make a difference in their community."

Another university convened faculty workshops that focused on the theme of "learning through writing." These workshops had an explicit focus on decoding the text of higher education. One workshop session focused on how faculty members can convey more clearly their expectations regarding audience, genre, and goals in the writing assignments that they design. Another workshop session focused on how faculty members can better incorporate peer feedback into the writing process.

Student voice was the theme of a number of workshop series. The faculty team at one university convened panels that included both faculty members and students, who spoke about the research that they had conducted on issues regarding race, ethnicity, and cultural differences. Faculty and students presented their work on equal terms. The student presentations were not simply extensions of a larger project directed by the faculty member; instead, students designed and conducted research on questions that they had identified themselves. These forums led to the creation of an annual faculty–student research conference, which continues to offer a venue for student-scholars to present their work.

Encouraging college students of color to conduct research on issues of race, ethnicity, and culture is one strategy to promote cultural integrity and validate students' cultures of origin. Several of the faculty development workshops that emerged from the grant-funded project discussed herein promoted the use of pedagogical practices that validate students' cultural identities. Workshop sessions at one community college, for instance, focused on how faculty members can create welcoming and supportive classroom environments. Similarly, a faculty discussion group at a liberal arts college focused on building trust in the classroom. As Kinzie et al. (2008) argue, "helping faculty members acquire approaches to validate students should be a priority for faculty development programs" (p. 33).

Strengthen Inclusive Educational Values

The goal of this grant-funded project was to foster more extensive use of pedagogical practices that promote inclusive teaching and learning. Organizational culture change was not an explicit focus of the project. Moreover, it would be overly speculative to claim that the project changed the cultures of these seven campuses, or that it effectively countered the problematic assumptions that were identified in the faculty culture. Nevertheless, evidence from our case study research does suggest that these faculty development programs reinforced a set of cultural values regarding teaching, learning, and diversity.

The members of the faculty teams at each of the seven participating institutions expressed several assumptions, which taken together, constitute a set of cultural values for inclusive teaching. Their assumptions were that all students are capable of academic success, that diversity enhances academic quality, and that diversity is relevant to teaching and learning in all fields and disciplines. These assumptions were codified in the set of guiding principles that these faculty teams used to design their faculty development programs and workshops (see Box 9.1).

Although only 51 faculty members participated in the teams at these seven institutions, several hundred faculty members engaged in the faculty development activities that these teams organized. Many of these new participants became energized by the experience, and many of the original 51 team members expressed an obligation to assume a greater leadership role on their campus in promoting the values of inclusive teaching. As a community college faculty team member explained:

> I guess the experience was sort of like being baptized into a new religion. Now I feel an obligation to go out and get other faculty involved in this work, and to give them an opportunity to grow and develop in the same way that I did.

In our interviews with faculty team members and workshop participants, we found that their references to a deepening commitment to inclusive teaching were often framed in terms of the tasks and work activities in which they were engaged. The strengthening of values regarding inclusive teaching was associated with the faculty members' involvement in collective experiences and actions. The workshops and forums encouraged faculty to take action, and the results of those actions strengthened their values for inclusive teaching. As a faculty member in the sciences explained:

> I was sitting there throughout most of the [inclusive teaching] workshop, thinking, "well, I am in science. I can't use this. This doesn't apply to me." It wasn't until I said, "I am going to try implementing a journal" that I really felt the impact of the workshop. So I tried it, quick little questions for students. The student feedback was that they loved the journals. It freed them to write whatever they wanted. It opened more doors to question things in the classroom discussion. So, I learned that just because I teach in the sciences, or just because you are in engineering or math, you can still use the same tools as the humanities and English professors are using.

To reiterate, the faculty team members identified several problematic assumptions in the faculty culture, but they did not directly seek to change those values. Instead, they created structures that embodied an alternative set of values. These structures enabled faculty members to share common experiences (workshop sessions, discussion groups, pedagogical innovations), and the positive effects of those experiences (such as higher levels of student engagement) deepened their commitment to the values that underlie those structures.

A prevailing assumption is that values drive actions and, if we can change people's values, then they will act in more appropriate ways. However, the prospects for changing other people's values are not particularly promising. Values are often deeply held (Schein, 1992), and efforts to change people's values may be viewed as antagonistic – that is, change agents may be perceived as espousing the notion that "my values are better than yours, so you should change." In contrast, we can think of actions as shaping values and beliefs (Weick, 1995). By engaging in new activities, individuals gain exposure to the underlying values of those activities. If a new activity produces a beneficial outcome for the individual, then he or she may develop a commitment to the values that underlie that activity (Seely-Brown & Duguid, 1991; Staw, 1980).

We acknowledge that enticing faculty members to participate in faculty development activities is a significant challenge (Sorcinelli, Austin, Eddy, & Beach, 2006). Those faculty members who adhere most strongly to problematic assumptions regarding diversity, teaching, and learning are probably the least likely to attend workshops on inclusive teaching. Nevertheless, if faculty development centers can focus on the tangible benefits of inclusive teaching, then they may be able to attract a wider audience of faculty participants who are committed generally to excellent teaching.

Some faculty participants whom we interviewed were initially attracted to the workshops and discussion groups out of an interest in teaching improvement generally, not a specific interest in inclusive teaching or students of color. Their commitment to inclusive teaching grew, however, as they engaged in faculty development activities that embodied those values.

Recommendations for Faculty Development Centers

In conclusion, we offer several recommendations for faculty development centers and the academic leaders who guide them. First, if faculty development centers are to harness the collective capacity of faculty to shape the cultures of their institutions, then faculty members themselves must be empowered to set the direction for the faculty development programming on their campuses. Rather than rely on outside consultants or external guest speakers, the seven institutions in this project allowed a group of faculty members to assess campus needs and design faculty development programming. This approach fostered a high level of faculty ownership and commitment to the initiative. Thus, we recommend that faculty development centers appoint a faculty team to guide the development and implementation of new programs and activities that advance the goals of inclusive teaching.

The faculty team also served as a means to connect faculty who are deeply committed to issues of equity and diversity in higher education. In many instances, supportive faculty may be isolated or marginalized within their own departments, and they may encounter numerous obstacles as they seek to improve the prospects for all students to succeed (Turner, 2003). Such obstacles are not only frustrating for the supportive faculty member, but also potentially debilitating in terms of institutional outcomes for students. If ideas to support the success of diverse students remain on the periphery of institutions, then the potential for meaningful improvements in student outcomes is severely compromised.

Therefore, we recommend that faculty development centers make inclusive teaching a central focus of their ongoing programming. Too often, faculty development priorities shift from one year to the next – instructional technology one year, service-learning the next, diversity the year after. These shifting priorities make it difficult for new cultural values to take hold. Instead, we argue that inclusive teaching can become a central organizing principle for all faculty development activities. Moreover, faculty development programs can be designed specifically to enhance faculty members' roles as cultural agents. Workshops, forums, and faculty discussion groups could be organized around each of the four dimensions of the cultural agent role that we outlined in this chapter.

Notes

1 Code-switching is a skill set individuals must have to maneuver between spaces that differ in race, class, and culture through mastering different styles of speaking and presentation of self.
2 The project described in this chapter was supported by grant number 1040-0275 from the Ford Foundation. The contents of this chapter are solely the responsibility of the authors and do not necessarily represent the official views of the Ford Foundation.

References

Akerlind, G. S. (2005). Academic growth and development: How do university academics experience it? *Higher Education, 50*, 1–32.

Allison, D., Wee, L., Zhiming, B., & Abraham, S. (Eds.). (1998). *Text in education and society*. Singapore: Singapore University Press.

Altman, I., & Taylor, D. A. (1973). *Social penetration: The development of interpersonal relationships*. Austin, TX: Holt, Rinehart, & Winston.

Astin, A. W. (1993). *What matters in college? Four critical years revisited*. San Francisco: Jossey-Bass.

Barefoot, B. & Fidler P. (1996). *1994 national survey of freshman seminar programs: Continuing innovations in the collegiate curriculum*. Monograph Series No. 20. Columbia: University of South Carolina, National Resource Center for the Freshman Year Experience and Students in Transition.

Bensimon, E. M. (2007). The underestimated significance of practitioner knowledge in the scholarship on student success. *Review of Higher Education, 30* (4), 441–469.

Bloland, H. G. (1995). Postmodernism and higher education. *Journal of Higher Education, 66*(5), 521–599.

Bourdieu, P. (1986). The forms of capital. In J. Richardson (Ed.), *Handbook of theory and research for the sociology of education* (pp. 241–258). New York: Greenwood Press.

Brown-Glaude, W. R. (Ed.). (2008). *Doing diversity in higher education: Faculty leaders share challenges and strategies*. Piscataway, NJ: Rutgers University Press.

Chang, J. C. (2005). Faculty–student interaction at the community college: A focus on students of color. *Research in Higher Education, 46* (7), 769–802.

de Anda, D. (1984). Bicultural socialization: Factors affecting the minority experience. *Social Work, 29*(2), 101–107.

Dee, J. R., & Daly, C. (2009). Innovative models for organizing faculty development: Pedagogical reflexivity, student learning empathy, and faculty agency. *Human Architecture: The Journal of the Sociology of Self-Knowledge, 7*(1), 1–21.

Derrida, J. (1976). *Of grammatology*. Baltimore, MD: John Hopkins Press.

Deyhle, D. (1995). Navajo youth and Anglo racism: Cultural integrity and resistance. *Harvard Educational Review, 65*(3), 403–444.

Duponte, J., & Dee, J. R. (2009, November). *The role of community college faculty in organizational change: Pedagogical reform and professional development*. Paper presented at the Annual Meeting of the Association for the Study of Higher Education (ASHE), Vancouver.

Foucault, M. (1986). Disciplinary power and subjection. In S. Lukes (Ed.), *Power* (pp. 229–242). New York: New York University Press.

Garcia, J., & Hoelscher, K. (2010). *Managing diversity flashpoints in higher education.* American Council on Education (ACE) Series on Higher Education. Lanham, MD: Rowman & Littlefield.

Gilley, J., Quatro, S., Hoekstra, E., & Whittle, D. (2001). *The manager as change agent: A practical guide to developing high-performance people and organizations.* Cambridge, MA: Perseus Publishing.

Giroux, H. A. (1992). *Border crossings, cultural workers, and the politics of education.* New York: Routledge.

Gonzalez, K. P. (2000/2001). Toward a theory of minority student participation in predominantly white colleges and universities. *Journal of College Student Retention, 2*(1), 69–91.

Katz, D., & Kahn, R. L. (1978). *The social psychology of organizations* (2nd edn.). New York: John Wiley & Sons.

Kingston-Mann, E., & Sieber, T. (Eds.). (2001). *Achieving against the odds: How academics become teachers of diverse students.* Philadelphia: Temple University Press.

Kinzie, J., Gonyea, R., Shoup, R., & Kuh, G. D. (2008). Promoting persistence and success of underrepresented students: Lessons for teaching and learning. In J. M. Braxton (Ed.), *The role of the classroom in college student persistence* (New directions for teaching and learning, no. 115, pp. 21–38). San Francisco: Jossey-Bass.

Kuh, G. D. (2003). What we're learning about student engagement from NSSE: Benchmarks for effective educational practices. *Change, 35*(2), 24–32.

Kuh, G. D., & Love, P. (2000). A cultural perspective on student departure. In J. Braxton (Ed.), *Reworking the student departure puzzle* (pp. 196–212). Nashville, TN: Vanderbilt University Press.

Lam, A. (2000). Tacit knowledge, organizational learning, and societal institutions: An integrated framework. *Organization Studies, 21*(3), 487–513.

Lamport, M. A. (1993). Student–faculty informal interaction and the effect on college student outcomes: A review of the literature. *Adolescence, 28*, 971–990.

Lieberman, D. (2005). Beyond faculty development: How centers for teaching and learning can be laboratories for learning. In A. Kezar (Ed.), *Organizational learning in higher education* (New directions for higher education, no. 131, pp. 87–98). San Francisco: Jossey-Bass.

Museus, S. D., & Quaye, S. J. (2009). Toward an intercultural perspective of racial and ethnic minority college student persistence. *Review of Higher Education, 33*(1), 67–94.

National Science Foundation. (2009). *Women, minorities, and persons with disabilities in science and engineering.* Arlington, VA: NSF. Retrieved August 15, 2010, from www. nsf.gov/statistics/wmpd/pdf/nsf09305.pdf.

Pascarella, E. T., & Terenzini, P. T. (2005). *How college affects students: A third decade of research.* San Francisco: Jossey-Bass.

Rendón, L. I. (1994). Validating culturally diverse students: Toward a new model of learning and student development. *Innovative Higher Education, 19*(1), 33–51.

Rendón, L. I., Jalomo, R. E., & Nora, A. (2000). Theoretical considerations in the study of minority student retention in higher education. In J. Braxton (Ed.), *Reworking the student departure puzzle* (pp. 127–156). Nashville, TN: Vanderbilt University Press.

Rhoads, R. A. (1994). *Coming out in college: The struggle for a queer identity.* London: Bergin & Garvey.

Schein, E. H. (1992*)*. *Organizational culture and leadership* (2nd edn.). San Francisco: Jossey-Bass.

Seely-Brown, J., & Duguid, P. (1991). Organizational learning and communities of practice: Toward a unified view of working, learning, and innovation. *Organizational Science, 2*(1), 40–57.

Sorcinelli, M. D., Austin, A. E., Eddy, P. L., & Beach, A. L. (2006). *Creating the future of faculty development: Learning from the past, understanding the present.* Bolton, MA: Anker Publishing.

Stanton-Salazar, R. D. (1997). A social capital framework for understanding the socialization of racial minority children and youths. *Harvard Educational Review, 67*(1), 1–38.

Staw, B. M. (1980). Rationality and justification in organizational life. In L. Cummings & B. Staw (Eds.), *Research in organizational behavior, volume 2* (pp. 45–80). Greenwich, CT: JAI Press.

Tierney, W. G. (1992). An anthropological analysis of student participation in college. *Journal of Higher Education, 63*(6), 603–618.

Tierney, W. G. (1999). Models of minority college-going and retention: Cultural integrity versus cultural suicide. *Journal of Negro Education, 68*(1), 80–91.

Treisman, U. (1992). Studying students studying calculus: A look at the lives of minority mathematics students in college. *College Mathematics Journal, 23*(5), 362–372.

Turner, C. S. (2003). Incorporation or marginalization in the academy: From border toward center for faculty of color? *Journal of Black Studies, 34*(1), 112–125.

Weick, K. E. (1995). *Sensemaking in organizations.* Thousand Oaks, CA: Sage.

Wellman, B. (1983). Network analysis: Some basic principles. In R. Collins (Ed.), *Sociological theory* (pp. 155–200). San Francisco: Jossey-Bass.

10

CULTIVATING CAMPUS CULTURES THAT SUPPORT RACIALLY DIVERSE AND OTHER UNDERSERVED STUDENTS

A Model for Multi-Institutional Transformation

Glenn Gabbard and Sharon Singleton

> When academic problems appear intractable, it is often because an underlying systemic element is responsible, but no one quite sees what or where that element is. People who work in the academy, like people in any institution or profession, are socialized to operate in certain ways. When they are called upon to alter their practices, they sometimes find that they lack a compass to guide those changes. Some of the reasons why "this is the way things are" in American higher education are still good ones, some almost certainly obsolete. (Menand, 2010, p. 17)

In his exploration of sources of resistance to broad-scale reform in higher education, Louis Menand (2010) notes a distinct cultural aspect to the barriers to transformative change, many of which are embedded in the history of colleges and universities. One of these cultural barriers is the internalization of assumptions about the purpose and structure of higher education, which may often include deeper presuppositions about the incapacity of new populations of students to succeed. Fortunately, the national conversation about ways in which college campuses can more effectively promote success among racially diverse and other underserved students has moved beyond discussions of the compatibility between students and their campuses or the efficacy of specific programmatic interventions. That is, an increasing number of campuses are engaged in equity-based examinations of the ways in which campus culture as a whole may be impeding the success of racially diverse and other underserved students.

A cultural perspective on change efforts to support underserved students' success underscores the importance of campus-wide ownership of this challenge, ideally resulting in institution-wide responses (Tinto, 2006–2007). This holistic perspective is supported by a more detached view of student departure through the lens of "new institutional theory," which focuses on the study of "that which persists organizationally despite efforts toward change and that which seems to be deeply embedded in organizational structures and procedures" (Laden, Milem, & Crowson, 2000, p. 236). New institutional theory, for example, can be used to view formal or informal organizational practices related to student departure from four distinct but sometimes over-lapping vantage points: (1) the view that such practices encourage and impede departure, instilling a particular value or set of values within the organization, (2) the view that such practices enhance a shared sense of reality and purpose for the organization, (3) the view that such practices are perceived by those within the organization to legitimate or rationalize its existence and ongoing survival in the larger social milieu, and (4) the view that such practices relate to the shared perceptions of the larger social purpose of the organizations of which they are a part. Such an institutional perspective takes into account the features of college and university culture, which Kuh and Hall (1993) refer to as:

> the collective, mutually shaping patterns of institutional history, mission, physical settings, norms, traditions, values, practices, beliefs, and assumptions which guide the behavior of individuals and groups in an institution of higher education and which provide frames of reference for interpreting the meanings of events and actions on and off campus. (p. 2)

How do campuses acknowledge and assess their respective institutional cultures and then transform "the way things are" into an institutional culture that is better oriented to support increasingly diverse student populations?

In this chapter, we explore the design, function, and formative outcomes of Project Compass, which is a multi-institutional, multi-year initiative that is aimed at facilitating institutional transformation to increase the success rates of racially diverse and other underserved students at four 4-year public institutions. Project Compass provides a potential model that can facilitate institutions' exploration of their respective cultures so that they may be more responsive to diverse student populations. Before discussing the history, structure, formative outcomes, and implications of the project, however, it is instructive to briefly review what scholars and practitioners know about transformative efforts of any kind on college campuses.

Transformational Efforts on Campuses

To distinguish "transformation" from ongoing organizational change in colleges and universities, Eckel, Hill, and Green (1998) identify four facets of transformational action characterized by (1) a focus on altering the culture of the institution by changing select underlying assumptions and institutional behaviors, processes, and products, (2) deep and pervasive influences on the whole institution, (3) intentionality, and (4) emergence over time. The problems impeding broad-scale transformation in colleges and universities are well documented, whether they focus on the structural barriers that impede collaboration between student affairs and academic affairs or the cultural elements that dictate how colleges work and that often hinder their ability to move toward common goals (Bergquist, Pawlak, & Bergquist, 2008). Lessons learned about transformational change from the Kellogg Foundation Higher Education Transformation (KFHET) Project illustrate the depth of investment required of institutions that are engaged in transformative, multi-institutional initiatives. Authors of a KFHET (2001) summary report raise an important point that distinguishes between institutional change and institutional transformation. They assert that institutions that attempt transformation are values-based – rather than efficiency-based, for example – and are willing to ask which kinds of learning, scholarly, and community outcomes should be sought. Indeed, transformation processes require that campuses be self-conscious about the values and assumptions that underpin serious efforts to increase the retention of underserved students.

Campus transformation must be systemic and of a magnitude that affects *all* aspects of institutional functioning, rather than a single part or few parts of an institution. It is deep in that it affects values and assumptions in addition to structures and processes. Campuses that seek to transform must be specific and intentional about the purpose and the direction of the transformation, even though the details of the change evolve over time. Finally, transformational change is cultural. It affects the underlying assumptions and deeply embedded values and meanings attached to what institutional members do and believe about their institution. Transformations that "alter the culture of the institution" require "major shifts in . . . the common set of beliefs and values that creates a shared interpretation and understanding of events and actions" (Eckel, Hill, & Green, 1998). In deep and pervasive institutional transformation efforts, "institution-wide patterns of perceiving, thinking, and feeling; shared understandings; collective assumptions; and common interpretive frameworks are the ingredients of this 'invisible glue' called institutional culture" (p. 4). Moreover, transformation occurs when shifts in the institution's culture have developed to the point where they are both pervasive across the institution and deeply embedded in practices throughout the institution. Transformational change also "involves altering the underlying assumptions so that they are congruent with the desired changes" (p. 4). In sum, organizational transformation is, by nature, a cultural process.

Addressing equity and inclusion in systemic, more complex, and more transformative ways requires not only deep and pervasive change, but also a comprehensive, integrative approach. Organizational integration is the process by which multiple innovations are undertaken in many units across the campus and their linkages are identified and activities are connected with a clear coordinating purpose. It has been apparent for some time that "our inability to build integrated links among . . . reform efforts, in their conception and in their practice, ultimately limits our ability to effect the kind of transformative change that we might have hoped for" (Schoem, 2002, p. 52). With organizational integration, innovations that have developed within isolated units, creating program specific infrastructure and resources, and involving targeted populations, are transformed into coordinated efforts intended to fundamentally change the existing operational model of higher education. It requires restructuring, strategic reallocation of resources, redefinition of roles, and deep and pervasive culture change.

Project Compass: A Multi-Institutional Model Addressing Retention of Racially Diverse and Other Underserved Students

Facilitating the transformation of campus cultures so that they provide environments that are more responsive to racially diverse and other underserved students and promote the success of those undergraduates is a highly complicated effort. The context, history, structure, and core assumptions of Project Compass respond to this complexity and offer a feasible, constructive approach to organizational transformation that (1) focuses on student success, (2) emphasizes the important role of faculty in student success through formal and informal teaching- and research-related relationships with students, (3) involves faculty in collaborative roles with colleagues, students, and the external community that extend beyond the traditional domains of teaching and learning, research, and service, (4) aligns institutional action with the campus mission, and (5) relies on extant literature to expand evidence-based practices and proposed interventions (Braxton, Brier, & Steele, 2007–2008).

Project Compass is an effort by the Nellie Mae Education Foundation to encourage colleges and universities to scale up and institutionalize retention programs, practices, and policies that had proven effective in retaining racially diverse and other underserved students. As a long-time funder of campus-based retention projects, the Foundation noted over time that those retention efforts seldom influenced the culture, structure, and mission of the institution as a whole. Rather, the work of retaining marginalized students often fell to successful programs that were themselves marginalized from the campus mainstream. Often funded through external, time-limited grants, the direct impact of these programs dissipated quickly once funding expired, leaving few cultural or structural vestiges to influence subsequent change at the institution.

In an effort to encourage state colleges and universities to scale up and institutionalize retention initiatives, the Foundation sought out an intermediary to design a multicampus project that would encourage public 4-year institutions to engage in campus-wide cultural transformation, grounded in a commitment to graduating increased numbers of low-income students, students of color, and students who are first in their families to attend college. For Project Compass, the Foundation selected the New England Resource Center for Higher Education (NERCHE) as an institutional intermediary, an emerging role that offers both engaged support for institutional change and "effective external accountability" (p. 271).[1] Sturm (2006) describes "institutional intermediaries" as:

> public or quasi-public organizations that leverage their position . . . to foster change and provide meaningful accountability . . . [I]nstitutional intermediaries use their ongoing capacity-building role within a particular . . . sector to build knowledge (through establishing common metrics, information pooling, and networking), introduce incentives (such as competition, institutional improvement, and potential impact on funding), and provide accountability (including grass roots participation and self-, peer- and external evaluation). (p. 251)

Working collaboratively with NERCHE, the Foundation developed an approach to institutional change, both structurally and culturally, in support of racially diverse and other underserved students. This approach acknowledges that, in order for change to be truly systemic, implementation of retention practices must be aligned with the larger cultural transformation efforts at the institutions. Indeed, this change approach suggests a bold hypothesis:

> If institutions develop programs and services systemically, which result from the collaboration of leaders from campus stakeholder groups (including administrators, faculty, students, community members); examining local data and current literature on retention, and aligning the implementation of new programs and services for underserved students with current campus policies, practices, and procedures that support academic success; then, underserved students will experience higher levels of persistence and success. (New England Resource Center for Higher Education Project Compass, 2011)

The Project Compass change approach is guided by six core assumptions:

1 An ongoing culture of evidence and inquiry where quantitative and qualitative data from both internal and external sources are collected, interpreted, and analyzed is essential to the formulation, implementation,

and ongoing improvement of practices and policies supporting racially diverse and other underserved students.

2   Sustained, institution-level change supporting increased success and retention of underserved students requires ongoing collaboration from across the college – including executive leadership and students – and can benefit from external engagement with the community.

3   In and of themselves, "islands of excellence" that help retain racially diverse and other underserved students in larger numbers, but exist at the margins of the institution, will not result in broad cultural change unless they are scaled up, both in scope and in function, and connected to other institutional change initiatives.

4   Change in institutional culture – including practices, policies, and other conditions – supporting the success and retention of underserved students must be supported by extant research in the field.

5   Colleges and universities committed to institutional change to better serve underserved students will benefit from ongoing collaborative relationships with peer institutions that espouse similar commitments.

6   Racially diverse and other underserved students are an asset to the institution and present opportunities for broad-based institutional change in policy and practice, benefiting all of the institution's students.

Context: Why Public 4-Year Institutions?

State colleges and universities are at the center of the current controversy over whether higher education is considered a public entitlement or a private service. The steadily increasing pool of low- and middle-income applicants at 4-year public colleges reinforces the importance of integrating access and excellence nationwide, a hallmark of the non-flagship, regional 4-year public institution. A highly competitive marketplace and radical cuts in public funding have forced many public institutions to adopt policies, practices, and strategies – such as raising tuition and fees – that undercut the mission of what have been historically known as "people's colleges." This picture is especially clear in regions, such as New England, where demographic reports sound the warning of a rising number of young people who find college unaffordable and a shrinking number of college graduates who stay in the region and join the workforce (Jobs for the Future, Nellie Mae Education Foundation, 2008; Kirsch, Braun, & Yamamoto, 2007). The role of public 4-year institutions is equally vital in economically challenged urban areas (Little, 2010).

In an attempt to maintain commitments to access, public institutions commonly develop specialized retention programs for students from racially diverse and other underserved populations. Despite their positive impact, however, such programs often get relegated to "boutique" status, existing on the margins of the campus organizational structure, with minimal funding.

At the same time, the literature on retention and student success suggests that campuses can achieve sustained effectiveness only if retention efforts are scaled up as a critical priority that permeates the institution. In this way, underserved student populations present continuing opportunities for organizational learning and improvement. The public 4-year institution was the logical cohort of campuses to participate in broad-scale transformation intended to support large numbers of racially diverse and other underserved students. Underserved students already constitute a significant proportion of their student populations, and ongoing change in response to these populations is consistent with their history of affordable, high-quality public higher education that is easily accessible to students within the immediate community.

A Transformational Assumption: Racially Diverse and Other Underserved Students as Assets to Transformation

Although a critical examination of the institutional systems for student success is essential, that examination, as Green (2006) notes:

> is not possible unless administrators, policymakers, and researchers first scrutinize their over-reliance on a deficit model, in which minority, low-income, and first-generation college students are characterized as lacking the skills and abilities necessary to succeed in higher education. This focus on deficits emphasizes students' inabilities rather than their abilities, and encourages policies and programs that view racially diverse and other underserved students as less than their peers who have traditionally populated colleges and universities. (p. 25)

Educational deficit thinking is a form of blaming the victim. Such a perspective holds underserved students and their families primarily responsible for their school problems and academic failure, while often failing to acknowledge the role of structural inequality in hindering success among diverse populations (Valencia, 1997).

To move away from a deficit orientation, Project Compass is grounded in research that advocates for a strengths-based model in which high schools and colleges "identify the positive qualities and human potential each student brings to learning . . . The student strengths model builds learning strategies around the personal skills, interests, abilities, language, and culture of individual students" (Sautter, 1994, p. 4). As Green (2006) writes:

> moving to an asset model requires educators to investigate the circumstances under which minority, low-income, and first-generation students succeed academically. For example, which curricular efforts facilitate academic advancement for underserved students? Which pipeline sequences

help underserved students achieve academic success? Which strategies complement their strengths and career goals? Which systemic approaches minimize deficit thinking and emphasize students' strengths? (p. 26)

Institutional change that centers specifically on the success of racially diverse and other underserved students should engage those individuals through institutional practices that validate their contributions and strengths. Beyond campus celebrations of diversity, which tend to fall short of true integration of diversity into campus cultures, valuing the cultural and intellectual contributions of underserved students requires the institution to see students as informants and assets in cultural change (Torres, 2006). Indeed, students are often the first to know when programs are failing to meet their needs. Similarly, students who engage in dialogue with practitioners who convey genuine interest in their success can be quite articulate about barriers to learning and what they need to help them succeed.

Project Implementation and Planning

Informed by the six core assumptions and this commitment to racially diverse and other underserved students as assets to the organizational change process, Project Compass initiated a rigorous selection process to identify six public 4-year institutions based, in part, on their readiness to engage in transformational cultural change in response to the presence of increasing numbers of racially diverse and other underserved students. Institutions participated in a planning year, the outcome of which was a proposal for funds to support key interventions aimed at campus-wide cultural transformation and the retention of underserved students. Four campuses received implementation funding for four subsequent years to target different populations. The different target populations, as well as the diversity of approaches utilized, reflects the unique cultural and structural context of each of the funded campuses:

1   A small, rural campus in a low-income area of a rural state created multiple opportunities to distinguish itself as the institution of choice for "first-in-family, modest income" students.
2   A mid-sized, suburban campus focused on deepening its institutional commitment to diversity and inclusivity by developing a multimodal retention approach for students of color, first-generation, and low-income students. Efforts are directed at faculty development, creating a system of documenting co-curricular outcomes systematically, and increasing awareness of culturally responsive practices in advising within the academic disciplines.
3   An isolated rural campus aimed to reclaim a positive relationship to recruiting and supporting Native American students from the local area

by creating learning communities, cultural events, faculty development, and curricular change within its developmental offerings.

4 A semi-rural, public liberal arts institution intended to develop a predictive model for identifying likely variables contributing to student departure and using that model to provide incoming students who are most likely to leave with intensive advising and academic support.

Responding to Tinto's call for an "institutional model for action" to address retention challenges (Tinto, 2006–2007, p. 6), the design of Project Compass imposed a set of parameters for guiding both the planning and implementation of project-funded interventions for these four campuses. These parameters anticipated core challenges to any transformation effort in higher education, including:

- the common imposition of a deficit model in interpreting the educational and personal experience of students;
- the tendency for retention solutions to be defined in terms of existing organizational "silos," thereby limiting the pervasive effect of implementation across campus subunits;
- the inconsistent use of quantitative and qualitative institutional data as the basis for interpreting student behaviors on campus and determining related institutional responses;
- the desultory attention paid to extant research on critical institutional change issues in colleges and universities;
- the propensity of colleges and universities to compete with institutional peers rather than participating in collaborative learning communities; and
- the relegation of responsibility for "fixing" racially diverse and other underserved students to marginalized subunits of the institution, often in student affairs and well beyond the central core of the academic mission.

Key Project Features

Project Compass consists of four primary features, each of which is grounded in the aforementioned six core assumptions and responds to the preceding institutional challenges. In this section, we discuss these structural features, including a rationale explaining how each feature is grounded in a specific core assumption. Preliminary outcomes from campus work will be used to illustrate the impact of the Project Compass Model on campus culture.

Feature #1: The Community of Practice

Each funded Project Compass campus was required to create a "community of practice" designed to promote cross-institutional collaboration and dialogue. This model for organizing individuals to develop a shared reper- toire of resources – experiences, stories, tools, ways of addressing recurring problems; in short, a shared practice (Wenger, Arnold, & Snyder, 2002) – was deemed an especially valuable structure to facilitate problem identification and solving. Each community of practice was required to include key administra- tors, faculty, and staff engaged in the work of retention of racially diverse and other underserved students at their respective institutions. Membership in the group was mandated to include representation from across typical institutional "silos," such as:

- the senior administrative staff, with particular emphasis on participation from the President, Chief Academic Officer, Chief Financial Officer, and Chief Student Affairs Officer;
- faculty in various academic departments; and
- frontline managers of retention and/or student success projects.

Campus groups ranged in size from 10 to 15 members. One of the guiding organizational principles supporting the development of a community of prac- tice is that membership is driven by assembling individuals who are best suited to respond to a particular problem. Given this, membership in the groups changed as the project developed over time, and was somewhat fluid. Though a core group of members was constantly involved over time, new members representing the evolving needs of the group were included as needed. The intermediary encouraged campus groups to include additional members based on the potential assets each might bring to the table. As a result, the membership of each campus community of practice differed, some including community leaders and students in addition to the required representatives.

Communities of practice were required to convene six to eight day-long meetings, including a 2-day planning meeting held at the beginning of the academic year. Premised on the notion that innovation requires dedicated time "away" from established work routines, the meeting regimen provided a self-enforced opportunity to commit intensive amounts of time to exploring the complex antecedents and context for the underserved student retention challenge, allied with individuals from a variety of sectors of the institution who shared a commitment to creating effective institutional responses.

Rationale for the Community of Practice

Requiring campuses to take part in a community of practice is a response to the tendency of college campuses to define retention problems and solutions in terms of existing organizational "silos," thereby limiting the possibility for campus-wide ownership of student success policies and practices. Such requirements also encourage campuses to "scale up" initiatives beyond the boundaries of existing organizational structures in order to avoid marginalizing efforts for change. Kezar and Eckel (2002) emphasize the centrality of staff development across the broad spectrum of campus constituents for (1) drawing forth and enhancing existing skills, (2) developing new skill sets, orientations, and perspectives, and (3) sustaining intellectual and personal investment in institutional transformation. Staff development in the form of a community of practice equips participants in institutional change with the language and knowledge needed to "personalize" the change effort according to their institutional roles and identities.

It is unlikely that public institutions will enjoy a windfall of state support any time in the near future – a reality that justifies the need for institutional change that capitalizes on existing resources, especially human resources. Although much can be learned from the experience and expertise of practitioners and staff in the process of institutional change, much is also being asked of them. Thus, opportunities for professional development or designated activities that are meant to enhance each individual's understanding of and participation in the change process may be required. For example, some staff may lack experience with asset-based approaches or tools for meaningful collaboration and will therefore need to acquire appropriate skills to implement such approaches as part of their change initiatives. Personnel in offices that frequently interact with increasingly diverse audiences of students may need specific training to assess their assumptions about and perceptions of behavior of students whose cultural contexts differ from their own. For instance, one Project Compass campus has adopted new "high touch" advising practices for students of color in the college's new student success center, based on recommendations from professional staff advisors whose expertise is embedded in theoretical frameworks related to intercultural communication. In this same center, a panel of student advisors, comprising students of color who have demonstrated academic success and can identify effective support practices that encouraged that success, inform advising practices.

Institutions aiming to create institutional transformation will need to structure multiple opportunities for intra-institutional communication, such as intentionally including a mix of people from across divisions in planning processes. Replacing a faculty senate with a university senate, for example, allows for broad representation. Where individuals are physically located within the institution and how they are connected through networks of communication matter.

In a study of six institutions that were part of the ACE Project on Leadership and Transformational Change funded by the W. K. Kellogg Foundation, Kezar and Eckel (2002) repeatedly emphasize the importance of involving individuals, divisions, and other subgroups within the institution in effecting organizational learning. Most significantly, the study identifies "sensemaking" – that is, the ways that participants understand the *how* and *why* of change – as central to the process of institutional transformation. The study also maintains that any new or revamped campus structure for supporting change must build in opportunities to reflect on practice – structured time for participants to assess, revise, and incorporate new learning. Both communication and collaboration are components of the community of practice.

Preliminary Outcomes of the Community of Practice

The community of practice is a structural construct, grounded in management science, which facilitates in very practical ways the call for campus-wide "ownership" of retention and student success challenges. Because of the opportunity to define, discuss, and resolve retention issues that extend beyond the influence and authority of any one organizational silo, campuses reported that the community of practice was an authentic problem-solving strategy that clarified the complex sources and characteristics of protracted campus problems. Using input from an array of campus constituencies, the groups could then devise potential solutions grounded in an information and resource base from across the campus, rather than relying solely on one campus unit. In addition, campuses were able to enlist the direct support of various constituencies that were not usually involved in understanding retention issues, and combine existing resources in new, more efficient ways.

By bringing together multiple campus units during the planning year, for example, one campus mapped out the various offices, programs, and projects that offered some form of academic support for racially diverse and other underserved students. Discovering that over 65 different opportunities existed, most of which operated without any overall coordination, the community of practice was able to better understand student complaints of confusion in finding appropriate supports during particularly challenging junctures in the academic term. By convening senior leaders responsible for these multiple academic support efforts in discussions about potential integration of services and resources, the campus was able to create a unified student success center, offering a streamlined set of academic support services, staffed by individuals from multiple units across the campus, and unified by a common theory of practice in student support. Another campus has used the community of practice model to engage community members who represent the leadership of Native American students who have historically been underrepresented. The campus has also initiated an advisory council of Native elders that advises the institution's senior cabinet on collaborative opportunities to better support Native American student retention. A third campus has successfully acquired external funding for a regional Center for Rural Students, the mission of which is to research local rural communities and their relationships to education.

Feature #2: The Logic Model

Each Project Compass institution was required to submit a detailed logic model, which was used to guide campus work throughout the duration of the project. The logic model is an integrated framework that can be used to explain how a proposed intervention will yield results corresponding to a clearly articulated educational problem for campus constituencies and external audiences. A common approach from the field of program evaluation, logic models typically include a definition of the educational problem, critical contextual assumptions that influence the history of the problem and how it plays out on campuses, proposed strategies to respond to the problem, intended outcomes that will result from the successful implementation of the strategies, data-based measures of success that will document the degree of intervention effectiveness, and the long-term impact of intervention outcomes over an extended period of time (W. K. Kellogg Foundation, 2001). The Project Compass logic models were required reference points for campuses to guide their work at the beginning of each project year. They also served as actively changing portraits of the structural change processes over the course of multiple project years. Because the models were updated frequently to reflect the evolution of ongoing modifications to the funded interventions as efficacy and feasibility data were collected, they functioned as a visual map by which campus members could better understand the nature of proposed interventions with measurable outcomes and adjust these interventions to reflect the ongoing learning of campuses as they navigated their change efforts and processes.

Rationale for the Logic Model

Institutions have long been in the habit of responding to multiple requests for data – from faculty surveys and surveys of student engagement to accountability requests from external agencies. Too often, however, largely because institutional research offices are underresourced, data are gathered but not intentionally and strategically deployed to inform change efforts. Bringing about the cultural and structural changes to support the success of underserved students requires institutions to become intentional about what data are gathered, how the analyses are shared across the campus, and how those analyses are managed and disseminated throughout the institution to assess and inform changes in institutional practice. Being strategic about the uses of data involves first creating cross-campus consensus on which data are valuable and meaningful, and then supporting institutional entities with the responsibility for collection, management, and dissemination. The use of logic models induces this intentional and important use of data in transformation efforts.

Preliminary Outcomes of the Logic Model

The logic model has allowed Project Compass institutions to further advance their efforts at fostering a culture of evidence and inquiry aimed at supporting the success of racially diverse and other underserved students. Through the use of the logic model, campuses were better able to integrate innovations for retention across existing organizational silos and determine campus-wide outcomes that reflected the contributions of multiple collaborating partners across campus. This was accomplished by using the logic model as a mapping process, matching agreed-upon retention problems with potential sets of solutions and interventions for which responsibility was shared across organizational units. For example, one campus addressed the need for increased awareness of culturally responsive practices, both inside and outside the classroom, by linking a freshman orientation process, sponsored by student affairs, with ongoing academic efforts to create discipline-based learning communities. Campuses developed refined data collection instruments to better understand the educational contexts that influence initial motivations to attend college, as well as the educational and other cultural experiences that affect persistence and attainment.

Logic models provided a unified map encouraging representatives of key offices across the organization to link meaningful data-based observations with operationalized activities and related measures of success. Some campuses refined their admissions materials to collect more finely grained student data highlighting previous educational experience, while others designed predictive models that identified factors that contribute to student success and students whose profiles may indicate a call for more intensive interventions. Faculty discussed a general shift in the quality of campus conversations addressing a variety of topics, including, but not limited to, retention and student success. Specifically, campuses reported that common practice had changed so that most discussions about institutional issues inevitably involved the interpretation of available data. In instances in which existing institutional research resources were limited, campuses sought out faculty whose disciplinary focus naturally included an emphasis on data collection and analysis. For example, an applied mathematician and an exercise scientist at different campuses became deeply engaged in the nature of student retention problems, applying their expertise in statistical analysis to designing instruments and/ or refining data sets that would facilitate a better understanding of various aspects of retention problems on their respective campuses. Thanks to the logic model, campuses were able to use data to better understand factors contributing to complex retention problems and link them to strategies that involved collaborative participation from various organizational subunits on campus.

Feature #3: Cross-Institutional Learning Community

Project Compass campuses were required to participate in a learning community, comprising selected representatives from each of the funded communities of practice at each campus. Designed to facilitate cross-campus collaboration, the learning community was convened twice annually. At each meeting, the project intermediary organized a series of opportunities for sharing emerging practices related to funded interventions. In addition to the learning community meetings, campuses were encouraged to participate in a series of virtual "think tanks," dedicated to emerging issues related to institutional change and underserved students. National experts helped the learning communities to focus on cross-cutting campus issues, such as the need to build newly conceptualized advising models to better meet the needs of underserved students, qualitative research strategies aimed at improving dialogue between campus staff and faculty about better understanding students and their home communities, and reorienting campus culture to authentic "learner-centered" environments. The virtual think tanks provided opportunities to discuss strategies for inclusive and culturally responsive faculty development initiatives, money management issues for underserved students, and changing the faculty reward structure to acknowledge and honor high-impact faculty practices which encourage underserved student persistence and success.

Rationale for Cross-Institutional Knowledge Communities

A multi-institutional approach to change in higher education enhances opportunities for institutional and industry learning. An initiative that involves multiple institutions sharing a similar goal creates opportunities for institutions that include but are not limited to learning from one another, sharing strategies and resources, and increasing opportunities for professional development (Thomas, 1999). A multi-institutional approach supports the collaborative and collective generation and sharing of knowledge among campuses with similar commitments. It also combats institutional isomorphism by supporting the uniqueness of structure and culture of each institution while providing a collective context for sharing information and resources that support what these institutions have in common. In essence, a multi-institutional approach provides the context for a learning community of campuses, dedicated to the common purpose of institutional change. By creating a set of "peer" institutions that are focusing on similar issues but embedded in different institutional contexts, multicampus models can yield a richer, more diverse set of potential responses to complex organizational challenges.

Cross-institutional collaboration is an effective approach for facilitating communication and exploiting the ingenuity of members of the campus, particularly as they attempt to resolve the complex, interrelated factors linked to any systemic challenge. Such collaboration accomplishes three important functions: (1) it locates individual innovations in an institutional context as part of a broader transformation effort, (2) it strengthens individual innovations within departments and offices, and (3) it increases the openness of departments and offices to new mental models that guide the work colleges do around retention – such as a model that shifts from a focus on underserved students' deficits to a focus on their assets. Some examples of influential cross-institutional collaboration include the following:

- Institutional researchers from each of the four campuses met periodically through the year to compare methodological designs and share strategies for responding to emerging data-collection challenges. Through this informal collaboration and learning from one of the participating institutions, some other campuses adopted their predictive modeling strategy – an approach to use limited resources effectively in responding to student support needs for new populations of racially diverse students.
- Influenced by a peer institution that developed a summer institute for faculty committed to culturally responsive teaching, one campus enhanced its own approach to faculty and staff development through the creation of a similar multi-year effort, linking student and academic affairs in a Native American student success center.
- By sharing challenges to effective advising, all of the campuses have created an array of practices that respond to a range of nationally shared issues, including the need to create a network of coordinated advising centers relying on the expertise of both professional and faculty advisors, as well as carefully designed early alert systems that integrate high-tech, "high-touch," and discipline-based supports once students enter the major.

Preliminary Outcomes of Cross-Institutional Learning Communities

Establishing a cross-institutional learning community has resulted in structural changes on individual campuses. The learning communities have also created opportunities for knowledge dissemination beyond the scope of the initiative itself. The most compelling evidence of benefit from cross-institutional interaction through Project Compass has been the aforementioned adoption of proven strategies and practices at one campus by other campuses participating in the project. Equally important, however, has been the participation of campuses in presenting preliminary findings related to their funded interventions at local, regional, and national meetings. For example, representatives from all four campuses presented individually and collectively at a national meeting of the American Association of Colleges and Universities, presenting on data collection, faculty development, and the creation of specialized student success centers. Institutional researchers at one campus, for instance, have presented on their efforts to create more responsive institutional data collection techniques so that more meaningful data related to underserved populations can affect the development of institutional policies and practices.

Feature #4: The Role of an External Intermediary

Project Compass campuses were funded to implement changes to practices, policies, and structures resulting in greater numbers of successful students from racially diverse and other underserved populations. To facilitate the possibility of cultural transformation resulting from the preparatory and implementation processes related to these interventions, the Project Compass model includes an intermediary role around capacity-building and accountability framed as an institutional coaching component. Campus coaches are individuals who have expertise both in organizational change in higher education and in various structural and cultural frameworks that would facilitate racially diverse and other underserved students' success. Each coach works closely with the chair of a campus community of practice and attends each of the required group meetings. The coach is charged with working collaboratively to support the successful implementation of funded interventions while at the same time stewarding the process of long-term organizational and cultural change in order to sustain these initiatives beyond the funding cycle of the overall project. In addition to providing resources about research and practice that help campuses to devise their own solutions, the coach is charged with working across the campus hierarchy to advise on issues of broad-scale change. Coaches also take an active role in facilitating specialized meetings and in brokering conflict among various campus constituencies in addition to organizing and implementing activities related to the learning community. Coaches had a diverse history of experience in both faculty and administrative roles and were knowledgeable systems thinkers in higher education with strong facilitation skills.

Rationale for the Intermediary Role

The Project Compass approach to transforming institutions in support of racially diverse and other underserved students combines best practices in the fields of both organizational change and retention in recognition of the fact that there are two levels of work happening simultaneously: (1) the conditions for successful, sustained change across the institution are being created, and (2) consistent with research findings, the approach to change rests on the principle that institutions undertaking major transformation will have a greater chance of sustaining their work if they receive skilled coaching from an outside entity and if they engage in exchanges with peer institutions committed to similar efforts. Thus, NERCHE has designed a coaching and technical assistance model that provides guidance tailored to specific concerns of individual campuses and at the same time promotes collaboration within and among campuses in a learning community structure.

Each funded institution articulated its objectives and strategies in the logic model submitted in the implementation proposal. NERCHE holds each institution accountable to these objectives and measures of success after an initial process of refinement. From that point, NERCHE will build on the institution's assets to foster the conditions that allow the best chance of success of the proposed initiatives. They include (1) understanding the best practices in the field, (2) effectively tapping internal and external sources of expertise, (3) practices supporting collaboration and system-level thinking, (4) a strong and growing base of support among stakeholders, and (5) strategic use of resources. The coaching model not only offers technical assistance toward achieving these conditions for success, but it holds each institution accountable to best practices in carrying out its implementation plan.

Preliminary Outcomes of the Intermediary Role

Though we cannot validate them as a critical variable in sustained cultural change, we believe that the coaches have been important ingredients to ongoing institutional transformation. Coaches have engaged in the following:

- facilitating and modeling group processes for planning and problem solving;
- acting as a "critical friend," asking critical questions about which insiders may not have thought or that may be difficult for insiders to raise, such as questions that probe how issues of race and class may be presenting barriers to moving forward;
- encouraging communities of practice to adopt strategies that are critical to the success of their initiatives, but with which they have no experience; for example, one coach worked with an institution to create an outreach plan to the surrounding community from which they draw many of the low-income, first-generation students that make up their target population;
- assessing participation of members of the community of practice and advising on roles;
- providing perspective on common challenges for organizational change; for example, coaches have begun advising campus teams about the range of approaches taken by peer institutions and strategies they might employ

to ensure that their faculty reward structures align with the commitment to teaching that fosters success among underserved students;

- providing assistance with translating theory into practice and practice into theory; for example, in conjunction with another national expert, one coach conducted a 4-day intensive faculty workshop in culturally responsive pedagogies;

- tapping practitioner expertise; guiding appropriate practitioners in a process of making explicit the kinds of practices and approaches they know work well with particular populations;

- identifying opportunities for creating sustainability; for example, a coach worked with a campus to link its Project Compass initiative to the institution's diversity efforts and restructured curriculum in ways that highlighted common objectives and created opportunities for pooling resources.

Conclusion

Transformational cultural change aimed at supporting the success of underserved students – and, by extension, all students – must necessarily include broad participation from every element of the college or university. Rather than viewing students as the object of change, institutions must learn to value students as assets; faculty, administrators, and staff as both learners and generators of practitioner knowledge, ingenuity, and creativity; and education itself as an ongoing process of change. Creating a culture of success for racially diverse and other underserved students requires a commitment to deep, pervasive, integrated institutional change. It also requires structural ways of approaching retention problems that diverge from the typical ways in which colleges "do business." By design, Project Compass attempts to create opportunities for campuses to find an innovative middle ground that provides the time and space to reflect and learn from a broad range of individuals in order to move toward transformation. Acknowledging the difficulty in assessing the extent to which any of the funded campus interventions has a direct impact on overall retention of the target populations at each campus, project staff are committed to documenting the ongoing evolution of cultural attitudes within each of these institutions that will provide the contextual framework for any retention to flourish and be sustained.

Note

1 NERCHE is a resource institute at the University of Massachusetts, Boston; founded in 1987, it is "committed to collaborative change processes in higher education to address social justice in a diverse democracy."

References

Bergquist, W. H., Pawlak, K., & Bergquist, W. H. (2008). *Engaging the six cultures of the academy: Revised and expanded edition of The Four Cultures of the Academy*. San Francisco: Jossey-Bass.

Braxton, J.M., Brier, E.M., & Steele, S.L. (2007–2008). Shaping retention from research to practice. *Journal of College Student Retention: Research, Theory and Practice, 9*, 377–399.

Eckel, P., Hill, B., & Green, M. (1998). On change: En route to transformation. An occasional paper series of the ACE project on leadership and institutional transformation. Washington, DC: American Council on Education.

Green, D. (2006). Historically underserved students: What we know, what we still need to know. In D. D. Bragg and E. A. Barnett (Eds.), *Academic pathways to and from the community college* (New directions for community colleges, no. 135, pp. 21–28). San Francisco: Jossey-Bass.

Jobs for the Future, Nellie Mae Education Foundation. (2008). What it takes to succeed in the 21st century – and how New Englanders are faring. Retrieved June 1, 2011, from www.nmefdn.org.

KFHET (Kellogg Forum on Higher Education Transformation). (2001). *What have we learned about transformation in higher education?* Battle Creek, MI: National Forum on Higher Education for the Public Good.

Kezar, A., & Eckel, P. (2002). Examining the institutional transformation process: The importance of sensemaking, interrelated strategies and balance. *Research in Higher Education, 43*(3), 295–328.

Kirsch, I., Braun, H., & Yamamoto, K. (2007). America's perfect storm. Ewing, NJ: Educational Testing Service. Retrieved June 1, 2011, from www.ets.org/stormreport.

Kuh, G. D., & Hall, J. E. (1993). Using cultural perspectives in student affairs. In G. D. Kuh (Ed.), *Cultural perspectives in student affairs work* (pp. 1–20). Lanham, MD: American College Personnel Association.

Laden, B., Milem, J., & Crowson, R. (2000). New institutional theory and student departure. In Braxton, J. M. *Reworking the student departure puzzle: Vanderbilt issues in higher education* (pp. 235–256). Nashville, TN: Vanderbilt University Press.

Little, D. (2010). Equity and excellence from three points of reference. In D. Little and S. Mohanty (Eds.), *The future of diversity: Academic leaders reflect on American higher education* (pp. 74–75). New York: Palgrave Macmillan.

Menand, L. (2010). *The marketplace of ideas: Reform and resistance in the American university*. New York: W. W. Norton.

New England Resource Center for Higher Education Project Compass. (2011). About Project Compass. Retrieved May 25, 2011, from http://bit.ly/jRIRr6.

Sautter, R. C. (1994). Who are today's city kids? Beyond the "deficit model." *CITYSCHOOLS, 1*(1), 6–10.

Schoem, D. (2002). Transforming undergraduate education: Moving beyond distinct undergraduate initiatives. *Change Magazine,* November/December.

Sturm, S. (2006). The architecture of inclusion: Advancing workplace equity in higher education. *Harvard Journal of Law and Gender, 29*, 247–334.

Thomas, N. L. (1999). *An examination of multi-institutional networks*. Working paper #23. Boston: New England Resource Center for Higher Education.

Tinto, V. (2006–2007). Research and practice of student retention: What next? *Journal of College Student Retention, 8*(1), 1–19.

Torres, R. J. (2006). Being seen, being heard: Moving beyond visibility in the academy. *Journal of Latinos and Education*, *5*(1), 65–69.

Valencia, R. (1997). *The evolution of deficit thinking: Educational thought and practice*. The Stanford Series on Education and Public Policy. Bristol, PA: Falmer Press.

Wenger, E., Arnold, R., & Snyder, W. (2002). *Cultivating communities of practice: A guide to managing knowledge*. Watertown, MA: Harvard Business Press.

W. K. Kellogg Foundation. (2001). W. K. Kellogg Foundation Logic Model Development Guide. Retrieved May 25, 2011, from http://www.wkkf.org/.

CONTRIBUTOR BIOGRAPHIES

Estela Mara Bensimon is Professor of Higher Education and Co-Director of the Center for Urban Education (CUE) at the USC Rossier School of Education. Dr. Bensimon has published extensively on issues of equity, organizational learning, practitioner inquiry, and institutional change. She has also conducted research on leadership in higher education and is the author and co-author of several publications on college presidents, department chairs, and administrative teams. Her publications have appeared in *Change*, *Review of Higher Education*, *Journal of Higher Education*, *Liberal Education*, and *Harvard Education Review*. Dr. Bensimon held leadership positions in the Association for the Study of Higher Education (President, 2005–2006) and in the American Education Research Association – Division on Postsecondary Education (Vice-President, 1992–1994). She also served on the boards of the American Association for Higher Education and the Association of American Colleges and Universities, and was named an AERA Fellow in recognition of her sustained excellence in research in 2011. She earned her doctorate in Higher Education from Teachers College, Columbia University.

Stephanie H. Chang is a third-year doctoral student in the College Student Personnel Program at the University of Maryland. She studies diversity, social justice, and qualitative research methods. She also teaches undergraduate courses on human diversity, advocacy, and leadership. In her professional experience, she worked in Lesbian, Gay, Bisexual, and Transgender Resource Centers at multiple institutions. Chang earned her bachelor's degree in African & Afro-American studies from the University of North Carolina at Chapel Hill and her master's degree in College Student Affairs from The Pennsylvania State University.

Cheryl J. Daly is Assistant Professor of Education at the University of New Hampshire. Her scholarship addresses organizational leadership, college learning environments, faculty careers, and faculty development, examining the ways that organizational structures and cultures shape both faculty roles and teaching/learning contexts.

Jay R. Dee is Associate Professor of Leadership in Education at the University of Massachusetts Boston. He also serves as Co-Director of the New England Center for Inclusive Teaching, a multi-institutional faculty development network that links pedagogical practices to an understanding of student diversity. His research interests include college and university governance, higher education accountability systems, and faculty careers and faculty development.

Glenn Gabbard is Co-Director of the New England Resource Center for Higher Education at the University of Massachusetts Boston, where he also serves as Director of Project Compass, a multi-institutional initiative designed to increase the success of students of color, first-generation college students, and those who come from low-income backgrounds. He is an academic leader, administrator, faculty member, and researcher with experience in community colleges, universities, and non-profit organizations. Throughout his work as a faculty member, department chair, dean, and director of national change initiatives, Glenn has focused on issues related to forging stronger collaborative efforts within and across institutions that acknowledge the contributions of individuals who are labeled "underserved." His areas of interest include developmental education in multicultural settings, seamless linkages between public schools and higher education, inclusive policy and practices related to individuals with disabilities and their families, and the skills, knowledge, dispositions, and vision required for transforming colleges and universities as democratic institutions. Dr. Gabbard holds a doctorate in Higher Education. He is a faculty member in the Higher Education Administration Program at UMass Boston.

Douglas A. Guiffrida is Associate Professor of Counseling and Human Development in the Warner School of Education and Human Development at the University of Rochester. His research focuses on understanding the experiences of college students of color who attend predominantly White institutions, in order to support them more effectively. He also studies constructivist approaches to counselor education and supervision. He is a nationally certified counselor and a licensed mental health counselor in New York State, and serves as Associate Editor for Best Practices for the *Journal of Counseling and Development*.

Shaun R. Harper is on the faculty in the Graduate School of Education, Africana Studies, and Gender Studies at University of Pennsylvania, where he also serves as Director of the Center for the Study of Race and Equity in Education. He has published nine books and more than 75 peer-reviewed journal articles, book chapters, and other academic publications. He has also delivered over 50 keynote addresses and presented more than 130 research papers, workshops, and symposia at national education conferences. The *Review of Higher Education*, *Journal of Higher Education*, *Journal of College Student Development*, *Teachers College Record*, and several other well-regarded journals have published Dr. Harper's research. He received the 2010 Outstanding Contribution to Research Award from the National Association of Student Personnel Administrators and the 2008 Early Career Award from the Association for the Study of Higher Education.

ChuYu Huang is a recent graduate of the College of Liberal Arts and Asian American Studies Program at the University of Massachusetts Boston. She has a double major in Sociology and Asian American Studies. She is engaged in the Boston Chinatown community. In her professional experience, she worked in multicultural settings with immigrant youths in several non-profit organizations.

Uma M. Jayakumar is an Assistant Professor of Organization and Leadership in the School of Education at the University of San Francisco. She also holds a Faculty Associate position with the Education and Well Being program in the Survey Research Center (SRC) at the Institute for Social Research (ISR) at the University of Michigan. Jayakumar's scholarship examines race, equity, and diversity issues in higher education, with a focus on how institutional environments such as campus culture and climate, and organizational practices shape access and success among college students of color. Her work is featured in journals such as the *Harvard Educational Review* and the *Journal of Higher Education*, reports to foundations and educational institutes, and numerous national conference presentations. Dr. Jayakumar is recipient of the 2007 Bobby Wright Dissertation of the Year Award by the Association for the Study of Higher Education and was named Exemplary Diversity Scholar by the National Center for Institutional Diversity in 2010. She received her Ph.D. in Higher Education and Organizational Change at the University of California, Los Angeles.

Pratna Kem is a first-year graduate student in the Graduate College of Education at the University of Massachusetts Boston. He completed his bachelor's degree in English and a program of study in Asian American Studies from UMass Boston. He is now working toward his M.Ed. in hopes to become a high school teacher in urban and underserved communities.

Adrianna J. Kezar is Associate Professor of Higher Education at the University of Southern California. Her research focuses on leadership, organizational theory, change, and diversity and equity in higher education.

Judy Marquez Kiyama is Assistant Professor of Educational Leadership in the Warner School of Education and Human Development at the University of Rochester. Her research interests include college access, outreach, choice, and transition, with particular interest in underrepresented students, their families, and their communities. Kiyama's community-based approach to research engages asset-based theoretical frameworks to better understand collective knowledge and resources present in communities. Kiyama is currently involved in a collaborative research project with the Ibero-American Action League examining the state of Latina/o education in the Rochester City School District. Specifically, this project examines the resources that promote and the barriers that prohibit Latina/o students from progressing through school.

Sơn Ca Lâm is currently pursuing a master's degree in the Applied Linguistics Program at the University of Massachusetts Boston. She received her dual bachelor's degree in Environmental Science and Comparative Ethnic Studies, with a focus on Asian American Studies, at UMass Boston. She is interested in social justice and the intersections of space, language, and culture.

Samuel D. Museus is Assistant Professor of Educational Administration at the University of Hawai'i at Manoa. His scholarship focuses on college access and success among underserved populations. He has produced over 80 publications and national conference presentations on the factors that influence college enrollment and completion among racial minority, low-income, and first-generation students. This includes publications in journals such as the *Review of Higher Education*, the *Journal of College Student Development*, and the *Journal of Diversity in Higher Education*. He received the Emerging Scholar Award from the American College Personnel Association (ACPA) in 2009. He also received the Outstanding Contribution to Asian Pacific Islander American Research Award from ACPA's Asian Pacific American Network in 2010 and the Research of the Year Award from ACPA's Multiracial Network in 2011.

Joanna N. Ravello is a third-year doctoral student in the Higher Education Administration Program at the University of Massachusetts Boston. Her research interests include the experiences of racially and ethnically underrepresented students in higher education. Specifically, she is interested in the impact of high-impact co-curricular practices on the persistence of underserved students in urban areas. In her professional role, she works for the University of Rhode Island's Talent Development Program, a program designed to recruit, admit, support, and retain in-state students of color and students from disadvantaged backgrounds. Ravello earned her bachelor's degree in Human Development and Family Studies and her master's degree in College Student Personnel from the University of Rhode Island.

Stephen John Quaye is an Assistant Professor in the College Student Personnel Program at the University of Maryland. He is the recipient of the 2009 NASPA Melvene D. Hardee Dissertation of the Year Award for his dissertation, "Pedagogy and Racialized Ways of Knowing: Students and Faculty Engage Racial Realities in Postsecondary Classrooms." In addition, he is a 2009 ACPA Emerging Scholar. His research concentrates on the influence of race relations on college and university campuses, specifically the gains and outcomes associated with inclusive racial climates, cross-racial interactions, and racially conscious pedagogical approaches. At the University of Maryland, he teaches courses in student development theory, facilitating student learning, qualitative research, and race/ethnicity, class, and gender issues in higher education. Quaye earned his bachelor's degree in Psychology from James Madison University, his master's degree in College Student Personnel from Miami University, and his Ph.D. in Higher Education from the Pennsylvania State University.

Sharon Singleton is a Senior Program and Research Associate at the New England Resource Center for Higher Education at the University of Massachusetts Boston. She has more than 20 years of experience in as a project director, administrator, and researcher, with a particular focus on qualitative studies and program evaluation. Among her research interests are systemic organizational change to support the academic success of college students from underserved populations; faculty, administrator, and staff workload issues in the context of institutional change; and scholarly engagement with communities that is guided by the principles of reciprocity, social justice, and democracy. Sharon holds a master's degree in Education from Harvard University.

Kevin Tan is an undergraduate student at the University of Massachusetts Boston. He studies international business management and Asian American Studies. He currently works for an NIH grant-funded project studying health disparities amongst Southeast Americans.

Blanca E. Vega is currently a doctoral candidate in the Higher and Postsecondary Education program at Teachers College, Columbia University. She simultaneously works as Director of the Higher Education Opportunity Program

(HEOP) at Marymount Manhattan College. Her research interests include examining the role of higher education on the construction of race and racism, exploring racial dynamics in state political culture and their effects on higher education policy, and studying policies affecting undocumented immigrant students in higher education. Blanca earned her bachelor's degree in Anthropology from Brandeis University and a master's degree in Higher Education at New York University.

Stephanie J. Waterman, Onondaga, turtle clan, is an Assistant Professor in Educational Leadership in the Warner Graduate School of Education & Human Development at the University of Rochester. She began her formal education at the Onondaga Nation School located on the Onondaga Nation. She was a 2005 National Academy of Education/Spencer Post-Doctoral Fellow. Her research interests are Native American college experiences, retention, and staff involvement in student retention. Dr. Waterman serves on the editorial board of the *Journal of American Indian Education*, and is co-chair of the National Association of Student Personnel Administrator's Indigenous Peoples Knowledge Community Scholarship & Research Committee.

Keith A. Witham is a doctoral student at the University of Southern California's Rossier School of Education. He is also a research assistant in the Center for Urban Education, where he works on implementing and evaluating the use of CUE's Equity Scorecard and benchmarking tools in higher education institutions and systems. Prior to coming to USC, Keith was Senior Research Analyst at Complete College America, a non-profit organization that works with state policymakers to implement policies aimed at improvements in college completion rates. His research interests center around the interaction of state/federal policy and institutional initiatives, as well as factors that promote postsecondary and workforce success for low-income, adult, and first-generation students.

INDEX